A SENSE OF
WONDER

"Maybe the best thing to say about Van Morrison's Ireland is that there's more of it than we think." Glenn Patterson

A SENSE OF
WONDER

VAN MORRISON'S IRELAND

DAVID BURKE

For Shirley, my wife, best friend, muse and the finest person I've ever known. With love, always.

And in memory of William and Marion Burke, my grandparents and blood source of the music.

A SENSE OF WONDER
VAN MORRISON'S IRELAND
by David Burke

A Jawbone Book
First Edition 2013
Published in the UK and the USA by Jawbone Press
2a Union Court,
20–22 Union Road,
London SW4 6JP,
England
www.jawbonepress.com

ISBN 978-1-908279-48-4

EDITOR Tom Seabrook
DESIGN Paul Cooper

Printed by Regent Publishing Services Limited, China

1 2 3 4 5 17 16 15 14 13

CONTENTS

FOREWORD
'BLUES FOR VAN MORRISON'
A POEM BY JOSEPH O'CONNOR

Down the Cypress Avenue, Belfast,
Through the fog from off the river,
A pale boy comes searching
For bottle-tops of song.
The wind from off the Lagan
Brings the voice of Muddy Waters.
Wonder who/
Gonna love yuh/
When you sweetman gone.

City of enmities,
In an island of rain,
The staunch granite buildings,
Dampened flags, broken looms.
But America comes drifting.
From the river's grey mists
Bessie Smith is singing
Got the Mean Man Blues.

And over in St Dominick's,
The choir is rehearsing
Amazing Grace
And *Abide With Me*
While the banners of war
Tell the story of betrayals,

Of The Somme, and of Ypres,
And of doomed Gallipoli.
At nights he has the radio,
Hilversum, Lille.
Luxembourg, Warsaw.
He isn't alone.
Ray Charles on American Forces Network.
Mahalia Jackson.
Moscow, Athlone.

The bitter, Belfast winter
Of 1956.
The boy is aged eleven
In a city iceberg-hard,
But maybe there'll be nights
For a moondance, he dreams,
As he gazes at the cranes
In the shipbuilding yard.
The phrase 'Harland and Woolf'
Brings a bluesman to his mind.
Great Chester Burnett,
The Howlin' Wolf.
'No Surrender' daubed
On the gables by the mart.
In his head, Hank Williams sings
'Your Cheatin Heart'.

Loner. Gospel moaner.
William Blake with the shake.
Sax voiced soul-man; too cool to play games.
In your slim black tie and your pork-pie hat.
High on John Lee Hooker, Ledbelly, Etta James.
And the voice rising up like a rumour of hope,

7

Thunder-blasted, love-struck, witnessing the joy
That only exists in the country of song,
Where the flags are made of yearning
And trumpets cry like Otis Redding,
And redemption comes in grace notes
Falling like brave angels,
Even as the tawdry cling to fake celebrity.
The healing is begun. Sweet Lord, how long?

I glimpse an awkward, moody boy,
In a city long gone.
Linen-skinned, Ulster,
Hard to impress.
Around him waif the spectres
Of those radio nights,
Voices once encountered through the spinning of a dial
On a crackling old wireless in his mother's front room,
Where he learnt that a song lights our walk from the tomb,
That healing comes in mercies you couldn't afford,
In Sam Cooke singing 'Darling, You Send Me',
In the sacred alleluia of a minor seventh chord.

A boy on Royal Avenue pauses in the rain,
And the memory of the Lagan is the Lakes of
Pontchartrain.
And the ghosts of Belfast rebels
Swirl with the rest;
The Hurricane Higgins.
Handsome George Best.
Quietly distaining
Mediocrities and fools,
Saying *Keep Your X-Factor*.
I don't live by your rules.

Where Lagan streams sing lullabies
There grows a lily fair.
The twilight gleam is on her eyes;
The night is on her hair.
And Madame George arises
Like a phantom, and she stops.
'Hush, love,' she murmurs. 'Be cool. It's the cops.'

Wet October leaves on an Orangefield day,
And a boy born in Belfast walks on his way,
As the brown-eyed girls make their beautiful choices,
The greatest voice ever in a land of great voices
Rises up a memory he didn't think he knew.

What about ye, Van? Rave on, Rave on.
Have we told you lately that we love you?
We do.

INTRODUCTION

"You get these biographies that claim to be about me. They come up with stories and some of it is partial truth, some of it's completely made up. It's all third-party stuff. They interview people from years ago who know nothing about me now and probably didn't know much about me then. Then there's books that say things about my music, like they know where the songs have come from. It's all bullshit."

Van Morrison to *Uncut*, 2005

"I think the guys who wrote the last couple of books were complete ignoramuses, not qualified for the job. If anybody told them anything, they believed it, they didn't question it."

Van Morrison to *Mojo*, 2006

Another ignoramus peddling bullshit, or someone earnestly endeavouring to understand the misunderstood Mr Morrison, to explore his particular Ireland? You decide.

He doesn't make it easy for those of us who want to get close enough to the man and inside the music, to reify the impulses that impel him to create a spellbinding tableau out of language and sounds. Not that it is the duty, either, of an artist like Van The Man to explain or assist in the explanation of his art. And let's clarify this from the off: Morrison is an artist rather than an entertainer, performer, song-and-dance man, or whatever other designation has been imposed on him by the real ignoramuses.

There's certainly no reason why he should reveal anything about himself just because he happens to be a recognisable figure. Famous, in other words. Indeed, his rejection of the fame that accompanies his success, his apparent discomfort with it, his refusal to play the game, to conform to the expectations of a capricious medium, his fidelity to his own truth, is impressive. Curmudgeonly, cantankerous, recalcitrant, obnoxious—mad, even—are some of the words used by journalists and company men and women over the years to describe Morrison.

Stories of his, let's say, idiosyncratic behaviour are legion. The dining companion, a long-time associate, who committed the grievous error of calling him "my son", only to feel the full import of Morrison's rage, replete with threats of physical violence. The terror among record company employees whenever he dropped into their office, "usually to harangue somebody about some imagined slight—people would literally hide in the cupboards so as not to have to confront him", according to a former press agent. The warning of legal action against the Belfast Blues Appreciation Society over its erection of a plaque outside his childhood home to commemorate his contribution to Irish music. (When I informed a colleague that I was writing a book about Van, he quipped, "I hope you have a good lawyer!"). Or the humiliation of one interrogator, upon the release of *Irish Heartbeat*, his album with The Chieftains, of whom Morrison asked, three questions in, "Is it OK if I go to sleep?"

"Hello," he added, "have you got your pound of flesh? I don't have to prove anything." Followed by, "Do you want me to stand on my head?" And finally, "These questions, God they're unanswerable. 'Why those songs?' We've been asked that all day. I mean, 'Why get up in the morning? Why, why, why?' There is no why. You just do something because at the time that's the thing to do. There's nothing to read into it at all. There's no mystery. What I do is very simple. My songs, my music, my whole shtick, is not something that's mysterious."

And then there's the one about the post-gig, wee small hours exchange of views with a band-member. This hapless individual argued the toss on a particular point until, exhausted, he conceded that Van was right. Van paused momentarily before snapping, "Well, in that case … you're wrong!"

Not even the literati escape Morrison's wrath. Salman Rushdie once told of encountering Van in Bono's living room—a mental picture I struggle to bring into focus, the gobshite messiah from U2, human balm to the tired, poor, huddled, wretched masses, chowing down with a misanthrope from the school of Jean-Paul Sartre—and being subjected to "the rough edge of the great man's tongue". Van, Rushdie observed, "has been known to get a little grumpy toward the end of a long evening". No shit. Mahatma Ghandi, bless him, would have had difficulty suppressing his hackles in this company.

Unlike Bruce Springsteen, the subject of my previous book, *Heart Of Darkness: Bruce Springsteen's Nebraska*, Morrison doesn't buy into the myth about himself. He's a songwriter, not a sage. He's a musician, not a mystic. Mention of Springsteen reminds me of another Van yarn. They were once on the same flight. Springsteen, a Morrison acolyte whose first two albums, *Greetings From Asbury Park, NJ* and *The Wild, The Innocent & The E Street Shuffle*, were cut from the same R&B and soul prototype, wanted to meet him, to say hello. Van was having none of it. Humbug to all that celebrity fraternity nonsense.

Of his contemporaries, only Bob Dylan has maintained a consistent line of declining to feed off the fatted calf of his own legend, of leaving interpretation to others, of keeping schtum about matters that may occasion an invasion of his right—like the right of everyone—to privacy. Dylan achieves this mostly through being disarmingly mischievous: "All I can do is be me, whoever that is"; "I write songs because nobody says I can't"; "Some of them are three minutes, some of them are four," this in response to the query, "What are your songs about?" Morrison, on the other hand, is menacing. Bob would at least tickle your funny bone; Van would probably break your bones.

He can be amusing, too, although admittedly it sometimes translates as unintentional amusement. Showing up to an interview with *Mojo* on a warm summer's evening in sleepy Suffolk in 2012, he was dressed in "heavy coat, scarf, shades and a cap with large ear muffs ... avoiding all attempts at eye contact, he moves through the tables and selects a seat with his back to the crowd, suspiciously eyeballing a frothy coffee that sits before him". It's a comical picture, to be sure, yet one that belies an almost torturous timorousness. Being Van Morrison, public figure, is something he finds tough. As Colin Irwin wrote in the same *Mojo* piece, "The music is it: the beginning, middle, and end of what he does. He doesn't understand why writing songs and making records should inspire curiosity about lifestyle and personality; or even interest in the motivation, events or mental state that induced him to make that music. 'Why would you talk about your private life?' he asks ... 'Does a carpenter? Does a plumber? Do you?' And you find yourself thinking that, after all, it may very well be Van who's the normal one and everybody else—especially the music industry itself—that's weird."

That's probably the most acute reading yet of the Morrison enigma.

Barry Egan, columnist with *The Sunday Independent* in Ireland, allowed that Morrison could be "rude and bad-tempered" but claimed the sway he held over others was due "not to his temper, but to a sweetness that emanates from him unexpectedly, like perfume from a thorny rose. Once you get past the protective barriers— difficult admittedly—he will not stop talking".

○

So, here I am, the latest in a procession of inquirers trying to make head or tail of Van, in this case through the Ireland from which he comes; how and to what extent that Ireland moulded his artistic vision—in other words, how he then remade Ireland in his music— and the minor role he played in bringing together a nation divided. A Belfast Prod claimed by the south as one of its own, he is a Northern Irishman and an Irishman—sometimes an Irish exile—who has rejected the hateful, twisted ancient rivalries that continue to poison the blood of a post-conflict society; one who has rejected this or that

13

God, this or that flag, and instead rejoiced in a kind of aesthetic oneness, a coalition of cultures.

He embodies, too, the idea of the black Irish, not as that term denotes the dark-haired phenotype descended from prehistoric Iberian migrants, nor even as metaphorical shorthand for the shared experience of peoples cast out into the wilderness of their own ethnicity (it wasn't so very long ago that English landlords tacked the prohibitive notice, 'No Irish, No Blacks, No Dogs', to their rental properties), but rather in his use of what chin-stroking musicologists categorise as black music—a social construct—as "simultaneously the conduit to the world outside Ireland, and the conduit back to Ireland".

Van Morrison's Ireland is also, if you like, a journey through the subject's Irish experience, a map of the people and places he has encountered along the way.

David Burke
April 2013

CHAPTER 1
TWO TRIBES

Van Morrison's Ireland is a mythical place. It exists in the fertile ground of the imagination engendered by song. It realises the fears of one tradition while concurrently realising the dreams of another, uniting orange and green. It embraces the soul of a people liberated from denominational dogma. It has a singular voice comprising many different accents. It eschews designations contrived to divide—north and south represent compass points and cultural diversity rather than declaring allegiance to this or that principle. The triumphalism of 'The Sash My Father Wore', a rallying cry to the reactionaries with bigotry in their blood from the sour-faced, bowler-hatted old men banging the Lambeg drum for God and Queen and country, is subverted by Morrison collaborators The Chieftains, musicians from a part of the island once in thrall to Rome, now servile to Brussels. It is Cyprus Avenue and Raglan Road. It is Georgie Best and Paddy Kavanagh. It is Ireland as Ireland could be; not, lamentably, as Ireland is.

In the real world, however, Van Morrison is of Northern Ireland. He belongs to Belfast. East Belfast to be precise—the citadel of Northern Irish Protestantism, Unionism, Loyalism. Part of the Six Counties. He is not Irish at all, but British. Or, in the context of the Good Friday Agreement, both British and Irish, with said concord recognising that it is "the birthright of all the people of Northern Ireland to identify themselves and be accepted as Irish or British, or both, as they may so choose, and accordingly confirm that their right to hold both British and Irish citizenship is accepted by both governments and would not be affected by any future change in the status of Northern Ireland". Neither fish nor foul, then, but of amorphous identity. (And I haven't even mentioned a long-ago acquaintance of mine—English—who wouldn't be divested of the notion that Van The Man was actually an American.)

This vexed question of identity seems like a good place to begin, particularly in a dominion such as Northern Ireland, where, once upon a time, the mere disclosure of your given name, school, or locale could get you killed. So what is this country that Van The Man comes from? What is Northern Ireland? And what constitutes Northern Irishness?

"Northern Ireland has two tribes, so trying to define Northern Irishness seems pretty well impossible," Irish historian Ruth Dudley Edwards wrote in response to an email requesting an interview for this book. Instead, she referred me to *Aftermath: The Omagh Bombing And The Families' Pursuit Of Justice*, her study of the 1998 Omagh bombing, then described by the BBC as "Northern Ireland's worst single terrorist atrocity". The book, she said, was her "most recent attempt to understand what Northern Ireland is about".

Dudley Edwards's version of Irish history essentially refutes the Republican credo that Ireland was something of a Gaelic Utopia until the English invasion in the 12th century, and that in the 800-plus years since, "Irish men and women resisted British rule and attempted to assert Irish independence". This last line is quoted from the website of Sinn Fein, widely acknowledged as the political wing of the IRA, or the Irish Republican Army. Dudley Edwards goes so far as to accuse Irish Republicans of revelling in necrophilia in martyring those killed while serving the cause. Such claim, and the inevitable counter-claim (known colloquially as "what aboutery"), accentuates Dudley Edwards's tribal perspective of Northern Ireland. Each faction—manifest variously as Protestant/Catholic, Loyalist/Republican, Unionist/Nationalist, British/Irish—obdurately adheres to its own narrative. Therein lies the big problem in nailing down Northern Irish identity: it all depends which side you're on.

First, some incontestable facts. Northern Ireland, situated in the northeast of Ireland, is part of the United Kingdom, sharing its border with the Republic of Ireland. The 2011 census numbered its population at 1,810,900—about 30 percent of the island of Ireland's overall population, and approximately 3 percent of the UK population. Of those, 48 percent are either Protestant or brought up Protestant, a drop of 5 percent from the 2001 census; 45 percent are either Catholic or brought up Catholic, an increase of 1 percent. One reason for the decline in Protestantism is that it's an older population with higher mortality rates. Other factors cited include migration, and an upsurge in those who claim to belong to another religion (or none at all). In this census, for the first time ever, statisticians asked about national identity. Two-fifths, or 40 percent, of respondents regard themselves as British only; a quarter, 25 percent, as Irish only; and just over a fifth, 21 percent, as Northern Irish only. According to the BBC, these figures illustrate "the danger of trying to equate someone's religion with their political identity". Largely self-governed by the Northern Ireland Assembly, a devolved legislature, Northern Ireland cooperates with the Republic on some policy areas, while others are reserved for the UK government.

Next, the facts outlined by history. In the early 17th century, King James I seized some four million acres in the province of Ulster and offered them to Scots and English settlers. The arrival of these immigrants, largely Presbyterians, forced the native Irish onto inferior land, or into work without land, thus creating the conditions for tribalism to which Dudley Edwards alluded.

Ireland officially became part of the United Kingdom in 1801. The following century was characterised in parliament by Protestant pressure to retain the status quo—namely, UK citizenship—and Catholic lobbying for Home Rule, punctuated by the occasional rebellion. In 1914, the Catholics got what they wanted, though the implementation of the Home Rule Bill—which included provision for a "temporary" partition of Counties Antrim, Down, Armagh, Londonderry, Fermanagh, and Tyrone—was suspended with the outbreak of the First World War. During that conflict, a group of

Nationalists in Dublin initiated what became popularly known as the Easter 1916 Rising, forming a provisional government of the Irish Republic before they were finally defeated by Crown forces. By the end of the war, the demand for Home Rule had been superseded by the demand for full independence. In 1919, a new bill was introduced by Prime Minister David Lloyd George, separating Ireland into two Home Rule areas: 26 counties ruled from Dublin, and the aforementioned six counties ruled from Belfast. Ireland was partitioned between north and south in 1921. A treaty in 1922 gave Northern Ireland autonomous status within the newly independent Irish Free State, yet with the proviso that it had the right to opt out— a course of action duly taken later that same year.

Northern Ireland functioned as a relatively peaceful entity under the auspices of the United Kingdom until the Troubles erupted in 1969. Before that, in 1967, the Northern Ireland Civil Rights Association—modelled on the US civil rights movement— spearheaded a campaign of civil resistance to what it saw as anti-Catholic discrimination in housing, employment, policing, and electoral procedures. Within a couple of years, armed paramilitary groups usurped the campaign, calling for an end to British rule in Northern Ireland and the unification of Ireland's 32 counties. During the Troubles, 3,254 people were killed. Finally, in 1994, the IRA announced a ceasefire, its leader Gerry Adams promising peace in our time. The Good Friday Agreement, a multi-party consensus between most political parties in Northern Ireland, was ratified in May 1998.

O

This streamlined account of how Northern Ireland came into being is admittedly light on detail and requires greater exposition. But that's another tome entirely—unravelling such a tangled web is the responsibility of more methodical (and indeed mightier) minds.

The relationship between north and south since the split in 1922 has been contentious or cordial, acrimonious or accommodating. It has always been ambivalent. The Troubles were a constant theme during my childhood in the 1970s and 80s as a native of Mullingar, the main town in the Irish Midlands, and a favourite commuter outpost of Dublin when the Celtic Tiger was at its most bloated. It seemed as though every news bulletin on state broadcaster RTE was helmed by a story detailing the latest atrocity—Derry, Dublin, Monaghan, Eniskillen, Birmingham, Guildford, and on and on. Then there were the hunger strikes by Republican prisoners in 1981, which resulted in the deaths of ten men. Margaret Thatcher, then the incumbent at 10 Downing Street, became the bete noir of not just Irish Republicans but a majority of Irish people—or at least those not of the Loyalist persuasion.

Before the hunger strikes there was, in the south, some empathy with the disenfranchised Catholic minority up north, but such solidarity had been tempered by a philosophy of self-interest, which later became more grotesquely pronounced during the boom period of the 90s and the early 21st century. But the hunger strikes, and especially Thatcher's intransigence, her absolute refusal to negotiate with a body of men that she termed terrorists, revived southern antipathy toward the formerly oppressive neighbours across the water, and for a time stimulated Sands's aspiration for "the rising of the moon" (namely, "the day ... when all the people of Ireland will have the desire for freedom").

Much as with internment in 1971 and Bloody Sunday in 1972—the murder of 13 unarmed civil rights marchers in Derry's Bogside by the First Battalion of the Royal Parachute Regiment, a 14th victim dying several months later from injuries he had received—IRA recruitment arguably received a temporary boost. However, a momentous shift in southern sentiment didn't endure, as we returned to being preoccupied with our own doings, while becoming evermore conditioned to the increasing death toll north of the border. Indeed, those of us in the Republic of Ireland became jaded—probably not unlike those on the English mainland—as paramilitary factions from Nationalist and Loyalist communities fought against each other and among themselves. It was all a bit too barbarian and regressive, an increasingly ugly spectacle that was a stain on Irishness internationally. We were better off washing our hands of "that lot up there". It was, literally, another country.

This was a point reinforced by Mike Nesbitt, leader of the Ulster Unionist Party, whose ex-leader, David Trimble, was one of the chief architects of the Good Friday Agreement.

"Northern Ireland is a country, one of the four constituent countries of the United Kingdom, with whom we share common history, heritage, and culture," he explained, dismissing any historical or cultural connection to the Republic of Ireland. Expanding on the entity of Ulster—which is made up of six counties that belong to Northern Ireland and three counties affiliated to the Republic of Ireland—Nesbitt described "an ancient province which has meaning for me mainly in sporting terms. The three Ulster counties that rest in the Republic use a different currency, and have a foreign feel.

"I can do no better than to quote John Hewitt, that great Ulster poet of the last century, who said, 'Firstly, I am an Ulsterman steeped in the traditions of this place. Secondly, I am Irish, of this Ireland. Thirdly, I am British. And finally, in a more diffuse way, I am European. It may make it easier for you to understand if you remove one of those elements, but if you do, you are no longer describing who I am.' More challenging for Unionists, he went on, 'I always maintained that our loyalties had an order to Ulster, to Ireland, to the British Archipelago, to Europe; and that anyone who skipped a step or missed a link, falsified the total. The Unionists missed out on Ireland; the Northern Nationalists couldn't see the Ulster under their feet; the Republicans missed out both Ulster and the Archipelago; and none gave any heed to Europe at all.'"

For Northern Ireland First Minister Peter Robinson, the entities of Ulster and Northern Ireland were interchangeable.

"Historically, the term Ulster—a half-Germanic and half-Gaelic word—has been applied to various geographical forms—ten, nine, and even two counties. So it has always been a flexible term. The nine-county definition is the most common one. This was actually the definition of Queen Elizabeth I's officials when they formally defined the 32 counties of Ireland [as] the four provinces. When the Ulster Covenant (endorsed by just under half a million men and women from Ulster on 28 September, 1912, in protest against the British government's Third Home Rule Bill proposing the establishment of a Home Rule parliament in Dublin) was signed by Unionists, it was the definition that was used. The official definition of Northern Ireland has always been the six counties of Antrim, Down, Armagh, Fermanagh, Tyrone, and Londonderry.

"However, the difficulty in differentiation between Northern Ireland and Ulster is that all six counties are within the common definition of Ulster, but not all of Ulster is within Northern Ireland. Thus you could legitimately talk about Belfast, Ulster, and Belfast, Northern Ireland … while the new state was not called Ulster, many of the public bodies the Northern Ireland government created were given the name Ulster rather than Northern Ireland. The Cabinet did also consider formally changing its name. In speeches the terms were used interchangeably. There are even simple issues, [such as] that headline writers prefer a six-letter word to two seven-letter words."

The outsider's somewhat simplistic view of Northern Ireland tends to associate Protestantism with Britishness and Catholicism with Irishness. While Robinson agreed that there was a strong correlation between the two, he rejected them as absolutes.

"It was Daniel O'Connell [aka 'The Liberator' or 'The Emancipator', the iconic Irish political leader of the first half of the 19th century, who campaigned for the right for Catholics to sit in Westminster] who first drew the direct connection between religion and identity, in this case between Catholicism and Irishness. Later, with the Gaelic revival, this got added to the list. In British history, Protestantism has played a central role, and is still recognised in the constitution with the Established Church and the Act of Succession.

Indeed, one academic argued that Britishness was built around a Protestant empire and a dislike of the French.

"However, through history there have been those who did not follow the simplistic view. Some have not seen Irishness and Britishness as a choice, but that they can identify with both. This is common in unitary states—you can be Scottish and British. A similar comparison is the strength of state identity in the USA and its co-existence with a strong national identity. It should be noted as well that while religion has declined, the belief or attachment to Britishness and Irishness has continued."

Professor Marianne Elliott, director of Irish Studies at the University of Liverpool, said that while in the past "you could be 70 percent sure" of the Protestant/British and Catholic/Irish characterisation, this had changed since the arrival of peace.

"The Troubles alienated Protestants, and there was a real decline in those accepting Irish identity. Today, far more people would accept both [British and Irish] identities—though still not the politicos—and there is a rise in the number calling themselves Northern Irish, the middle way."

The provision in the Good Friday Agreement that allows Northern Irish citizens to define themselves as Irish, British, or both has, said Mike Nesbitt, "given people the confidence and permission to prioritise their feeling of being of Northern Ireland, Ulster, Britain, and Europe". Elliott considered the provision "a recognition of reality" that has "made it easier for the middle ground, who feel a bit of both". Robinson refused to attach any significance to the provision at all. It wasn't new, he said. "This was the position in Northern Ireland before the Agreement was reached. It was a re-statement of fact."

Clare Bailey of the Green Party of Northern Ireland regarded herself as Northern Irish, even though she thought of it as "a kind of invented, artificial identity. No one really wants us. We are isolated by everyone we are supposed to be connected to: an orphan of the isles." Nesbitt maintained that many Catholics, "perhaps even the majority in Northern Ireland, would vote to keep Northern Ireland in the UK in a border poll".

This appears to be borne out by a 2011 Northern Ireland Life and Times Survey, a rolling record of public opinion that found more than half of Catholics in Northern Ireland—52 percent—want Northern Ireland to remain as part of the United Kingdom long term. This compared with just one in three Catholics who would support a united Ireland. Dr Peter Shirlow, a senior lecturer in law at Queen's University, Belfast, said it wasn't that Northern Irish Catholics "don't feel culturally Irish, but it is a material economic argument for them that this is a better place to live".

It may not be long before Catholics form the majority in Northern Ireland. There are now significantly more Catholics than Protestants in nursery, primary, secondary, and third-level education. Gerry Moriarty, in *The Irish Times* after the publication of the 2011 census findings, wrote, "If that trend continues, and it's difficult to see a reason why it should not, then in another generation or so the majority population should be Catholic or from a Catholic background—people of voting age, most of whose immediate antecedents are Nationalist in their political outlook. The figures clearly indicate shifting religious and political sands in Northern Ireland which First Minister and DUP [Democratic Unionist Party] leader Peter Robinson implicitly acknowledged recently by making a direct pitch to Catholics to hold with the north's union with Britain."

Dr Shirlow believed there was "a growth in people who feel politics is too sectarian or too Nationalist. They are operating a civic-shared identity through their lifestyle. They will socialise together, inter-marry, go to gigs together. They are in many ways—but not completely—sectarian blind, or tradition blind. It was primarily within the Unionist electorate, but from my observations it is starting to grow within the Nationalist community. It is neither Unionist nor Irish, it is identity-less, at most pale orange or green."

Monica McWilliams, co-founder of the Northern Ireland Women's

Coalition with Pearl Sagar, and now Professor of Women's Studies at the University of Ulster, felt more people "have become more comfortable with the term Northern Irish—or is it because the Irish passport is cheaper, and you get more money from the [Republic of Ireland] President if you live to 100 years?!"

Rather than exacerbate the problem of identity, the Good Friday Agreement's acceptance of people's right to be Irish, British, or both had made it easier, McWilliams suggested.

"More people are now carrying both passports. I tried to enshrine this into the Bill of Rights when I was Chief Commissioner [of the Northern Ireland Human Rights Commission], and it is probably one of the few rights that all sides accept as being a basic human right in Northern Ireland. They will contest most other rights, but the right to vote and this right are taken now as given."

Peter Robinson accepted that more people were at ease with being identified as Northern Irish, "in much the same way as Scots being British but also Scottish".

Susan McKay's excellent book, *Northern Protestants: An Unsettled People*, was based on more than 60 in-depth interviews with a wide range of Protestants. It's a candid analysis of a people—McKay's own—that wrestles with the myriad issues Northern Irish Protestants are having to confront since the end of the Troubles and the implementation of the Good Friday Agreement, through the testimonies of victims, perpetrators, and observers of violence. The late David Ervine, visionary leader of the Progressive Unionist Party, hoped that McKay's investigation of the Protestant psyche would "allow people to begin to recognise the degrees of denial that we have of ourselves, which is not shared by others".

Identity is a recurring theme in *Northern Protestants*. David Dunseith hosted *Talk Back* on BBC Radio Ulster for over two decades until 2009 (he retired in May 2011, and died within a month at the age of 76). He talked about how Protestants in the north were "an embattled minority":

"They see that Britain was willing to send a task force to defend the concept of Britishness in the Falkland Islands away off near Argentina. They see the way Britain fights to keep Gibraltar from Spain. And then they listen to the British political leadership saying that Britain has no selfish or strategic interest in remaining in Northern Ireland. They ask, 'What do they care about their kith and kin here a few miles from them?' They fear the imperial power of Rome. They dread the Republic. They feel they are losing everything. It almost reaches the level of hysteria. The sense of identity among Catholics is much stronger."

Mervyn Long, a former soldier in both the British Army and the Ulster Defence Regiment, saw himself as "very, very much Irish. It is crap to say you have to be a Catholic to be Irish". John Gray thought it "an extraordinary reflection on the social strictures of Northern Ireland" that he didn't meet a Catholic until he was 16. Now, when he went to England, he said, "It is not exactly a foreign country, but it is not my country. My imagined identity is Irish, and my desired identity is Irish, but I am very specifically Northern Irish."

Pearl, who described herself as a liberal Unionist, was proud to be Irish and British. "I feel I can be both," she said. "We are going into a more federal sort of United Kingdom anyway." And Ian Young, a Derry businessman, identified himself as Irish, though his Protestant heritage was important to him. "I always thought the Protestants had made a very big contribution to this country," he said. "We are all born innocent. We become victims of our tradition."

For Peter Robinson, identity was a matter of self-definition that could transcend indicators such as faith or geography. "As each identity is defined by the individual, each person will choose different elements to compile their identity. I can make a case for what makes Ulster distinctive geographically, socially, culturally, etc, from elsewhere in Ireland. Many others may share that view, but others may not reach the same conclusion, despite drawing their identity from the same elements."

During the writing of this book, Loyalists took to the streets in violent protest over what they saw as a threat to their identity with the decision to fly the union flag at Belfast City Hall only on designated days. Nationalists had wanted the flag taken down altogether, but they eventually voted in favour of the above compromise proposed by the Alliance Party. The latter bore the brunt of Loyalist discontent. A petrol bomb attack on the office of East Belfast MP Naomi Long was treated as attempted murder by police. There were also attacks on Alliance councillors' homes in Bangor and Newtownards. Old enmities die hard.

A reasonable case could be made for the irrelevance of local or national identity in an increasingly globalised world, although both Robinson and Marianne Elliott refuted this. "Global identities have tended to be over-arching or complementary rather than replacements," said Robinson. "There is nothing to prevent a Northern Irish identity coexisting with a global one. Northern Ireland has a growing British identity. I don't detect any growth or even semblance of a European identity in Northern Ireland. Well, unless one of our local golfers is playing in the Ryder Cup!"

For Elliott, identity in Ireland remained so controversial "that it needs to go through a rethink, a redefinition, before any other identity can realistically be espoused". Not so, according to Gerry Moriarty of *The Irish Times*, who contended that, irrespective of complications in nomenclature, "there is a real sense of a changing Northern Ireland, that there are people here who have resolved or are resolving within themselves the nationalistic conundrums that for centuries caused trouble and discord. Are they Irish, British, or Northern Irish? Some people can manage the trinity of allegiances, some two, some one."

The author Glenn Patterson, a winner of the Rooney Prize for Irish Literature for *Burning Your Own*, his 1988 novel about a young boy coming of age in Belfast before the Troubles, went further than this "trinity of allegiances" outlined by Elliott.

"In my early teens, I would probably have said I was British," he said. "Mind you, my mother always said she was Irish, and as I got to the other end of my teens I was starting to come to the realisation—it took a bit longer to get there—that it wasn't a question of choosing between one and the other, but embracing both together. More than both, actually. I was—am—Irish, British, Northern Irish, European … Finally though, I am from Belfast. I like the word 'citizen'."

The Newtownards-born, Bangor-raised novelist Colin Bateman, whose 14 novels include *Divorcing Jack*, gets the final word on identity, if only because his view encapsulates the absurdity of trying to define such a thing in this troubled outpost of the United Kingdom.

"Van isn't Irish, but very definitely Northern Ireland—and there's a huge difference," he asserted. "He doesn't—despite where he might have ended up—come from a Celtic tradition, and his references and influences are absolutely working class Protestant Belfast. He's not really a product of the Troubles, because he was away before they started. But Northern Ireland relishes its heroes, and they are generally troubled heroes and extreme personalities. If you think of the Protestants who have made it as international stars, they are George Best, alcoholic; 'Hurricane' Higgins, alcoholic; James Galway, ex-Loyalist flute band-member; and even Blair Mayne, one of the founders of the SAS, one of the most significant killing machines of World War Two, and another heavy drinker who killed himself in a drunken car crash. And Van, certainly, is extreme in his own way. We celebrate that.

"Growing up in Northern Ireland, these were our heroes. The Irish Republic was different. Their heroes were Joyce, Yeats, Wilde, all from a literary tradition, which the north just didn't have. Instead, we worshipped sportsmen and singers and warriors. It's worth remembering also that Northern Ireland has an inferiority complex. We generally don't believe that we are good or capable, so when someone does do well, they are immediately lionised and excused bad behaviour. We're also a very negative people. 'No' is a word you hear bandied about—Ulster Says No, No Surrender, etc."

CHAPTER 2
FUNKY NEIGHBOURHOOD

The name Belfast has its origins in the Gaelic Beal Feirste, alternately translated as 'mouth of the sandbars', 'mouth of the sandy ford', or 'mouth of the Farset', because of its position on the old River Farset, a tributary of the River Lagan now contained within a tunnel under the city's High Street. The banks of the Farset became the first quaysides of the developing metropolis, and in the 18th century was one of several Belfast rivers to provide the power for early industrialisation. Benefiting enormously from location, it also gained prominence as one of the world's premier shipbuilding centres.

Belfast's history can actually be traced back as far as the Bronze Age. During the Industrial Revolution, the leading citizens declared it the modern Athens, their civic pride reflected in the construction of lavish buildings, including the Custom House (where Victorian author Anthony Trollope once kept an office), the Grand Opera House, the Ulster Hall, and Queen's University. City Hall—with its great dome, Portland stone façade, and marble halls—was erected to celebrate the granting of city status by Queen Victoria in 1888. Thirty-three years later, Belfast was made capital of Northern Ireland.

East Belfast was subsumed into the city following an extension of the municipal boundary taking in the former townland of Ballymacarrett on the County Down bank of the River Lagan in 1853. The area established pre-eminence with the growth of its shipyards, and contributed further to the success of the burgeoning conurbation with a glassworks, foundry, and ropeworks. The shipyards fostered a closeness among the local community. Thousands of households were brought together at Harland & Wolff, which at its peak had 30,000 employees. The doomed Titanic came out of Harland & Wolff, as did other White Star vessels, Olympic and Britannic. Short Brothers (now known as Bombardier), pioneers in aviation and the company behind the Sunderland flying boat and the Stirling bomber, formed their aircraft factory there in 1936.

The birthplace of *Narnia* author C.S. Lewis, it was also home to football legend George Best and George Ivan Morrison—Van The Man to you and I. Morrison was born at 125 Hyndford Street on August 31 1945, the only child of George, an electrician in the nearby docks, and Violet, a mill worker. The small two-bedroom terraced house was where Violet herself had grown up. A short stroll away is the opulent, tree-lined Cyprus Avenue, immortalised in Morrison's song of the same name on *Astral Weeks*.

"I come from a working-class background," Morrison said in 1993. It is an environment that remains important to him, almost five decades after leaving it—"the source", as he described it to John Bennett in 2012. "You see that when you go away," he said, "I remember going to other places. I always remember being in Greece. I felt really homesick and thought, I need to go back. I went back and I thought, Yeah, this is the source. My source is not, you know, somewhere else. This is it. This is where my source is here."

And what thoughts went through the sixtysomething Morrison's mind as he roamed around the haunts of his formative years—landmarks like Woodcot Avenue, the Gospel Hall, Elmgrove?

"Well, I go back to childhood and beyond, and I go back to what it is now, because it's all in present time. You've got the past, the present, and that's it, because you don't know what the future is. Sometimes you know what you might be doing tomorrow, or your plan [for] next week, but you've just got the past and the present. It's all happening now. It's like in the poem I wrote … I wrote a poem called 'On Hyndford Street'. It's all in that."

This poem is actually a song on his 1991 double-album, *Hymns To The Silence*. Over Derek Bell's meditative synthesizer accompaniment,

Morrison spirits himself back to Hyndford Street, where the silence was tangible on long summer nights, the wireless tuned to Radio Luxembourg, the voices whispered across Beechie River. On sunny afternoons, he walked up Cherry Valley from the North Road Bridge, picking apples that spilled onto the railway tracks from the gardens of the posh dwellings on Cyprus Avenue. He caught the bus to Holywood, went down to the seaside, stopping off at Fusco's for ice cream. There was laughter and music and singing, jazz and blues, Debussy. And reading—tomes on Jelly Roll Morton, Big Bill Broonzy, 'Mezz' Mezzrow's *Really The Blues*, Jack Kerouac's Zen novel *The Dharma Bums*. Mostly, Hyndford Street meant "feeling wondrous", alight inside, possessed of "a sense of everlasting life".

If the Van Morrison of 'Astral Weeks'—the opening track on the album of the same name—feels like "a stranger in this world", he belongs on Hyndford Street, the place of his awakening. This isn't a nostalgia trip. His reflections aren't mawkish—they're too rooted in ordinary experience—yet they convey a sense of rapture that you feel Morrison has never recaptured as an adult being. The world beyond Hyndford Street—a world of backbiters, copycats, hustlers, ignoramuses; a world of alienation—is a crushing disappointment by comparison. It's on Hyndford Street that the essence of Van Morrison can truly be found. Here, he is a man-child all caught up in the amazement of discovery.

Morrison's father, of Scottish stock but raised on Lord Street, was a man of few words, completely irreligious—the polar opposite to his wife, an ebullient character who liked to sing and tap dance. While she joined the Jehovah's Witnesses at a point in Morrison's childhood, she wasn't, he claimed, that religious.

"She was a free-thinker," he said in 1997. Morrison's father, meanwhile, was an atheist. As a consequence, his religious sense didn't come from the church but from music—specifically gospel music. His was a much more universal spirituality.

"When I was young in Belfast, I saw so many Catholics and

Protestants for whom religion was a burden. There was enormous pressure and you had to belong to one or the other community. Thank God my parents were strong enough not to give in to this pressure."

Rather than a burden, Peter Robinson saw Protestantism—and indeed Catholicism—as "very strong forces in our society" at that time. "Attendance at Sunday school and church were the norm," he said. "Midweek mission meetings would have been part of the weekly social calendar. In working class communities, the evangelical mission halls would have been a significant presence."

East Belfast was staunchly evangelical territory during the 40s and 50s, but it hadn't yet been overtly infected by the disease of sectarianism that became viral throughout the Troubles, as Paul Bew, Professor of Irish Politics at Queen's University, explained.

"When Van was growing up, East Belfast was distinctive politically in that it was represented by Labour in the Northern Ireland Parliament, and leaned toward a progressive, secular—at least by Northern Irish standards—culture. The school he was at [Orangefield School for Boys], the local football team, all operated in this context. In other words, while the constituency was Unionist and Protestant, it was somewhat removed from the normal Unionist/Protestant, Nationalist/Catholic divide in the rest of Northern Ireland. Morrison is inexplicable, unless one understands that he emerges from this culture of relative openness."

Yet according to Peter Robinson, a young Protestant man growing up in East Belfast during the 1950s would have identified himself, in order, as "British, Ulsterman, and Protestant". While Morrison himself conceded that East Belfast then was "totally Protestant", with only a handful of Catholics, "there wasn't any problems, there wasn't any friction or anything like that".

In 1972, he told John Grissim of *Rolling Stone*, "I wasn't even aware of religious prejudice until one day a couple of kids I'd never seen before came up to me and two friends and started swinging. They were going around punching out Catholics. Or Protestants. I

31

forget. It was weird, 'cos at the same time we were fighting them, we were asking why they were trying to beat up on us. They stopped when we said we weren't whoever they thought we were. The whole thing was unreal. I really feel for what the people are going through over there [in Belfast]."

George and Violet's boy had no truck with prejudice, even rebuffing an approach to join the Orange Order as a teen. The Order, a Protestant fraternal organisation dedicated to making "a stand for truth in an age of sectarianism ... to defend our culture and traditions", has strong links with Unionism. Critics say it is triumphalist, and make comparisons with the Ku Klux Klan, American advocates of white supremacy. Brian Dooley described the Order as "so bare-faced and confident enough in the bigoted status quo that they wore bowler hats and sashes rather than white robes and painted hoods".

An academic survey of 1,500 Orangemen, conducted by Professor Jon Tonge of Liverpool University in 2011, revealed that some 60 percent thought "most Catholics are IRA sympathisers". Only six percent of respondents would be happy for their son or daughter to marry a Catholic, while more than half of those polled agreed that the Order was anti-Catholic. Professor Tonge described his findings as "depressing" and "outdated". The views of Orange Order members, according to the report, "are infused by a conservative social outlook, regular religious worship and a sense of cultural and religious threat. Almost two-thirds of Orange Order members claim that religion is more important than politics, and the themes of religion and constitutional defence are intertwined to produce a cautious political outlook, which opposes Catholic political and religious encroachment. For many Orange Order members, Republicans have merely changed tactics, but the political basis of the previous 'war' remains unchanged". In this context, "a discourse of 'siege' and 'need for vigilance' remains apparent within the Order". Members' main concern was to bring a halt to what they saw "as the removal of symbols of British faith and culture".

"When I was growing up in Belfast, I was lucky, because I knew all kinds of people," said Morrison. "I wasn't on any side when I grew up, so consequently I never really thought about it. I never had any of the ingrained hatred inside of me. I was conscious of it in other people, but that was very foreign to me."

He did listen to gospel, but that had nothing to do with religion. As a kid, Van "couldn't get plugged in. I went once or twice to Bible class, but there was no singing there anyway. I just never got into it. I went with my mother to a faith healing thing once, but that just turned me off. There was a lot of fear".

Novelist Glenn Patterson, whose fiction is predominantly an aperture for the Protestant experience in Northern Ireland, found it depressing that religion has "bled into so many other aspects of our lives, so that your religion at birth is still a fairly reliable indicator of everything from the football team you support to the party you vote for. And then you have to accept that many of our big social occasions are inflected by religion, the 12th being the obvious one, although for me, especially as a teenager, it was the 11th night that was the highlight—bonfires and illicit alcohol and '12th kisses'. That said, I think a great many people—and I could include myself in this as I got older—lived in at least two worlds at once. Many interests, music being an obvious one, were independent of that faith-fellows worldview. I am struck by the fact that not only did many of the Them-era R&B bands come from East Belfast, but a large number of the punk bands did too.

"If religion was an ever-present cloud—or a cloud you could always see coming, as you can see the cloud on summer days massing on Black Mountain—then there was an awful lot going on beneath it."

○

Ballymena is 24 miles and half an hour's drive from Belfast. A mainly Protestant town, it was where the actor, Liam Neeson, a Catholic, grew up in the 50s and 60s. Looking back on that time, he recalled "very,

very happy memories", with "no feeling of opposites" in his immediate community.

"We were working class, quite poor, as was everybody in our street. There were Protestants; there were two or three Catholics living there. As kids, July 12 was still a festive occasion. We weren't excluded, because all our mates were Protestants. It never entered my mind, that whole political side, as a child.

"My grandfather had a pub in the middle of the town called the Coronation Bar. We used to go there and lean out the windows and see the bands marching on July 12. Pipe bands, you name it— extraordinary bands. It was real exciting."

July 12, popularly known as the Glorious 12th or Orangemen's Day, is a yearly celebration of Protestant King William Of Orange's victory over Catholic King James II at the Battle of the Boyne in 1690. It became a particularly divisive date during the Troubles, with the Orange Order exploiting the occasion as an opportunity to stoke up virulent anti-Catholic rhetoric.

Now living in and a naturalised citizen of the United States, Neeson is one of Hollywood's most bankable box-office stars, having appeared in the likes of *Schindler's List*, *Michael Collins*, *Star Wars*, and the *Taken* franchise. Yet for all of the commercial success and critical plaudits that he has enjoyed during a career spanning some five decades, being afforded the freedom of Ballymena in 2013 was, you sense, an honour that meant just as much, if not more, to him. Only three people had previously been given such recognition—the Reverend Ian Paisley, rugby legend Syd Millar, and former Mayor Sandy Spence. Neeson was actually proposed for the award in 2000, but the proposal was withdrawn following an objection from Democratic Unionist Party councillors over remarks he had made to an American magazine about being made to feel like a second class citizen as a Catholic youngster in Ballymena, and how he was compelled to stay indoors during the Orange parades on July 12. Obviously stung by the snub, Neeson wrote to the local council to emphasise his pride in his "upbringing in and association with the town and my country of birth, which I will continue to promote at every opportunity. Indeed, I regard the enduring support over the years from all sections of the community in Ballymena as being more than sufficient recognition for any success which I may have achieved as an actor".

Talking down the phone from New York a couple of weeks after being feted by Ballymena, Neeson's gratification with the accolade was still palpable.

"My town is extraordinary. My mate is the Lord Mayor, a Catholic. It's changed. I was sitting at a table with Ian Paisley and his wife, and his son, Ian Jr, was there. Changed times. I'm very proud of that. I helped Ian on with his coat, wished him well. We posed for photographs. God, how things change."

Here's a curious fact: Paisley, for so long the bogeyman of many Irish Catholics/Nationalists/Republicans north and south of the border, played an unsuspectingly influential role in Neeson's decision to become an actor.

"When I was a younger, a couple of times I crept in to his—I don't know what you'd call it—church or place in Ballymena just to see him. He was an amazing orator, full of fire and brimstone. He was a big man with this huge voice. He was powerful; he was riveting. He's like something out of some fucking weird novel."

Glenn Patterson was raised in the 60s on the Erinvale housing estate in Finaghy, a southern suburb of Belfast, built at the same time as Orangefield in the east and by the same developer.

"My parents had emigrated to Canada in the 1950s—all my brothers were born there—and came back because they had heard things were 'looking up' at home," he said. "Belfast could be bleak and grimy—my mum's family are all Shankill and Woodvale, so I was familiar with the Victorian industrial landscape—and the weather was then as the weather is now: a defiance of supposed seasonal norms. But I do think there was something going on then: a sense of possibility, perhaps, which is not to be confused with a widespread acceptance of the Unionist government. I think you see it in the buildings of that late 1950s, early 1960s period, in the housing estates themselves, poorly served though many of them were—my own included—by shops and buses."

Patterson's novel *The International*, which he wrote in the 90s, is set in the Belfast hotel of the title in January 1967, on the eve of the first meeting of the Northern Ireland Civil Rights Association.

"On the evening before that meeting, the leader of the Nationalist Party in Northern Ireland, Eddie McAteer, was addressing a meeting in Cork and spoke of 'a faint feeling of lightness in the air' up north. I liked that, and I think that faint feeling of lightness has sometimes been written out of the narrative."

O

Morrison started school in 1950 at Elmgrove Primary. It was here that he interchanged his first and middle names and became known as Ivan. An isolationist young boy, he was given to the occasional astral projection—he saw things.

"I can never remember talking about it with anyone when I was a child," he said in 1985. "It was something I kept to myself because I didn't feel there was even the possibility of talking to anyone about this. I also didn't really feel the need. All I was interested in was somewhere to put my experiences."

He wasn't alone among his contemporaries in having visions—Bob Dylan and Patti Smith had similar experiences as kids. The poet and artist William Blake (very much a touchstone for Morrison) encountered a tree "filled with angels, bright angelic wings bespangling every bough like stars" as a child on Peckham Rye, London, according to his first biographer, Alexander Gilchrist.

The artistic antennae seem to be particularly attuned to the possibility of such apparitions. Irish singer-songwriter Damien Dempsey—part-Bob Marley, part-Luke Kelly (the late frontman of legendary folkies The Dubliners)—admitted to me in a 2012 interview that he has seen "some beautiful things" both while meditating and swimming in the sea off Howth Head in Dublin.

"When I hit that sea water, I feel really spiritual," he said. "I've seen things, had little glimpses of things. Things I can't explain, feelings. I've gotten these five-minute blasts of euphoria for no reason. It's like someone trying to tell you something, like a message trying to get through to you, telling you it's going to be OK.

"I've had little tiny visions. I've disregarded them for years. If you say anything to people, they think you're lying or you're fucking mad. People can be closed minded, so I keep it to myself mostly."

The post-Second World War environment in Belfast, like most of Europe, was a place of austerity. Food and clothing was rationed, while queues formed for utility goods. In the liner notes that accompany *The McPeake Family Of Belfast*, folk outfit The McPeakes painted a less than alluring picture of a city that was "bleak, grimy ... windswept and cheerless in the winters, and wet and cloud-hung in the summers". Yes, the countryside around it was "a beautiful landscape of small farms and rolling hills, with the coast and mountains not far away, but Belfast seems itself apart from the beauty, as it huddles against its riverside tangle of shipyard building cranes. Its only picturesque neighbourhoods are the slums behind Sandy Row. If it were not for Belfast's people, both Irish and Scottish, there would be as little music in its streets as there is in Birmingham or Liverpool".

George Morrison left for America in the early 50s to find work. He ended up on the railroad in Detroit. "He went to check things out," said Morrison. "Later, he was supposed to bring the rest of the family over, but it didn't work out."

George's record collection was the talk of Belfast—well, Hyndford Street at least. Originally a fan of big bands and swing, he went on to consummate his love of Americana with country (Hank Williams, Jimmie Rodgers), gospel (Mahalia Jackson, Sister Rosetta Tharpe), jazz (Charlie Parker, Louis Armstrong), and blues and R&B (Lead Belly, Muddy Waters).

"I was lucky to grow up in a time and a place where a lot of people had music," Morrison told *Mojo* in 2006. "My dad had records, and my friends did too. Plus, people around me were always playing music of their own. It was nothing out of the ordinary to be surrounded by music … I grew up listening to Hank [Williams] and then to Webb Pierce—I think he influenced me the most—Ray Price, Faron Young, and The Browns, who had a song called 'Looking Back To Sea'. And Jimmie Rodgers, of course—he was actually the first person that I heard."

George subscribed to *Jazz Journal* and tuned the radio to AFN, the American Forces Network in Germany. One night, Van was lying in bed, after midnight, when he heard 'What'd I Say' and "just knew it was Ray Charles", even though he'd never heard anything by him before.

Charles became a touchstone to Morrison the younger. He bought a copy of *Ray Charles Live At Newport* in McBurneys, a Belfast treasure trove of US imports. It became "like the Bible" to him.

Down the street from the Morrisons was a saxophonist, George Cassidy, who mimicked the style of Lester Young. There was a guy who played guitar and knew every Hank Williams song, and another guy well versed in obscure Appalachian folk music. Others had classic country records. So Van was exposed to a pretty eclectic mix of music in this small pocket of East Belfast coming up—a fact he didn't think unusual until discovering, later on, that this wasn't the experience of many people.

The first record he ever bought was 'Hootin' Blues' by Sonny Terry. "It cost 1/6d in Smithfield," he told John Kelly in *The Irish Times*. "I think the shop was called Smith's. There were rows and rows of records there. And I got my first guitar in Smithfield too—it must have been in Joe Kavanagh's place. It was called I Buy Anything."

When talking to Happy Traum for *Rolling Stone* in 1970, Morrison emphasised Belfast's separateness from both the rest of the United Kingdom and Ireland.

"Memphis Slim has been in Belfast. Jesse Fuller, Champion Jack Dupree—John Lee Hooker's been there," he enthused. "They've got folk clubs and rock clubs there, but it's got nothing to do with the English scene. In fact, I'd go so far as to say it doesn't have much to do with the Irish scene either. It's just Belfast. It's got its own identity, its own people. It's just a different race, a different breed of people."

Morrison came up in "a pretty funky neighbourhood … a white collar district" where "people weren't involved in any other place but Belfast". If George was the primary source of his son's obsession with the sounds of America, Violet imbued him with a sense of Irishness through the songs of traditional players like The McPeake Family from Antrim, Na Fili from Cork, and John McCormack from Westmeath. Mick Cox, a guitarist who first worked with Morrison in 1967 and appeared on his later albums *Common One* and *Poetic Champions Compose*, was impressed by Violet's "incredible knowledge of Irish music".

The McPeakes are renowned for their arrangement of the Scottish lament, 'Wild Mountain Thyme' (also known as 'Purple Heather' and 'Will Ye Go Lassie, Go'), one of the most successful songs to emerge from the folk revival of the 50s. Their combination of close harmony singing, accompanied by pipes and harp, proved an influence on groups such as Planxty and Horslips in the 70s. But it was the tenor McCormack whom Violet championed on the informal sing-alongs she hosted at 125 Hyndford Street, leading the assembled throng through 'I'll Take You Home Again, Kathleen', 'Danny Boy', 'She Moved Through The Fair', and 'Star Of The County Down'. These last two songs were covered by Morrison with The Chieftains on their collaborative album, *Irish Heartbeat*.

"Relatives would come around on a Saturday evening," Morrison remembered. "They'd go to a club first and then come back and have a few drinks and sing songs. My mother sang, played piano and harmonica."

John McCormack was born in Athlone, a provincial market and garrison town in the Irish Midlands, on June 14 1884. Music was a feature of his home life from a young age, and the remarkable qualities of his voice earned him a gold medal at the 1903 Dublin Feis Ceoil—a cultural festival of song and dance—and brought him to the attention of James Joyce, who himself had ambitions to be a singer, and who gives McCormack a mention in *Ulysses*. A year later, McCormack's voice led him to Milan, to be trained by Maestro Vincenzo Sabatini. After hearing McCormack's audition, Sabatini informed his new charge, "I can do little except teach you how to use your voice properly. God has done all the rest."

McCormack made his operatic debut at Covent Garden, London, in a 1906 production of Pietra Mascagni's *Cavalleria Rusticana*. Further operatic engagements followed in New York, Chicago, and Boston, and there was an Australian tour in 1911. He quit the opera stage to begin a second career as a concert singer—appearances which were enhanced by some 541 recordings, many of them ballads and sentimental Irish airs. According to Gordon Ledbetter, author of *The Great Irish Tenor*, a large swathe of McCormack's audience "wanted to hear him in little else, and few singers have approached the freshness and enchantment of his singing of Irish songs". McCormack was the first artist to record 'It's A Long Way To Tipperary' (in 1914), and also sang songs expressive of Irish Nationalism, one of which, 'The Wearing Of The Green', about the Irish rebellion of 1798, became an unofficial anthem for the Home Rule lobby.

He sang with operatic luminaries such as Nellie Melba, Geraldine Farran, and Luisa Tettrazini, as well as crooner Bing Crosby, counted the great Enrico Caruso among his admirers, and was granted American citizenship in 1919. "This and his support of the cause of Irish independence annoyed some early British admirers," writes Peter Costello in *The Irish 100: A Ranking Of The Most Influential Irish Men And Women Of All Time*, a list that includes a certain Van Morrison. "However, this did not seem to affect his general popularity when he returned to England in the 1920s and during World War Two he injured his health by singing at Red Cross concerts, at one of which he collapsed."

A devout Catholic, McCormack was made a Papal Count by Pope Pius XI in 1928 for his charitable efforts in several countries. He had earlier received three Papal knighthoods: Knight of the Order of the Holy Sepulchre, Knight of the Order of St Gregory the Great, and Knight of the Order of St Sylvester.

Music and faith came together in 1932 on the occasion of the Eucharistic Congress, a gathering of clergy, religious, and members of the laity to bear witness to the real presence of Jesus in the Eucharist, an important Catholic doctrine. McCormack sang Cesar Franck's 'Panis Angelicus' at the outdoor mass in Phoenix Park, Dublin, before a million-strong crowd and worldwide radio and cinema audiences. It was a pivotal moment. He died on September 16 1945.

A few days after his passing, McCormack's widow Lily discovered the following words in a notebook: "I live again the days and evenings of my long career. I dream at night of operas and concerts in which I have had my share of success. Now like the old Irish Minstrels, I have hung up my harp because my songs are all sung."

American music critic Max de Schauensee described McCormack as "truly a singer for the people" and "the surest technician".

"Like Caruso," de Schauensee continued, "he had a forthright charm that, free of any complications, made its effect with a minimum of time and effort. People who listened to McCormack were drawn to him. Let us call this personal magnetism. We are apt to refer to people we are drawn to as 'warm' or 'genuine'. McCormack was just that. Even when he was singing in a huge auditorium, he always gave me the sensation of person-to-person intimacy.

"McCormack had a sense of the power of language such as few singers have possessed. In this he was like the bards of ancient Ireland. He could tell a story. He could paint pictures. His enunciation was so clear that every syllable reached the last row of listeners."

English critic Ernest Newman was equally generous in extolling McCormack's virtues.

"He was a supreme example of the art that conceals art, the sheer hard work that becomes manifest only in its results, not in the revolting machinery that has produced them. He never stooped to small and modest things; he invariably raised them and with them the most sophisticated listener, to his own high level. I never knew him in his public or his private singing, to be guilty of a lapse of taste, of making an effect for mere effect's sake. He was a patrician artist, dignified even in apparent undress, with a respect for art that is rarely met with among tenors. There is no one to take his place."

O

While McCormack undoubtedly made an impression on Morrison the younger, it was a former convict turned iconic folk and blues musician—and virtuoso of the 12-string guitar—who exerted a greater influence. Huddie William Leadbetter, aka Lead Belly, was born on a plantation in Louisiana and brought up in Texas. As a teenager, he did time with a chain gang for the offence of carrying a pistol. In 1918, he began a seven-year sentence for killing a relative, Will Stafford, in a fight over a woman. Five years after his release, Lead Belly was back behind bars for attempted homicide. It was while in Angola Prison Farm, Louisiana, that he met folklorists John Lomax and his son, Alan. They recorded him singing 'Goodnight Irene' for the American Library of Congress. A free man again, Lead Belly joined the Lomaxes as their driver and assisted them in their folk-collecting through the southern states. He was, in a sense, the conduit through which the aforementioned 'Goodnight Irene', along with 'Midnight Special', 'The Bourgeois Blues', 'Where Did You Sleep Last Night?', and countless others became standards.

"My major influence was Lead Belly," Morrison said in 1970. "If it wasn't for him, I may never have been here." He has often credited Lead Belly with inspiring him to pick up the guitar as a kid, even though the instrument was anything but cool in the 50s.

"I can remember when I started playing, there weren't any guitars around, apart from on the records by Lead Belly, Josh White, Sonny

Terry and Brownie McGhee," he told Paul Lewis for *Now Dig This* in 1991. "You never really heard guitar. You saw it on television—somebody like Ivor Mairants, or you saw people like Elton Hayes. And there were some comedians who played guitar—like I saw Max Wall play guitar once. But it wasn't 'in' then by any means."

Folk music, said Morrison, was "your entrance into playing guitar", but "it wasn't something that was everywhere—not where I was. You couldn't just walk in and hear it, as you walk in and hear rock'n'roll later on, when the guitar became fashionable and all the teenagers were getting the records."

He listened to folk singers like Rory McEwen, who appeared on television "every night when I was a kid" and would often perform Lead Belly songs.

"That's when I became interested in it," he continued. "That was a key factor … I was planning to be a folk singer. When I was still in school, I actually had an audition with the BBC on Ormeau Road. I don't know what happened to the tape, but I never heard anything. That was it. That was the end of my folk singer career."

It was skiffle protagonist Lonnie Donegan who, in the UK and Ireland, "brought the guitar in". Skiffle—a hotchpotch of jazz, blues, folk, and other roots forms using homemade or improvised instruments—may have been the hep new craze sweeping across the UK in 1956, but to Morrison it was merely the diversification of a source to which he was already connected.

"For me, skiffle tapped into the Lead Belly thing," he told *Uncut* magazine in 2005. "When Lonnie Donegan started coming out with versions of Lead Belly songs, that's when it all kicked in for me." Donegan, Morrison said, never received his due as a singer or as a guitarist. "He could do more with three chords than most people could do with 50 chords. People tend to dismiss skiffle as DIY music. It can be that. It all depends who's doing it. Skiffle stands on its own. It was never a poor cousin to rock'n'roll. America never produced anything that was close to Donegan."

The Scottish-born Donegan was part of Ken Colyer's Jazzmen. He would entertain audiences during intervals at Jazzmen gigs, playing Lead Belly and Woody Guthrie songs accompanied by a washboard, a tea-chest bass, and a cheap Spanish guitar. Donegan had a huge hit in 1956 with his version of 'Rock Island Line', another Lead Belly favourite. Four years later, he shifted a quarter of a million copies of 'My Old Man's A Dustman', something of a novelty song on which Donegan came over as a diamond geezer, a cheeky chappie—a cuddly sprite, if you will. This was all artifice, according to Patrick Humphries, author of *Lonnie Donegan & The Birth Of British Rock & Roll*, who attaches words like negative, prickly, rude, difficult, mean, moany, suspicious, and bitter to his subject's persona. The late jazzman and surrealist George Melly found him "incredibly big-headed, conceited, arrogant, and patronising". Morrison, though, never forgot Donegan's formative influence on him.

"Van always spoke fondly of Lonnie," Humphries told me, "[and] always cited Lead Belly as 'the' influence. While I was talking to musicians for my book, whether it was Brian May, Dave Cousins, Mark Knopfler, or Bill Wyman, they all testified that it was Lonnie who first made them aware of Lead Belly—and Hank Williams, The Carter Family, Hank Snow, and Woody Guthrie. So Van would have been aware of Lonnie since he was a teenager."

In later years, Morrison organised a tribute concert to Donegan, and recorded an album with him, *The Skiffle Sessions—Live In Belfast 1998*, also featuring Chris Barber and Dr John. Not that Donegan was enamoured with the results, feeling the album "too rough for public consumption", according to Humphries. "Occasionally, he became exasperated with his singing partner and could be heard at the bar pointing out that Morrison would never have had a career were it not for his pioneering work."

Despite the Glaswegian's conceit, Morrison knew there was at least a semblance of truth in his words, lauding him as "a man we're all in debt to" and declaring that Donegan "started the ball rolling" when presenting him with an Ivor Novello Lifetime Achievement Award in 1994.

"Aside from the truculence, which those who knew them both commented on, both had a real appreciation of musical history," said Humphries. "One thing which came across while I was researching my book, or talking to Lonnie, was his knowledge of the music he helped popularise. And this was, of course, in a pre-internet era. His research—and Van's only a few years later—was scouring record libraries, music papers, or talking to those with firsthand memories of the music they admired. Both men managed a unique fusion of music—today, what they call Americana. It draws on folk, blues, a hint of jazz, country … in Donegan's hands that became skiffle. Then Van took it one step further, particularly on that fabulous run of albums, *Astral Weeks* to *Veedon Fleece*, where he forged that incredible stylistic hybrid.

"Both men were pioneers. And the fact that Van effectively paid for the Donegan revival, with *The Skiffle Sessions* album, testified to Lonnie's influence. Both men drew from that deep, rich well of American music, but managed to infuse it with their own inimitable style. The one piece of music which came as a revelation to me while I was writing my book, was Lonnie's take on 'Ain't No More Cane On The Brazos'. I was familiar with it from Dylan's 1975 *Basement Tapes*, but hearing Lonnie's much earlier version was a revelation—such an impassioned, powerful performance from a Glaswegian cockney between pantomime appearances!"

Chris Barber saw similarities between Donegan and Morrison's personalities. "Lonnie was difficult, though," he told Humphries, "because like Van Morrison, he's inarticulate at explaining things to people." It was inevitable that the two grumpy old men would eventually have a falling out, which, according to Humphries's book, they did when Van told his senior, "You're a good singer, Donegan, but you're not a star." Donegan reportedly never spoke to him again. He died in 2002.

It wasn't only Morrison who dug the new skiffle breed—an early incarnation of The Beatles, The Quarrymen, was formed by John Lennon in Liverpool the same year.

"Everybody was in a skiffle group," George Harrison, who joined the band in 1958, would later recall. "All you needed was an acoustic guitar, a washboard with thimbles for percussion, and a tea-chest—the ones they used to ship from India. You just put a broom handle on it and a bit of string, and you had a bass. You only needed two chords."

Morrison formed his own skiffle outfit, The Sputniks, in the summer of 1957. The line-up featured his nextdoor neighbour, Walter Blakely, along with Gil Irvine—who, using lead pipe retrieved from the nearby Beechie River, invented a woodwind instrument known as the zobo—plus Billy Ruth and John McCullough. They played youth clubs, Women's Institute meetings, wedding receptions, church fetes, parties, and talent contests.

In 1959, Morrison drafted in singer-guitarist Bill Dunn in a bid to stretch The Sputniks—now renamed Midnight Special, according to Clinton Heylin, author of *Can You Feel The Silence? Van Morrison: A New Biography*—beyond the musical parameters of skiffle. It didn't make any difference. To local followers, they were still skiffle.

The story goes that Morrison began learning the saxophone after he was rejected by Deanie Sands & The Javelins, featuring Evelyn Boucher on vocals. When Boucher moved on to other things, the band became The Thunderbolts, an instrumental outfit, and Morrison was invited to join, brass instrument in tow. "I decided I wanted a sax when I heard Jimmy Giuffre doing 'The Train And The River," he said.

In 1986, Morrison told Mick Brown that he was 15 when his career as a professional musician began. "It started off as playing hospital stage productions and dances—local dances and local halls. One gig was the Brookeborough Hall. I remember we played there on Saturday nights. It was the Sandown Road in Belfast. Then there was a place on Chamberlain Street, the Hull."

The band, which according to Morrison had "all sorts of names, depending on which way the wind was blowing", played chart material of the day by Johnny Kidd & The Pirates, The Shadows, Cliff Richard, and Jerry Lee Lewis.

"It was mainly Jerry Lee, actually," he recalled. "I remember doing 'A Whole Lot Of Shakin'. That was a big one. We did some of the more esoteric type things that Jerry Lee did, because he put out a lot of singles then. I mean, it was practically a new single every couple of months from him. You really couldn't have played blues then. I think we did about one blues number."

○

Throughout this early period of Morrison's maturation as a musician, he was a fairly average pupil at Orangefield School for Boys, supposedly the jewel in the crown of Belfast Local Education Authority's experiment to provide more expansive, modern facilities for the city's increasing numbers of schoolchildren.

"The development of the Orangefield school site is a courageous venture," *The Belfast Newsletter* declared. "It means that thousands of children in the densely populated and rapidly growing district of East Belfast will have all the education the state can provide … on their doorsteps. Not only that, but on the vast site they will eventually have more playing space than their predecessors ever enjoyed."

Among his teachers at Orangefield was David Hammond, who went on to become a folk singer, guitarist, and collector of considerable repute. Hammond, who died in 2008, told Van biographer Johnny Rogan that he knew little of Morrison in those days, and that no other teacher "had striking memories of him".

"He slipped through school without making much impression," Hammond told Steve Turner. "I say that out of admiration rather than criticism. If he'd listened to people like me, he would never have written a line. He believed in nobody but himself."

Another unnamed teacher identified Van's vocal prowess early on,

47

predicting that he would eventually carve a career out of singing. Morrison had other ideas.

"I wanted to be a vet," he insisted in 2012. "And I was quite good at football, too. But one of the teachers at my school knew I'd be a singer before I did. I was about 15 and he pointed to me and said, 'This guy's gonna be a singer!' I think he heard me in a skiffle group at a school concert and he must have had some insight."

Morrison didn't engage with academia. The curriculum certainly wouldn't have satisfied his callow libertarianism, with its emphasis on all things British and its neglect of Irish culture.

"I didn't study poetry or read Irish writers," he said. "We didn't get Irish writers at school. All we got was Shakespeare, no Irish writers. There wasn't one book by an Irish writer in our school."

So while W.B. Yeats and Patrick Kavanagh are two names often mentioned in the same breath as Morrison, they had no bearing on his writing style whatsoever, because he never read them as a youngster learning his craft. The only way he could relate to them later was as other writers.

"I was just writing these songs instinctively," he told Victoria Clarke, "and then I read other things where people were making references, saying, 'This is sort of Yeatsian,' and I would go, 'Really?' Because I didn't know. I'd never read him. So I would go out and get Yeats and see, but I hadn't read him until I saw this article. Or some would say it was Joycean, so I would think, oh well, I must check Joyce out."

Peter Robinson confirmed that exposure to Ireland and Irish culture was limited when he was a lad.

"Most communication was face-to-face, and most areas were divided along religious lines, therefore exposure would not have been commonplace for an East Belfast Protestant. However, in rural Ulster this would not have been the case, as neighbours helped neighbours and children attended the closest school rather than the school of their faith."

Liam Neeson claimed to have read all of the major Irish

playwrights at school, along with the poetry of W.B. Yeats. His mother was a native of County Waterford, and he spent many summers in his boyhood there. As an amateur boxer from the age of 11, he regularly travelled down south to take part in competitions at Dublin's National Stadium.

"We'd be brought to the Garden of Remembrance, big tricolours, a couple of museums. I guess it was different. But I was very slow on the uptake, very slow in finding out about these revolutionary heroes from 1916 and stuff. I had, I guess, a very cocooned life. It revolved around school, the church—I was an altar boy—boxing and then eventually amateur drama."

Keith Donald, saxophonist with Moving Hearts, attended Methodist College—alias Methody—in Belfast. He remembered one particular history lesson when he was about 14.

"The teaching of the history of Ireland stopped at 1908. I asked why. The teacher blushed and stammered that that was what the curriculum dictated. When I arrived in Dublin in 1963 to go to Trinity [College], I wasn't aware of Irish geography, history, music, literature, and language."

As a youngster in the 60s, Glenn Patterson got his southern Irish fix mostly through song.

"My parents would have friends around, and there would be singing. My dad was known for singing 'Kevin Barry'. He didn't sing it mockingly, or ironically, and it was received with the same appreciation as the other ballads and standards that were the singsong's fare—there was respect for the song well sung."

In 1920, Kevin Barry was the first Irish Republican executed by the British since the leaders of the Easter Rising in 1916, for his part in an IRA operation that resulted in the deaths of three soldiers. Under torture, he refused to inform on his comrades. His death, at the age of 18, is regarded by historians as a watershed in the Ireland's fight for independence from Britain. It outraged public opinion at home and around the world because of his youth. Attempts were made by American and Vatican officials in Rome to secure a reprieve for him, but to no avail.

His killing, and the death by hunger strike several days earlier of Terence MacSwiney, the Republican Lord Mayor of Cork, precipitated an escalation in violence during Ireland's War of Independence. A celebrated Irish Republican martyr, Barry is immortalised in the ballad, 'Kevin Barry', with its avowed determination to liberate Ireland from Britain at all costs: "Lads like Barry will free Ireland / For her sake they'll live and die." It has been performed by Paul Robeson, Leonard Cohen, The Clancys, and The Dubliners.

"Outside the house, in contrast, as I got older, as the 1970s progressed, anything suggestive of Irish culture would have been regarded with suspicion, if not outright hostility," said Patterson.

○

Meanwhile, Morrison completed the Junior Technical Certificate, the most basic qualification available. "There was no school for people like me," he later boasted. "I educated myself."

To appease his parents, he set about finding a job—first alongside George at Harland & Wolff, then as an apprentice engineer at Musgrave & Co. There were also spells as a meat cleaner, chemist's assistant, and window cleaner—the latter immortalised in 'Cleaning Windows' from *Beautiful Vision*, a song that namechecks his shammy-wielding colleague, Sam Woodburn, a giant Teddy Boy with a proclivity for dressing in a kneelength drape coat and brothel creepers.

Really, Morrison was just biding his time. The music wouldn't let him alone, wouldn't give his head peace. His next move would take him into the twilight world of the showbands.

CHAPTER 3

KEEP IT SIMPLE, STUPID

Bob Geldof, a voluble spokesman on most things since his virtual canonisation post-*Live Aid*, described it as "a musical desert" inhabited by "crap" bands. Such disdain is not only the default position of an old punk rocker—albeit one for whom the transition to establishment figure appeared to cause barely a ripple of idealistic self-reproach—it is also a little unfair. The era of the Irish showbands has been much maligned by more measured critics than the scruffy-arsed former Boomtown Rats frontman.

Whatever the criticism of its human jukebox format, or its association with a backward Ireland—these were the days before we became, for a time, the coolest (and among the most affluent) people on the planet, which themselves were the days before the money and attention sent us pure wild and we ended up going to Brussels on bended knee, cap in hand, begging our prudent European peers for a few quid—it represented an important chapter in Irish music, and it can't just be consigned to the dustbin of a history. At which point I must declare a personal stake in restoring the reputation of the showbands: my own father, Gabriel Burke, was singer and guitarist with The Dinny Hughes Band out of Mullingar, joining their ranks at the age of 17. He cut a handsome figure in publicity shots, the small-town Irish approximation of an American teen idol, bequiffed and besuited behind a big electric guitar. Although less successful on a national scale than other Mullingar outfits like Joe Dolan & The Drifters or The Times Showband, the band, anchored by saxophonist Hughes and wife Bridie on accordion, did good business.

"Starting off, it was more or less once a week, maybe some weeks twice a week. Then it got busier," the old man said. "We could be playing anywhere from Cavan and Monaghan, to Leitrim, Roscommon, Longford, Meath, Tipperary, Kilkenny, Carlow, and bordering counties or townlands around that area. We did Dublin later on."

A typical gig would be a five-hour set with an interval. The musicians were expected to know anything the audience requested—and, for the most part, they did. Many of the contemporary hits of the day were learned straight from the vinyl records themselves, although Dinny Hughes would make the journey to Dublin every other week to buy sheet music from Waltons.

"We had a simple trick: to take things easy, the longer the night went on. We'd invent our own requests. What I found the most fatiguing were the guitar solos during The Shadows' stuff. It was frightening. I didn't read music. I was shit-scared of making a mistake, or breaking a string. What could you do then? You weren't a fully-fledged musician who could pick yourself back off the ground after falling."

The showbands liked a drink. The fact that the venues were unlicensed didn't matter. There were ways and means.

"You could get drink in the ballrooms, no problem—from rare old mountain dew to anything you wanted. It was brought up in cases before the gig and put behind the stage."

The clergy, who patrolled the dance floor like sentinels, ensuring that Catholic Ireland kept its knickers on and its flies firmly fastened, turned a blind eye to the contents of the musicians' riders. The nuns, however, were less inclined toward such leniency in imposing moral order. Moonlighting as a solo artist away from The Dinny Hughes Band for one night in Kilbeggan, Burke's performance didn't impress the several brides of Christ that were present.

"It wasn't looked upon as very decent," he laughed.

I grew up with his showband memories. I also grew up in the 70s, when the showbands were increasingly morphing into the kind of country-and-Irish combos that gave both country music and Irish music a bad name. Framed in this context, my father's memories were almost tainted by association. Considerably older, and hopefully somewhat wiser, my attitude is less derisive than it once was. Where once there was possibly embarrassment, now there is a sense of pride in my father's involvement with what was an important period in Ireland's social and cultural history. A period in which a young country began to experience the many splendid thrills to be had away from the dreary everyday regime manipulated by the dog collar dictators and their God-fearing political lackies. A period in which, if the Irish didn't discover sex, drink, and rock'n'roll, they at least embraced this unholy trinity with some zeal.

"You were bringing the radio, you were bringing the songs, you were bringing the names of the singers—you were bringing that all home in the dancehall. So the people were having their little fantasies, imagining it was Roy Orbison singing up on the stage, or Elvis. It gave a lot of happiness to people."

Whether Bob Geldof's musical anthology—derivative punk with designs on populist appeal and a tendency for bringing out the inner nihilist in bedroom rebels—prompts a similarly affectionate response is a debate for another day.

"It's impossible to explain to people today the kind of hysteria generated by the showbands. Nothing can compare with it now," Father Brian D'Arcy told Vincent Power in *Send 'Em Home Sweatin'*, his book about the showbands. Or, as Mark J. Prendergast puts it, in *The Isle Of Noises*:

"In the beginning you had the showband and very little else. The idea was that Irish audiences wanted entertainment first and last. The showbands dominated every town and city in Ireland. From the early 60s, they made fortunes from live appearances, playing covers of standard hits and the English Top 30 rather than original material. When The Beatles started in England, the Irish response was to cover their material within the showband format ... Ballrooms on the circuit

53

were packed out every night by thousands, to hear hours and hours of covers by the showband of the day. It was this popularity that led to their affluence. With their vast resources they controlled the dissemination of popular music throughout the country. Records were a secondary thing to the showband, since it was the live event that generated the money. Artistic integrity and creativity were subsumed under the primary motive of profit."

The late Jim Aiken, the promoter who brought The Rolling Stones, Bob Dylan, and Bruce Springsteen to Slane Castle in County Meath during the 80s, heralding a new era of unprecedented large-scale outdoor gigs, said in 1998 that the showbands played "an enormous part in taking a closed Ireland into an open Ireland ... to an Ireland that did what they wanted to do. And it's the children of those people who have produced the confident Ireland of today. It was an essential element in the evolution of Ireland".

John Coughlan, former editor of *Spotlight* magazine, the bible of the showband scene, described it as "probably one of the biggest industries in the country", with an estimated 600 bands at its peak, while for journalist and political commentator Sam Smyth, the showband years were "part of the passage of the people ... a period we had to go through. I think the country owes the showbands a hell of a debt. They did make growing up in Ireland a lot of fun at that time".

"Purists have argued that creativity in Irish music, if not dead in the 50s and 60s, was definitely in a coma," argued Gerry Gallagher, ex-member of The Magic Band, The Fair Ways, and Pat Ely & The Rocky Tops, and now curator of an excellent website that is an essential archive for anyone with even a cursory interest in showbands. "However, I take issue with this view of Irish music history, as I think the Irish showbands played an integral role in forming the foundation on which the success of the Irish artists that followed, was built.

"The musicians of the showband era were often much better than the music they played. They were highly trained musicians who could have played rings around Mr Geldof and the Boomtown Rats. However, Irish bands were often the only exposure to live music available in Ireland—and they were, after all, showbands. Their job was to entertain dancers with the music of the day, whether it came from Frankie Avalon, Elvis, Chuck Berry, The Beatles, or The Rolling Stones. Original music was at a minimum unless it was an Irish ballad type of song.

"As time went on, though, the bands got better, the equipment got better, recording became less expensive, and bands started to make their own music, with baby steps at first. However, in retrospect, it is interesting to consider that Queen never attempted to play 'Bohemian Rhapsody' live, but The Memories did. Bands like The Memories, Chips, and Tweed could have blown the Rats out of the water, musically."

The showbands, said Gallagher, fulfilled a role that was assigned to them by the punters. "Keep It Simple, Stupid—KISS—was the name of the game."

Gallagher joined The Magic Band in 1974. During rehearsals and soundchecks, the other members often played jazz. "It prompted me to go out and purchase a Wes Montgomery guitar book, so I could keep up with the rest of the lads, who were all very musically savvy. In fact, today many showband heads are playing jazz in pubs and clubs across Ireland."

According to Gallagher's account, the showbands were derived from the orchestras that travelled throughout Ireland in the years after World War Two: names like Maurice Mulcahy, Johnny McMahon, Tony Chambers, and Brose Walsh, who "led 10 to 18 piece orchestras in which musicians sat behind music stands and respectfully played a wide selection of music from big band standards to Irish folk and even ceili music.

"To some degree, this form of wholesome entertainment satisfied Ireland's dancing public," Gallagher continued. "There was something for everyone. Formal attire was mandatory and most orchestras wore dickey-bows and tuxedos. A few adventurous bands even tried coloured blazers! The key for the orchestras, to some extent, was to be 'all things to all people', and to their credit they generally did that very well.

"The orchestras were a reflection of the times in Ireland, simple and inoffensive. The clergy reigned supreme over the country to the extent that dancing was forbidden during Lent [an observance in the liturgical year of several Christian denominations], during which the Irish entertainment industry more or less closed down.

"Ireland was a very religious, parochial place in the 50s. The showbands started humbly enough, but actually were a driving force behind social change in the country. Suddenly ballrooms sprang up everywhere around the country, and the young people did anything— even riding bicycles 20 miles—to get to a dance. Although many of the dances were initially run by priests, who often separated couples that were seen as dancing too close, eventually as the clergy's grip faded, dance halls became the place to meet members of the opposite sex. Although probably tame by today's standards, the ballrooms brought many an Irish lad or lassie their first sexual experience. And there were hundreds of groupies."

In Northern Ireland, big bands and orchestras flourished— especially Dave Glover and Clipper Carlton out of Belfast, and Johnny Quigley from Derry. But as the 50s came to a close, dancehall punters were growing restless. Roused by the rock'n'roll revolution from across the Atlantic, they wanted something new.

"Bands like Bill Haley & The Comets were jumping around onstage, and lead singers wildly gyrated to the delight of young fans. It is The Clipper Carlton Orchestra that are first credited with kicking away their music stands in the 50s and incorporating their regular feature, 'Jukebox Saturday Night', into their act. Soon, every band was doing the same thing.

"However, it was Dave Glover who first used the name 'showband'. A new genre of music was finally christened. Across the country, on both sides of the border, bands did away with sheet music and donned colourful suits, dancing and jiving their way through the night's programme."

Northern Ireland had a thriving showband scene. Apart from The Clipper Carlton from Strabane and The Dave Glover Showband from Newtonabbey, there were The Melody Aces from Newtownstewart, Gay McIntyre's Showband from Derry, The Freshmen from Ballymena (who, fronted by Billy Brown and Derek Dean, were among the few bands that wrote and performed their own material), The Plattermen from Omagh, and The Skyrockets from Eniskillen. There was a plethora of venues to play as well. With maple dance floors, ladies' and gents' facilities, and a mineral bar, they were often more ostentatious than the venues down south. Belfast boasted the Boom Boom Rooms, the Orpheus, Romano's, the Fiesta, and the Plaza, while in the sticks you had the Floral Hall, the Savoy, the Pallidrome, and the Arcadia.

After leaving Orangefield in 1960, Van Morrison registered with the Musicians Union. His card meant he became a go-to guy for any showband that suddenly found itself a member down. According to Brian Hinton, author of *Celtic Crossroads: The Art of Van Morrison*, he could be drafted in for a dinner-and-dance in Coleraine on a Saturday afternoon, or a coming-of-age celebration over the border in Sligo.

The Javelins-cum-Thunderbolts evolved into The Monarchs with the addition of pianist Wesley Black in 1961, and learnt their trade on the showband circuit. A boisterous outfit, they had a residency at Thomson's Restaurant in Belfast, during which Morrison garnered a reputation for his madcap antics, including knee drops, scissor kicks, dancing on tables.

"They were wild," he told Jon Wilde in 2005. "You had to have an act then. You were judged by your last live show. And your show had to be something different, otherwise you didn't get booked. You almost had to kill yourself to be different."

The Monarchs would try things that nobody else was doing:

attention-grabbing gimmicks with the emphasis on entertainment.

"It was great training ground and good fun," he told *Mojo* in 2012. "We basically played the Top 20 for ballroom dancing. Lots of gigs in Belfast, and Derry had an American airbase, so they'd all come and see us. The Beatles killed all that."

Comedy was an integral part of the act. The band would do numbers like 'My Boomerang Won't Come Back' by English funnyman Charlie Drake (whose catchphrase—every comic needed a catchphrase then—was, "Hello, my darlings").

"We had a singer called George Jones," Morrison recalled, "and he was the real comedian. I was more like the fall guy." The Monarchs were "strictly a rock'n'roll band" to begin with, and only later became a showband. This change was born out of necessity. In Ireland, the more bodies in a band, the more work that band secured.

"You had to have a horn section; you couldn't really work properly if you didn't," he said. "All the showbands had horn sections and a lot of them were really good, like The Royal Showband, Dixielanders, Swingtime Aces, Clipper Carlton … The horn sections were the main thing, so you had to have at least a seven or eight piece band to work."

He was more effusive in his praise of the showbands when speaking to Tony Johnston on Ireland's national network, RTE, in 1973. Showbands, he claimed, were where it was at.

"That's how one got work if you were a professional musician, which I was at that point. You had to work with somebody, and showbands were probably the only entity in Ireland that were getting work. I mean, I don't know anyone that wasn't in a showband. It was revolving chairs. You'd either be in one or the other. It wasn't any big deal. There was so many then—there were like hundreds of showbands and there were gigs galore at that time. So you always knew you were going to get a gig with somebody. And the people that actually paid the money were showbands. Like, groups didn't make any money then. In fact, groups didn't even exist on a professional level at that point."

Morrison left The Monarchs briefly for stints in both The Great Eight and Harry Baird's Olympics. By the time he returned, the band had a new frontman, George Hetherington, and a new moniker, Georgie & The International Monarchs—a move perhaps designed to separate them from The Monarchs from the Republic of Ireland, formed by Waterford brothers Ray and Dermot Heraty. They trekked around Hetherington's native Scotland in an old van, backing rock'n'roller Don Charles, whose claim to fame was the single 'Walk With Me My Angel'. They found regular spots at some of Birmingham's Irish clubs, and were eventually contracted to do a season in Germany at Heidelberg's Odeon and the Storyville in Frankfurt and Cologne. Five sets a night in raunchy clubs populated by punters who "might've worked us over if we didn't do at least three encores of 'What'd I Say'". It was an instructive experience for a 16-year-old who had to secure permission from the British Embassy to play.

This was where, as George Jones told Johnny Rogan in his biography of Morrison, "Van became the basis of what he is today. For the first time in his life, he had met American coloured GIs who dug soul, blues, and all the music that he was weaned on. Van drifted away every day to get near coloured guys who talked the same language as him. He suddenly became a big influence on The Monarchs. We started playing all this soul music in the clubs of Germany."

It was while in Germany that Georgie & The International Monarchs got the opportunity to record a single, 'Boo-zooh (Hully Gully)', featuring Morrison on sax. He dismissed it as "a really bad song" with "a dynamite instrumental track".

It was in Germany, too, that The Monarchs, as Morrison would later claim, morphed from showband to R&B band. Whatever the veracity of this statement, Morrison's showband apprenticeship was coming to an end. The International Monarchs finally broke up in 1963, and he joined The Manhattan Showband for some UK dates in 1964, but was impatient to scratch his rhythm & blues itch.

"It was a completely different scene then," he said in 1972. "Things weren't so personal. We had a kind of showband where egos weren't involved, and people weren't getting uptight over small things. I played the guitar, sax, drums—we all swapped instruments and had a good time. But in no way was it my scene up front. I was riding on the side."

The undisputed kings of the showband period were The Royal Showband from Waterford, featuring country crooner Tom Dunphy and the charismatic Elvis doppelganger Brendan Bowyer on vocals. They had six number one singles in Ireland, among them 'The Hucklebuck'.

"The Royal were always seeking good dance numbers," Bowyer said from his home in Las Vegas. "We heard Frank Sinatra doing a swing version of 'The Hucklebuck', which we then adapted. We did it onstage for a few years. Then we were in Abbey Road studios recording a single, and we wrapped up 'The Hucklebuck' in one take at the end of a session."

Bowyer admitted that The Royal Showband "weren't the best musically", but they were big at the box office in all 32 counties throughout Ireland.

"We were especially popular in Belfast and Derry. The crowds there would thunder with applause. They responded far more strongly than in the south, where applause was an automatic roll of the hands after every song."

Indeed, The Monarchs supported The Royal in Belfast, though Bowyer had a hazy recollection of the diminutive ginger-haired saxophonist.

"But I was blown away when I heard him later with Them," he added. "I remember somebody asked him once about the success of The Royal, and Van spoke about the big fellow who sang 'Jerusalem'!"

This was a reference to Bowyer's show-stopping rendition of 'The Holy City', a Victorian ballad dating back to 1892, which was a regular feature of The Royal's set. The two men actually performed together in Dublin's Vicar Street following the release of Bowyer's 2001 album *Follow On*.

"It was probably the best album, technically, that I ever did—30 years of songs by Irish singer-songwriters. I did [Morrison's] 'Bright Side Of The Road'. We did it onstage together at Vicar Street. I just sang it the way I had originally recorded it, but Van ad-libbed on the side. I was totally amazed at what the song became—it became world class all of a sudden!"

They shared a coffee during the interval, but rather than reminisce about their common showband experiences, Morrison grilled Bowyer on Elvis Presley, a friend of the Waterford singer's during his Las Vegas residences in the 70s.

"I first met Elvis when he was doing a movie called *Spinout*. In later conversations with him, he wasn't very proud of a lot of those movies. Colonel Tom Parker [Presley's Svengali-like manager] told him I was Ireland's Elvis. He made reservations for our show in February 1971. He brought his whole entourage. I did a song, was a Marty Robbins country song, 'You Gave Me A Mountain'. We dramatised it a lot with brass up front. And Elvis was quizzing me about it afterwards. I told him what it was, and that the original version was different to ours. He later put it into his stage act."

The Beatles also passed through The Royal Showband's orbit, opening for them at the Liverpool Pavilion in 1961.

"John Lennon was questioned in the press in Ireland afterwards, when The Beatles came to play the Adelphi in Dublin. He was asked what he thought of 'our Royal Showband', and he said, 'We thought we were looking at a talent competition!' You see, we had four singers in the band, and we would all take turns singing songs."

○

The rise of the showbands in the 60s created an entire industry, employing some 10,000 people at its height.

"Ballrooms started to spring up all around the country as the old parochial halls could no longer cope with the huge crowds the bands were attracting," said Gerry Gallagher. "Most of these facilities were thrown up in a matter of weeks, with little in the way of creature comforts. They had one purpose and one purpose alone—to cram a many dancers into the hall as possible."

It was, said Sam Smyth, a total cash economy. "You paid cash into the ballrooms, the bands were paid in cash that night. It was a hip pocket economy. A lot of people had folding money to spend."

The halcyon days were between 1963 and 1968, when showband royalty included Brendan O'Brien & The Dixies, Dickie Rock, Joe Dolan & The Drifters, and Butch Moore & The Capitol. While Britain was swinging, and the counterculture was challenging the American agenda, Ireland was stuck in a time machine. But it couldn't last—and it didn't.

"The huge influx of copycat showbands led to a glut on the market," said Gallagher. "In fact, other than the distinct voices of a handful of stars, the showbands all began to sound and look the same.

"Another major change was also happening. The dancers that had been packing the halls in the late 50s and early 60s were moving on, getting married, having kids, and a younger set of dancers were taking their place. In this environment, bands like the Clippers and others started to look old and out of date. It signalled the end of the old showband era and the dawning of a new age."

Several bands were dissolved, and those that weren't set about reinventing themselves by introducing younger blood. The distinction between pop and country groups became more pronounced.

"The industry recreated itself in a new way. Showbands morphed into pop or country acts. A smattering of cabaret artists tried their hands in the ballrooms. The Beat groups of Dublin became the pop and rock groups of the 70s, and started to challenge for their piece of the pie."

For Gallagher, a brace of tragedies in 1975 ended the innocence of the showband age. Tom Dunphy, the first showband singer to release a record in the 1960s, was killed in a car accident on July 29. Two days later, three members of The Miami Showband—Fran O'Toole, Brian McCoy, and Tony Geraghty—were gunned down by Loyalist paramilitaries from the Ulster Volunteer Force on the A1 road at Buskhill, County Down, when they were travelling home to Dublin after a performance in Banbridge.

"Immediately after the Miami killings, almost all southern-based bands refused to travel north. This meant more bands vying for fewer gigs in the south. Disco started to creep into the ballrooms, initially as a cost-effective alternative to the groups put out of work. Eventually, though, they were able to draw their own crowds to greasy chicken bar exemptions which would fill every hotel across the country, further killing the ballrooms."

Twink—real name, Adele Condron-King—of the all-girl showband Maxi Dick & Twink remembered "a terrible sense of reckoning" with Dunphy's passing. The Miami tragedy, according to Sam Smyth, devastated the entertainment business in Northern Ireland and was "a very deep wound in the psyche of the whole entertainment business north and south".

Paul Charles, author of the showband novel *The Last Dance*, had another theory about the demise of the showbands. "Managers and ballroom owners' priorities did nothing to encourage the showbands to develop their own songwriting or recording careers," he told *R2* magazine in 2012.

Maybe not, but the showbands were a starting point for several musicians who later made the jump from being entertainers to artists—Eric Bell, Rory Gallagher, Henry McCullough, and, of course, Morrison. Bell, another Belfast native, was in The Atlantics Showband before getting his big break as part of The Deltones, moving on to The Dreams and The Bluebeats. He joined Thin Lizzy in 1970. Gallagher, Donegal-born but a resident of Cork, was a member of The Fontana Showband, with whom he headed over to Hamburg—where they were then known as The Impact Showband—in 1965. Gallagher and two of his Impact colleagues quit the band while in the seedy German port, going on to form Taste. McCullough, from Portstewart, County Derry, first played with The Skyrockets and a number of other troupes, including Gene & The Gents, until Joe Cocker's Grease Band came calling. There were subsequent stints in Paul McCartney's post-Beatles venture, Wings, and alongside Roy Harper, Marianne Faithfull, Ronnie Lane, Donovan, Eric Burdon, and Spooky Tooth.

O

For Gerry Gallagher, the showbands embodied a significant movement in the Irish cultural story.

"They had a much bigger impact on Irish culture than any other type of music or even religion may have had during their heyday," he said. "They provided employment for thousands across the country, made many a promoter—and a few musicians—wealthy beyond their wildest dreams. The dancehall became the centre of the life of a town or village. Dances provided a meeting place, a matchmaking service, and provided the ability to raise funds for all manner of local concerns, such as football teams or schools, and they exposed people to new kinds of music—and even fashion—in an era when TV was in its infancy in Ireland.

"At a time when the church had an iron grip on the young people of Ireland, the showband era provided the freedom and release where they could more fully express themselves, often to the dismay of their parents. Another important function of the showband era was that it provided an industry in which young musicians could learn their craft and flourish. It was the job of being in a showband that allowed Rory Gallagher to make the money to buy that Stratocaster that became world famous. Men, and some women, had a career in music because of the commercial success of the showbands, something that is sadly lacking for young musicians today. They also provided a career path for the budding music, from garage band to pub group to relief band to showband."

Yet for Niall Stokes, editor of Ireland's leading rock magazine, *Hot Press*, the showbands "operated a stranglehold in a way that stifled people's creative instincts. There were a lot of people in good rock'n'roll bands who were bought out by the showbands, put on good salaries in return for being in a mobile jukebox."

Meanwhile, the trajectory of Van Morrison's career path in 1964 would take him to a former police station in Belfast that had been converted into a rest home for visiting mariners. At the time, the Maritime Hotel—near the city's Queen's University—had a 200-capacity hall that was used by various Christian organisations and the Mothers' Union. It became the hub of a rhythm & blues scene in Belfast, mirroring what was happening across the water in cities like Sheffield (Bluesville), Swansea (the R&B Cellar), Newcastle (Downbeat), and London (the 100 Club). It also became the birthplace of Them.

CHAPTER 4
KICKING AGAINST THE PRICKS

Almost half a century on, Them remain synonymous with the Maritime. They made their debut at the former seamen's mission on April 10 1964—without Van Morrison. While Morrison was fulfilling an outstanding date with another group, The Golden Eagles, at the Plaza, Billy Harrison (guitar and vocals), Alan Henderson (bass), Eric Wrixon (piano), and Ronnie Millings (drums) were playing to an underwhelmed audience of around 60 people.

This quartet had been together as The Gamblers in East Belfast since 1962. Soon after Morrison joined on tenor sax, harmonica, and vocals, they changed their name to Them, in homage to the 1954 sci-fi film of the same name, directed by Gordon Douglas, about a man's encounter with a nest of giant irradiated ants.

The way Morrison told it to Paul Lewis in 1991, he was responsible both for the rebirth of the Maritime as an R&B venue and the emergence of Them as a band as one of only two people who responded to an ad in *The Belfast Telegraph* seeking musicians 'to start an R&B club'.

"So I went out and found this club," he said. "It was a seamen's mission called the Maritime Hotel and they had a room set up. That's where I really made it—well, it came out of that situation. I had to just get musicians in at short notice, so the people that I really wanted, I couldn't get. I got another lot of people and we went into this club known as Them, and then it built up from there."

Six years earlier, Morrison had told Al Jones on Danish radio that the Maritime era was of less significance to him than the period before it. "I'd already been playing in bands for five years, and this is just in Ireland," he said. "At that time, there were a lot of good bands and there were a lot of places to play. It was a very sort of positive period for working in Ireland. And then that period ended, like mid 60s, completely vanished."

In the early 60s, Belfast's nightlife largely consisted of a number of licensed cabaret clubs with genteel pianists and singers, and an array of sedate ballrooms where the showbands did their thing. The Maritime's reinvention as a rhythm & blues mecca changed all that. According to the website of the Ulster History Circle, an organisation that places commemorative plaques in public places throughout the province in honour of men and women who have contributed to Ulster's history, the Maritime "earned a reputation on a par with the famous Cavern Club in Liverpool, where the Mersey Sound was incubated, for highlighting a new generation of exotic musicians who were inspired by the traditional American rhythm and blues tunes, but who gave the music their own twist, laying the foundations for what would years later evolve as Celtic rock."

Poet Gerald Dawe recalled the Maritime as a place "for kids of every religion and none to get together", adding that for many "seeing students looking like 'beatniks' would have had a greater effect on them than wondering about what church they went to".

Maritime regulars from its 1964 heyday until the Troubles erupted in 1969 included Rory Gallagher and Taste, Just Five, The Lovin' Kind, The Mad Lads, The Alleykatz, The Interns, The Aztecs, The Deltones, Five By Five, The Method, The Few, and The Fugitives.

Four days from that first Maritime appearance, *The Belfast Evening Echo* ran an ad cryptically asking, "Who Are? What Are? THEM." The ads became still more cryptic in the following days: "When? And Where? Will you see THEM?" and "Rhythm and Blues and THEM. When?" The curiosity of hip young *Echo* readers piqued, the attendance at their second Maritime gig was up on the previous week. By the third date, the venue was packed solid.

"We were playing for a certain bunch of people. It was really like a cult following. It wasn't in any way a commercial trip," said Morrison.

According to academic Lauren Onkey, Them were indicative of "a hip, liberating, urban Irishness that was inextricably linked with America. Their setlists were entirely American music, plus original songs. They did not play any of the Irish kitsch songs of the showband era". Onkey viewed their "blackness"—their embrace of R&B—as "a challenge to—or at least an escape from—sectarianism. At their best, they offered alternatives to fixed ideas of Protestant/Catholic identity through their focus on American blues". Them's assertion of so-called black music, she argued, "and their right to play it without defensiveness or explanation, was not rooted in the rhetoric of shared oppression or tied to nationalist aspirations. Them signified liberation, modernity, a celebration of trans-national and transatlantic youth culture, and perhaps subtly, therefore, a challenge to essential Irish identities".

Irish identity was something with which Billy Harrison had a problem. Teased in a 1965 interview by Keith Altham, who told him that he came across as an angry young Irishman, Harrison retorted, "I'm not Irish! I'm an Ulsterman. Why does everyone insist on calling us Irish?" Morrison, in the same interview, said he didn't "see any harm" in being labelled Irish. Indeed, in a 1970 conversation with Happy Traum, Morrison noted how, "when we had a couple of hit records, they started calling us a British group ... then after that we became an English group! I don't know how in the world they mistook it for an English group, 'cos if they ever heard us talk, they'd know it wasn't. It was an Irish group!"

Them's Maritime shows were "more spontaneous, more energetic, more everything," said Morrison, "because we were feeding off the crowd". He improvised to the max, especially on 'Gloria', a song he'd penned at the precocious age of 18, which could stretch out for more than 20 minutes. This, according to Van The Man, was the apotheosis of Them, embodying a raw, undiluted, freeform sound that was never caught on tape.

"Them lived and died on the stage at the Maritime Hotel," he would declare in hindsight, refusing to attach any significance whatsoever to hit singles such as 'Baby, Please Don't Go', 'Here Comes The Night', and 'Mystic Eyes'.

According to Morrison, it all began to go wrong for Them when they started their gradual transformation from hardcore blues outfit to pop combo.

"Suddenly, it seemed like we were working to someone else's agenda," he recalled. "They expected us to be slick and showbizzy. Well, I was neither of those things. For me, that was going nowhere. I couldn't pull that off. It was an alien thing to me. I wanted to play blues music, pure and simple. I wasn't doing it for the money or the fame. I had no interest in being a personality. Them started out as something straightforward and it got twisted into something else. We became fodder."

They gained a reputation as bad boys, for kicking against the pricks during interviews, for not conforming to the demands of an industry that worked in tandem with a more pop-culture-savvy media. "They were the most boorish bunch of youngsters I'd come across in my short career," a reporter for *The Irish Independent* complained.

The medium of television, too, was beneath them. They considered *Top Of The Pops* and *Ready Steady Go!* a complete joke, despite the enormous exposure that accrued from appearances on those programmes. And as part of the line-up for the *NME* Pollwinners' Concert at Wembley Empire Pool—a line-up that also included The Beatles, The Rolling Stones, The Kinks, and Dusty Springfield—they subverted their rendition of 'Here Comes The Night' by segueing into a seven-minute 'Turn On Your Lovelight'.

It was around this time that Van first came to Liam Neeson's attention.

"I may have seen them on *Top Of The Pops* or something—one of those British TV programmes. And my elder sister said, 'Oh look, that's Them, and they're from Belfast.' I thought, my God! Belfast was just up the road. A Belfast group being on this hit show! That grumpy face of Van's, and the hair swept down the side of his face—long hair—a very moody guy. He was an Irish artist that had made it—even though I didn't know what 'made it' meant. He was on a bigger stage. He was an Irishman, and a Northern Irishman to be particular."

Keith Donald, meanwhile, "liked it that someone from Belfast was near the top of the charts in Britain" and was "proud of him in the same way I'd been proud of Ruby Murray in the 1950s". This sense of pride—Belfast pride, Northern Irish pride, Irish pride even—was of huge importance to the natives. It meant that "Irish rock music had not only arrived, but in one fell swoop it had become the hippest new sound in town, and this is why, despite Morrison's own reservations, Them remain one of the most important bands in the history of Irish rock".

Important but controversial. There was the near riot in Cookstown, County Tyrone, when some pissed-up boyos in the audience pelted the stage with coins after Them ignored requests and belligerently stuck to an R&B setlist. The crowd's animosity was further stoked when Morrison, near the end of the show, bellowed "Goodnight pigs!" into the mic. At this point, the coins were replaced by the heavier artillery of chairs.

A local newspaper described how about 300 people, "some armed with bottles and stones, gathered at the entrance to the town hall after the dance on Saturday night, at which the group received a poor reception. The group were locked in the building for about 30 minutes until police, under District Inspector James Faulkner, succeeded in getting the crowd to leave the vicinity of the hall. Them were then escorted out of the building to their van by police who accompanied them to the outskirts of the town. Using side roads, they returned to Belfast through Portadown as a large crowd, armed with bottles and stones, had gathered at the north end of the town, expecting the group to return home via Antrim".

Parochial journalistic hyperbole or accurate reportage? It does seem like an extreme reaction to what could be construed as a bit of (admittedly antagonistic) badinage from the pugnacious Morrison, but then when there's drink taken, the blood is up, and a kind of mob mentality takes hold, the atmosphere inclines toward unpredictability. As Clinton Heylin would later quip, it wouldn't be the last time Morrison "has felt compelled to inform one or more members of an audience exactly what he thinks of them".

O

Here's a theory. Van Morrison is inept at filtering his fury. He shoots from the hip without pause for rational analysis. He shoots at the same targets again and again: the record industry that ripped him off; journos and writers who just don't get it, and wouldn't get it even if it was spelled out to them in their own blood; copycats who plagiarised his songs; and so on. He has spent a career nurturing grudges, righteousness on his side, payback on his mind. He is the archetypal hard-done-by Northern Irish Protestant, all caught up in the twisted masochistic glory of martyrdom. Concurrently, he is the repressed Irish Catholic, the flaming red rawness of whose ejaculations is suggestive of emotional impotence. Consider Morrison the personification of the tortured Irish psyche.

Whatever the provenance of his borderline misanthropy, his and Them's reputation for mouthing off, for downright insolence, was exploited by Decca when it came to issuing their first album, *The Angry Young Them*. Morrison was not amused. In fact, by his own admission, he "flipped":

"I didn't want any of that stuff to go out. I thought it was stupid. But I was basically outvoted and couldn't do anything about it. I was just a musician. I didn't know anything. Other people were calling the shots. They were trying to sell us, you know? But I've never been into selling myself. It's always been about the music. That's all I know about."

It's hard to get a handle on a definitive history of Them. From their formation until very recently, they have undergone at least 15 line-up changes, some eight of them featuring Van Morrison between 1964 and 1966. At one stage, in 1965, there were only two members, Van The Man and Alan Henderson—Billy Harrison, Patrick John McAuley and Peter Bardens having quit. By September of that year, Morrison and Henderson had recruited Jim Armstrong from The Melotones on lead guitar, Ray Elliot of The Broadways on keyboards, and The Misfits' drummer John Wilson.

Morrison found an unlikely ally in the music when Them crossed the Atlantic in 1966, hailed as part of the British invasion. Jim Morrison of The Doors was a cartoon hedonist who, while he didn't necessarily court publicity, didn't exactly shun it, either. A lizard king in leather trousers, Jimbo was the rock star most women wanted to shag, while Van was the rock star (a shorthand designation he has consistently denied) most women mistook for the strange boy next door who hardly ever left his house—and, when he did, walked with a lumbering gait that discouraged any contact whatsoever. Yet the pair bonded at the Whisky, where The Doors opened for Them during a two-week engagement. On the final night, both bands dug deep into a 20-minute version of Van's 'Gloria' and Wilson Pickett's 'In The Midnight Hour'.

"Van Morrison was insane," The Doors keyboard player, Ray Manzarek, said in a 1983 interview. "You know how he got into just standing there and singing? I haven't really seen him in a long time, but when he was with Them, the guy was all over the stage, man. Absolutely insane. Did that thing of holding the microphone stand upside down and singing, and smashing the mic stand into the stage, and just ... God, was he incredible. He was so good. Then, the last night we played, we had a jam. We got a couple of photographs of that somewhere, but nobody recorded it."

The Doors' drummer, John Densmore, was baffled by Morrison's dependence on the demon drink before going onstage. Them "slammed through several songs one night after another, making them indistinguishable. Van was drunk and very uptight and very violent with the mic stand, crashing it down on stage. I didn't understand why a guy with so much talent had to drink to get up on stage, or why he was so self-conscious up there".

After Los Angeles, Them headlined San Francisco's iconic Fillmore. But the cracks were showing, with disputes over money and Morrison becoming increasingly more disillusioned with the direction in which Decca were trying to manipulate them.

It wasn't just Decca that got Them all wrong—American audiences wanted the group to be an Irish incarnation of The Rolling Stones. Morrison was having none of it. His behaviour became more erratic. He finally lost his rag at a show in San Luis Obispo and stalked Ray Elliot with a microphone stand.

"The band were cooking, it was a great gig, but Van just freaked," Jim Armstrong told Steve Turner. "He was getting very funny onstage by this time. One night he would perform well and the next night he would just glower at the audience. The band was now huge on the West Coast, and the crowds were screaming, but Van was going in a different direction, and he couldn't cope with it."

Back in Belfast, Morrison was replaced as singer by Kenny McDowell of The Mad Lads. He holed up in Hyndford Street and worked on his own material, some of which would become *Astral Weeks*. Morrison did assemble a shortlived outfit—Van Morrison And Them Again—comprising young musicians who could be found in Crymbles Music Shop on Saturday afternoons. Mike Brown played bass, Joe Hanratty was on drums, and Eric Bell guitar. A full house turned up at the Square One Club for their first show. Among them was Alan Henderson, who contributed double bass to 'Mystic Eyes' and 'Baby, Please Don't Go'.

"I had the list of the songs we were supposed to be playing on top of my amplifier," Bell told Steve Turner. "Then Van looked at me and said, 'Start a blues in E, man.' I went, 'But what about the list?' He said, 'Fuck the list and start a blues in E, man.'"

As far as Bell was concerned, Morrison was like a jazz musician. "That was his approach. He was inventing the lyrics as he sang, taking the volume right up and then bringing it back down again."

There were a handful of other gigs, but Morrison was outgrowing his Belfast roots. "I think he was a bit pissed off at being back in Belfast," said Bell. "It obviously wasn't the same vibe as in America. It was about 300 years behind the times, as far as he was concerned."

Morrison did return to the States later that year to record for Bert Berns, a songwriter and producer best known for 'Twist And Shout', 'Hang On Sloopy', and 'Here Comes The Night'. Berns had founded his own label, Bang, and he brought Morrison to New York for two days of recording. These sessions yielded 'Brown Eyed Girl', 'TB Sheets', 'Ro Ro Rosey', 'Goodbye Girl', 'Who Drove The Red Sports Car?', 'Midnight Special' (Van channelling Lead Belly), 'Spanish Rose', and 'He Ain't Give You None'. When 'Brown Eyed Girl' became a hit, peaking at number ten on the *Billboard* chart, Morrison flew back to New York for a promo campaign. According to Steve Turner, Morrison wouldn't play ball, and the "uncooperative and moody tendencies that had been observed since childhood surfaced with a vengeance. Bang didn't know how to handle him. They were hoping for a bright new pop star and found themselves with a temperamental Irish poet who couldn't be squeezed into a mould."

The relationship between the two men ended acrimoniously. Berns died suddenly of a heart attack on December 30 1967. Morrison, meanwhile, was moving on. He lit out for Cambridge, Massachusetts, to begin a new life with Janet Planet, a sometime actress he'd met in San Francisco, and signed to Warner Brothers Records.

○

In a 2012 interview with *Mojo*, Morrison disparaged whatever Them had accomplished. "We had three hits," he said. "Well, four ... but it didn't really mean anything." Them, he bristled, "wasn't really a band anyway".

And Morrison, you suspect, wasn't really a band kind of guy—at least not in the way that bands are like gangs, with that all for one and one for all mentality. By his own admission, when he was part Them, he was "still kind of on my own".

Despite its classic status, 'Gloria'—covered by Patti Smith, Jimi Hendrix, The Doors, and countless others—wasn't one of those hits. It was actually the flipside of 'Baby, Please Don't Go', first recorded by Big Joe Williams, he of the nine-string guitar, in 1935, and the single that broke Them in the UK. Gloria's identity remains a mystery. Eric Wrixon recalled a woman of that name who would "disappear from time to time" with Morrison during the band's Maritime period. Hyndford Street neighbours, however, were convinced that Gloria was Van's cousin, Gloria Gordon, who died of cancer while he was away with The Monarchs in Germany.

"They were very close, almost like brother and sister," childhood friend Walter Blakely remembered. "When she died, she was only in her mid-twenties and had a little baby daughter. It was a terrible shock for him."

CHAPTER 5
ELEGY FOR BELFAST

To listen to *Astral Weeks*, an impossibly precocious album by a 23-year-old, is to hear the ghosts of Van Morrison's childhood. It is to hear John McCormack and the jazz and blues absorption of his father's eclectic record collection. Not that these influences are manifest overtly. There is none of McCormack's mannered baritone delivery, nor is there the exuberance of, say, Louis Armstrong or Sidney Bechet, or the primal groove of Robert Johnson. But you can hear them all if you listen closely enough. It's there in what the late critic Ralph J. Gleason called the 'yarragh'. In a 1970 review of Morrison's *Moondance*, Gleason recalled, "I saw a film version of the life of John McCormack, the Irish tenor, playing himself. In it he explained to his accompanist that the element necessary to mark the important voice off from the other good ones was very specific. 'You have to have,' he said, 'the yarragh in your voice.'"

This was a concept developed by Greil Marcus in his book, *Listening To Van Morrison*, a quest to trace The Man's particular genius. To get the yarragh for Morrison, he wrote, "you may need a sense of the song as a thing in itself, with its own brain, heart, lungs, tongue, and ears. Its own desires, fears, will, and even ideas: 'The question might really be,' as he once said, 'is the song singing you?' His music can be heard as an attempt to surrender to the yarragh, or to make it surrender to him; to find the music it wants; to bury it; to dig it out of the ground. The yarragh is the version of the art that has touched him: of blues and jazz, for that matter of Yeats and Lead Belly, the voice that strikes a note so exalted you can't believe a mere human being is responsible for it, a note so unfinished and unsatisfied you can understand why the eternal seems to be riding on its back."

For the poet W.B. Yeats, the yarragh was a cry of the heart, a haunting, haunted sound in Celtic song and poetry—specifically, Irish song and poetry. To me, the yarragh is really just a made-up alternative name for soul. Irish soul, maybe. It works. It actually succeeds in expressing a nebulous notion in a very primordial way. The word 'soul' appears too lightweight, too ethereal when applied to something that is so inside out—so raw and charged and meaningful. The yarragh is the point at which the spiritual, the emotional, and the physical coalesce. It is the stuff of Van Morrison's songs when they emerge from his diminutive, almost pugilistic frame, untrammelled by the requisites of performance. Songs like 'Listen To The Lion' or 'And The Healing Has Begun'. Songs like the songs on *Astral Weeks*. Songs that become transcendent in their presentation—songs that, to slightly shift the emphasis of the Morrison quote deployed by Marcus above, sing themselves, the singer becoming a vessel. At such moments, the singer, the players, the listeners—all of us—are taken out of ourselves. We are liberated, loosed from the earth to which we're rooted. We are, put simply, sent.

In 2007, Morrison told Barry McIlheney that *Astral Weeks* was "like starting again", a reaction to producer Bert Berns's insistence on exploiting the popular success of 'Brown Eyed Girl'. He went back to his early days as a would-be folk singer in Belfast, learning the songs of The Carter Family and Lead Belly.

"I was getting fed up with groups and bands and producers and people imposing their ideas on me and trying to get me to make a chart record and all that shit," he said. "So I just started all over again, me and my guitar, and took it from there."

And where exactly did he take it? Well, he filtered the folk elements through a jazz medium—jazz in this instance representing the spirit of innovation rather than a genre label—an instinctual exploration of the words and the music. Again, we're back to the idea of the singer becoming the song, and the song becoming the singer, the line that separates the two rendered obsolete. Throw some intuitive musicians into the mix—jazz musicians with an innate understanding of how to play beyond what shapes they're given to play—and what you have is a phantasmal sound, a protean body of indeterminate appearance, a thing meant to be felt instead of rationalised or intellectualised.

"This is not an exaggeration, this is not just trying to be poetic," Brooks Arthur, the recording engineer on *Astral Weeks*, said in 2009. "A cloud came along, and it was called the Van Morrison sessions. We all hopped upon that cloud, and the cloud took us away for a while, and we made this album, and we landed when it was done."

Morrison, of course, has frequently dismissed such attempts to invest *Astral Weeks* with an air of the abstruse in the years since those three sessions at Century Sound Studios, New York, in September and October 1968. There was no magic involved. It had nothing to do with luck, as Jon Wilde had the temerity to suggest to him in 2005.

"That's one of the many myths," Morrison replied. In fact, he said, he'd been playing and rehearsing those songs for a long time before he came to record them in the studio. "I'd been playing them in dives in Boston and New York, just myself and a bass player and a flute player. They had been worked to death. The idea that *Astral Weeks* was some fluke, something done with smoke and mirrors, is complete bullshit."

Morrison had been writing his own songs since the days of The Monarchs in Germany, but audience demand for material that was familiar meant he never got to play them. "I wrote a couple of songs when I was in The Manhattan Showband," he said, "and I recorded those two songs on the second Them album." For a while, he was only writing the odd song here and there, and it was mainly the encouragement of others that spurred him to write more. "It was like, 'Oh, you should do this, blah blah blah', because I didn't think about it myself."

Some of the songs on *Astral Weeks* were written as early as 1966.

"They are timeless works that were from another sort of place, not what is at all obvious," he explained to *The LA Times* in 2008. "They are poetry and mythical musings channelled from my imagination. The album is about songcraft for me—making things up and making them fit to a tune I have arranged."

Producer Lewis Merenstein, who had a background in jazz, booked a bunch of jazz heads for the recording. Bassist Richard Davis, best known for his work with Eric Dolphy, shared the floor with guitarist Jay Berliner (Charlie Mingus, Ron Carter), percussionist Warren Smith Jr (Aretha Franklin, Nina Simone, Nat 'King' Cole), and Connie Kay of The Modern Jazz Quartet. The line-up was augmented by Larry Fallon on harpsichord, Barry Kornfield on acoustic guitar, and John Payne on flute and soprano saxophone.

"I have probably always been more advanced in my head, in my thinking, than the calendar age of 22," Morrison told *The LA Times*. "My thinking musically has always been more advanced. It is difficult to get it down on paper sometimes, even now. And the music on *Astral Weeks* required these great musicians, because no one else could have pulled it off like they did. There is another reason, too, and that is the fact I did not settle for anyone other than these guys. They were the ones I insisted on."

According to Merenstein, Davis became a de facto leader in the studio. "If you listen to the album, every tune is led by Richard, and everybody followed Richard and Van's voice. I knew if I brought Richard in, he would put the bottom on to support what Van wanted to do vocally or acoustically."

Davis wasn't the first and certainly wouldn't be the last collaborator to find Morrison something of an inept communicator. "He was remote from us," he recalled. "He came in and went into a booth. That's where he stayed, isolated in a booth. I don't think he ever introduced himself to us, nor we to him. And he seemed very shy."

John Cale, formerly of The Velvet Underground, was recording in the adjacent studio at the same time as *Astral Weeks* was being created. According to his account, "Morrison couldn't work with anybody, so finally they just shut him in the studio by himself. He did all the songs with just an acoustic guitar, and later they overdubbed the rest of it around his tapes."

True or false—who really knows? And, quite frankly, who really cares? It's all about what came out of those sessions rather than how it was put together.

Morrison admitted there was no rapport; that everyone just got on with it and that it worked because they were good enough as musicians to make it work. His intimation that *Astral Weeks* would have happened as it did with or without those particular musicians, though, was wide of the mark. It would have been a different album. It may not have been the expressive and hugely significant album it was, and still remains. In fact, despite his assertion that the band were out of sync a lot of the time or sometimes unsure where they were going next, the visceral interpretation of Morrison's songs by these guys effects a visceral response. If they were reading from charts, then either the charts were inadequately drafted, or the readers of said charts were inadequate readers, because there is a discernible tension between this singer and these musicians in this context that transforms *Astral Weeks* into a remarkable, compelling, sublime entity.

It's even more remarkable when you consider that Morrison was a 23-year-old Irish immigrant, an introspective young man with negligible social skills, probably daunted by both the environment— New York was and remains the coolest city on the planet—and the personnel, on whom he was reliant to enable him to actualise the sounds that were going on in his head, thus introducing a whole other form of tension into the equation. The loneliness of the immigrant— that hankering for home, for the lost familiar, even if it's not a conscious hankering—is audible in Morrison's vocalisation. Hardly surprising when you learn that the songs were written in and about Belfast, as he revealed to *Select* magazine in 1990.

"The songs came out of some inner expression of trying to cope with what was happening around me," he said. "It came out of people I knew, and snatches of conversation, snatches about people's lives. Parties. It came out of the spirit of what was happening. Most of it was capturing the spirit of what was going on with my peer group at the time in Belfast."

Not that you'd know it, apart from the explicit references to locations in 'Cyprus Avenue' and 'Madame George'. The former is set in the Belfast street near to where Morrison was raised, a street "with a lot of wealth ... a very different scene. To me," he said, "it was a very mystical place. It was a whole avenue lined with trees and I found it a place where I could think. Instead of walking down a road and being hassled by 40 million people, you could walk down Cyprus Avenue and nobody was there. It wasn't a thoroughfare. It was quiet and I used to think about things there."

Cyprus Avenue was "the street that we would all aspire to—the other side of the tracks", according to Roy Kane, former drummer with The Monarchs. And it was literally the other side of the tracks. The Beersbridge Road "had the railway line cut across it," he said. "Our side of it was one side of the tracks and Cyprus Avenue was the other." After rehearsing, The Monarchs would take a short cut through the avenue, "'cos that's where all the expensive houses and all the good-looking totty came from. And maybe you'd get a chance to talk to some bird from the other side of the tracks on the way up". Indeed, Kane told Clinton Heylin that on 'Cyprus Avenue', Morrison was singing about "the unobtainable totty".

Poet Gerald Dawe, in his book *The Rest Is History*, said that Cyprus Avenue was not just a place but "the idea of another place; the railway, the river: all are conduits through which Morrison's imagination is freed".

The opening line of 'Madame George' finds Morrison down on Cyprus Avenue again, a "childlike vision leaping into view", the protagonist of the song tramping through Fitzroy on high heels with a squaddie drinking wine. It's arguably the most intriguing lyric in his canon, a symphony of images that manage to be deliciously seedy and unbearably heart-breaking, Belfast coming over like some post-World War fleshpot in London's East End, where only a drop of the hand uncovers the gender identity of your lascivious conquest. Or it could just be about a Swiss cheese sandwich, as Morrison, in a moment of Dylanesque facetiousness, declared to Happy Traum.

Later in the same interview, Morrison tried at least to provide Traum—whom he admitted asked "a lot of good questions"—with some insight into 'Madame George', however flimsy.

"Just imagine we had a sponsor, and he gave you a plane ticket and me a plane ticket, two-way tickets from Woodstock to Ireland, and we got on a plane and we went from here to Belfast, and we hung out and came back, then you would know the song. But I don't think I could tell you about the song if we didn't do that."

'Madame George' was actually 'Madame Joy', a straight poem with music added subsequently. Morrison claimed to have written it as a stream of consciousness thing, only later realising what the song was about.

"I had a great aunt whose family name was Joy," he recalled, "and she lived in the Cyprus Avenue area. I only met her once when I was little. She was supposed to be very clairvoyant or psychic and lived in this old Victorian house. I just heard stories about her. That's part of it. It's about the other thing too. It's a sketch about a lot of various moods. The feeling of that song is very important because that enables the lyrics to come through."

Gerald Dawe drew a comparison with a fellow poet, the late Patrick Kavanagh, in his reading of the song, "with its storytelling and repetitions, the anarchic mantra of the love it seeks to express and its almost obsessive questioning". Furthermore, he made a connection between Kavanagh, Morrison, and the Beat poets in the United States, youngsters Kavanagh professed to "admire very much" when he crossed the Atlantic in 1965 for a symposium on Yeats.

"What Kavanagh saw in the work of the Beats is curious, given the Irish situation he had in his mind," Dawe concluded. "They had, he said, 'all written direct, personal statements, nothing involved, no, just statements about their position. That's all. They are not bores as far as I am concerned'. Kavanagh's voice of dissatisfaction with convention ('boredom'), strengthened by his subjective romanticism ('direct personal statements') is very close to the poetic vision of *Astral Weeks* and in particular to the voice which recites 'Madame George'."

Brian Hinton heard James Joyce in Morrison's stream of consciousness, a literary technique spearheaded by the *Ulysses* writer (along with Dorothy Richardson and Virginia Woolf) and characterised by a fluency of time and thoughts and images that don't always seem make sense. In Hinton's view, though, Morrison's technique was radically different from that of Joyce's. Where the latter "used the technique to show the fragmented inner life of his characters, with all kinds of base desires and thoughts", Morrison was "closer to the impressionistic style of Virginia Woolf, with her flows of feeling, and painterly abstractions". Where Morrison did correspond with Joyce, Hinton asserted, was in "this double vision, the love and compassion that both can bring to their portraits of others, Leopold Bloom [the central character in Joyce's *Ulysses*] or Madame George, seeing their tawdriness and defeats, but also the heroism with which they survive, and live out their lives".

Joyce, one of the chief architects of 20th century modernism, was Dublin born and educated, though he emigrated to continental Europe in his twenties, living variously in Trieste, Paris, and Zurich. After 1904, he only made four return visits to Ireland, the last of these in 1912. Yet Joyce insisted he never stopped writing about Dublin, reasoning that if he could get to the heart of Dublin, he could get to the heart of all the cities of the world, for in the particular was contained the universal.

In 1914, his first novel, *Portrait Of The Artist As A Young Man*, was serialised in a London magazine with the assistance of American expatriate poet and critic Ezra Pound. The same year, *Dubliners*, a collection of short stories, was published, while Joyce also wrote his only play, *Exiles*, at that time. It was then that he began to apply himself fully to *Ulysses*, a novel he had been fermenting in his imagination since 1907. Finally published in 1922 by Sylvia Beach, proprietor of the Shakespeare & Co bookshop in Paris, *Ulysses* (the Latinised name for Odysseus, the hero of Homer's *Odyssey*) chronicles the passage of Leopold Bloom through Dublin on June 16 1904.

"I want to give a picture of Dublin so complete that if the city suddenly disappeared from the earth, it could be reconstructed out of my book," Joyce said.

I confess to never having read *Ulysses* in its entirety—though in secondary school we did study a brief excerpt—and therefore am hardly qualified to comment on whether or not Joyce achieved his objective of vivifying Dublin. Virginia Woolf certainly wasn't impressed, calling the book "a misfire". And she didn't stop there.

"Genius it has I think; but of the inferior water," read her withering critique. "The book is diffuse. It is brackish. It is pretentious. It is underbred, not only in the obvious sense, but in the literary sense." Woolf's friend, the poet T.S. Eliot, disagreed. He held *Ulysses* to be "the most important expression which the present age has found; it is a book to which we are all indebted, and from which none of us can escape".

Joyce's next and final novel, *Finnegans Wake*, was published in 1939. Arguably this work is even more demanding for the reader than its predecessor, being composed in a predominantly idiosyncratic language—idioglossia—that pulled together composite words from between 60 to 70 world languages, combined to form puns or portmanteau words and phrases intended to convey several layers of meaning simultaneously. For all of its bewildering inventiveness, *Finnegans Wake* commands a pre-eminent place in the annals of English literature—77th in the Modern Library's 100 Best English-Language Novels of the 20th century—and was lauded by Anthony

Burgess, author of *A Clockwork Orange*, as "a great comic vision, one of the few books of the world that can make us laugh out loud on nearly every page".

But back to 'Madame George'. The song also name-checks Sandy Row, a Protestant working-class district in Belfast's inner city through which the train from Dublin ran, and makes reference to "throwing pennies". This Dawe identified as the ritual of throwing pennies into the River Boyne—"the iconographic site for the Protestant defence of the British Crown and faith in Ireland".

Ultimately, for Dawes, 'Madame George' was "an ashling"—a dream or vision in Irish folklore—"which portrays a world of loss and gain, ceremonies and evasions, past and present, shifting like a carousel between real and imagined people and places". It was "a portrait of a society about to withdraw from public view at the same time as the voice which describes it is also leaving the scene", a collage of pictures that was "identifiably Belfast".

The references to the city as it was before the Troubles "are textures of a recognisably 'ordinary' working-class lifestyle", according to Noel McLaughlin and Martin McLoone. "This is the key to understanding the music of Van Morrison over the last 40 years or so, and to assessing the importance in the cultural context of Northern Ireland. He, more than any other Irish (or British) rock musician, has maintained a strong sense of his roots while at the same time exploring—and extending considerably—the international rock idiom."

Astral Weeks remains unparalleled as "his most complete celebration of his Belfast roots, a collection of songs—of emotion recollected in tranquillity, as Wordsworth described it—which evokes a place that is real and yet is also a place of the imagination."

Morrison himself, borrowing from author Truman Capote, used the word 'faction', a hybrid of fact and fiction, to explain the lyrical inspiration behind *Astral Weeks*.

"Some of *Astral Weeks* is real," he said. "For sure. There's names of people—Huddie Ledbetter [Lead Belly's real name], that's real. There's place names—Cyprus Avenue, Dublin, Fitzroy, Sandy Row. They're real, OK. But they're also fictionalised … some of it's actual and some of it's dreamt up from somewhere. Fitzroy is actually a street but it could also be a person."

How about this? It's an elegy for Belfast, a city that was, at the time Morrison recorded 'Madame George', on the precipice of internecine warfare between its citizens east and west, Protestant and Catholic, Loyalist and Republican, British subjects and Irish Gaels. An elegy for another time, another place, where and when, according to Dawe, people "hung out and there was little aggro, except for the usual sort of fighting that made Belfast city centre a dangerous place some Saturday nights. But you could still walk through the wider city without too much anxiety or fear. But within a matter of a year or so, you took your life in your hands for so doing."

A Belfast forever preserved in the aspic of *Astral Weeks*. A Belfast every bit as wondrous as city contemporary C.S. Lewis's fictional landscapes in *The Lion, The Witch & The Wardrobe*. Indeed, Peter Mills, in *Hymns To The Silence*, sees a correlation between *The Lion* and *Astral Weeks* in "the idea of the unfound door that leads out of time and space". While Lewis discovers the marvellous "in and through the ordinary", Morrison offers "a similar magic door into another world; both works go into the mystic, a kind of nirvana that has to be defended but is never owned, a place built on feeling".

Mills concludes that the most profound similarity between the worlds imagined by Lewis and Morrison "is a feeling for the emotional weight of the Northern Irish landscape, and the sensed yet unseen power in its beauty". It is to this landscape—his Belfast, in particular—that Morrison has returned many, many times in his songs.

There is a certain symmetry here. *Astral Weeks* was birthed as an album when old Belfast was dying, soon to be dead. Nearly 30 years later, when American President Bill Clinton made an historic visit to Northern Ireland, the first incumbent American President to do so, in order to affirm his support for the peace process and the reincarnation of Belfast—albeit older, scarred, more cautious—his opening act onstage outside City Hall was Van Morrison, a Belfast Protestant, alongside Brian Kennedy, a Belfast Catholic, harmonising on 'No Religion'.

Liam Neeson still listens to *Astral Weeks* "at least once a week every fucking week. It still kind of inspires me in some way with the beauty of it. Every song is like a fucking classic. It's still breathtaking in its originality, its composition, its poetry—and there he is, essentially, singing a lot of these songs about Belfast. It's a local album.

"I definitely hear a nostalgia when I hear *Astral Weeks*, even though Belfast was 30-odd miles away from me. It was still a faraway place that you got to see now and again. Now that I'm 60 years old and I'm living in New York and I hear *Astral Weeks*, it's definitely nostalgic for me. Very much a connection with home."

The topography of Morrison's Belfast songs, and particularly those on *Astral Weeks*, is "prior" to Glenn Patterson, even though he wasn't born until 1961. This makes them, "in the way of all things relating to the world just before you entered it, instantly intriguing and always out of reach, and that's even before you take into account the yearning quality of so many of the songs. I would say that what I respond to is the street—and stream—level view of Van Morrison's Belfast. Even if it is cloud-hung—and sometimes especially if it is cloud-hung—there are, if it is not an oxymoron, ordinary wonders to be found.

"I have lived for the last ten years not far from Cyprus Avenue— drive up it, in fact, half a dozen times a week. Drive up it sometimes with *Astral Weeks* playing. And I have on occasion stopped the car and told my children to listen and look, that everything they need for art is right there."

○

If *Astral Weeks* came out of the ether, Morrison's next two albums, *Moondance* and *His Band And The Street Choir*, were made for the mainstream: blue-eyed soul infused with pop sensibility, but, most importantly, on his terms. On *Moondance*, the Belfast detail of 'Cyprus Avenue' and 'Madame George' is supplanted by the implicit imagery of fog horns blowing as the boats pull into Belfast Lough ('Into The Mystic'), winding streams, pipes and drum ('Everyone'), and the railroad track ('Brand New Day'). The joyous 'And It Stoned Me' is the evocation of a childhood experience, as he told Steve Turner.

"We used to go to a place called Ballystockert to fish," he said. "We stopped in the village on the way up to this place and I went to this little stone house, and there was an old man there with dark, weather-beaten skin, and we asked him if he had any water. He gave us some water, which he said he'd got from the stream. We drank some and everything seemed to stop for me. Time stood still. For five minutes everything was really quiet and I was in this 'other dimension'. That's what the song is about."

Ralph J. Gleason was euphoric about the collection in the *San Francisco Chronicle*, ranking Morrison alongside Bob Dylan, The Band, The Beatles, and John McCormack.

"He wails as the jazz musician speaks of wailing, as the gypsies, as the Gaels and the old folk in every culture speak of it. He gets a quality and intensity in that wail which really hooks your mind, carries you along with his voice as it rises and falls in long soaring lines. He sounds like a young Irishman haunted by his dreams, a poet, one of the children of the rainbow, living in the morning of the world."

According to Johnny Rogan, Gleason's hyperbole suggested Morrison had "just emerged from the Gaeltacht", the Gaelic-speaking region of the Republic of Ireland, whereas in fact he was "Northern, Orange-hued, and urban. He was a child of the shipyard rather than a child of the rainbow. He had never been exposed to Irish poets or Irish writers, and knew nothing of the Irish language. The rebellious literature that Morrison read came not from Ireland, but America".

Rogan chides American commentators' laziness in placing Morrison "in a misty-eyed romanticised Celtic twilight populated by

Irish stereotypes. From their descriptions he sounded something like a cross between *The Quiet Man*, *Darby O'Gill* and an extra from *Finian's Rainbow*".

Just as Gleason and his ilk had Morrison down as a nailed-on mystical Paddy, the Irishness in his songs became far less pronounced on *His Band And The Street Choir*. Indeed, only the closing 'Street Choir' could be heard as a paean to the singing sessions that were part of the social tapestry of Hyndford Street and its immediate environs back in the day. The imagery is universal rather than local. Gone are the gypsies and the foghorn, the familiar street names—those echoes of a Belfast childhood. These are songs from anywhere, about anything you want. There is nothing to connect Morrison—or the listener—to Ireland. Van was physically a long way from home, and at some remove artistically from the place that birthed him.

CHAPTER 6
AMERICAN EXILE

The pastoral and domestic bliss illustrated by the front cover of *Tupelo Honey* is, like the songs on the album, a lie. Morrison walks beside a white horse, bestride which is Janet Planet, his wife and the mother of his daughter, Shana, christened Shannon Caledonia Morrison (Shannon being a goddess in Irish mythology, her name meaning possessor of wisdom, and Caledonia reflecting her grandfather George Morrison's Scottish Presbyterian roots). The lie is accentuated on the back cover, which shows Morrison, bedecked in threads that are both Byronesque and Wild West gentry, sitting on a fence while Planet, in what looks like a Gingham dress, stands faithfully, even submissively, by her man. "I didn't have a ranch, I didn't have a horse," Morrison raged years later. "That is all part of the fuckin' mythology."

The lie is compounded by the songs, with titles such as 'You're My Woman', '(Straight To Your Heart) Like A Cannonball', and 'Starting A New Life'. Truth is, by the time Morrison's fifth album was released, things were far from idyllic on the home front. Relocating from Woodstock, where they'd been based since 1969, to Fairfax, California, only served to emphasise the fractures in his marriage to Planet. In 1998, she admitted that, after they went west, their life became "very traumatic and horrible. I couldn't stand any more of his rage as my daily reality. I worried about its impact on the children"— as well as Shana, Planet had a son, Peter, from a previous relationship. "I couldn't reconcile the fragile dream with the emotional chaos which kept intruding and crashing everything down."

Tupelo Honey was meant to be a country album—territory that Van Morrison would later explore on 2007's *Pay The Devil*. He had planned to record versions of standards like 'The Wild Side Of Life', 'Crying Time', and 'Banks Of The Ohio'. There are certainly elements of that country sound, notably on the bucolic 'When That Evening Sun Goes Down', but it's largely a collection of R&B-lite and MOR-ish balladry, and features Morrison the lyricist at his most banal. 'Tupelo Honey' itself is among his most beloved songs, and has aged well. Named for the buttery-flavoured, light-coloured honey of the tupelo tree, which grows along the rivers and creeks of the Florida panhandle, it could, at a stretch, be heard as an unwitting eulogy for Elvis Presley, the most famous ever resident of Tupelo, Mississippi. Such an interpretation resonated with Greil Marcus, who described the song as "a kind of odyssey. The constant evocation of 'Tupelo honey' couldn't not invoke Elvis Presley; he was smiling over the song's golden couple, as if they were living out all the best hopes of 'Can't Help Falling In Love'".

For Johnny Rogan, Morrison's songwriting on *Tupelo Honey* is focused "on his recent experiences in America. When he looked back nostalgically, it was no longer to Belfast, but to 'Old Old Woodstock'. Increasingly his new family life would take precedence over childhood memories".

O

The Belfast Morrison had left behind would have been unrecognisable to him. The campaign for civil rights by Catholics had mutated into a toxic sectarian conflict. The presence of British troops on the streets, initially as a mediating force, had exacerbated rather than calmed an already volatile situation.

The period from 1970 through 1972 saw an unprecedented eruption of violence. In 1972 alone, nearly 500 people—over half of them civilians—lost their lives. This was the greatest death toll in the three decades of the conflict.

Unionists claimed the main reason for this dramatic escalation in hostilities was the formation of the Provisional Irish Republican Army

91

and the Official Irish Republican Army, alias 'the Provos' and 'the Officials', or 'the Stickies' (a term coined for those committed to the ideals of the old IRA, namely the creation of a 32-county workers' republic in Ireland). The latter embraced non-aggressive civil agitation, while the Provisional IRA were intent on waging armed struggle against British rule in Northern Ireland. They saw themselves as defenders of the Catholic community.

Meanwhile, the Nationalist narrative pointed to a number of events in these years to explain the increased bloodshed, including Bloody Sunday (already detailed earlier in this book). Another such incident occurred in the Falls Road in July 1970, when 3,000 British troops imposed a curfew, firing more than 1,500 rounds of ammunition in gun battles with the Official IRA, killing four people. Another was the introduction of internment without trial in 1971. Out of 350-plus initial detainees, there wasn't a single Protestant among them. Many of those arrested weren't even Republican activists, but they went on to become so because of their experience. Between 1971 and 1975, 1,981 people were detained: 1,874 were Catholic/Republican, while 107 were Protestant/Loyalist. There were allegations of abuse and even torture of prisoners. The five techniques used by police and army—wall-standing, hooding, subjection to noise, deprivation of sleep, and deprivation of food and drink—were, in 1978, deemed by the European Court Of Human Rights to be "a practice of inhuman and degrading treatment" in breach of the European Convention On Human Rights.

In 1972, the Provisional IRA killed some 100 soldiers, wounded 500 more, and carried out an estimated 1,300 bombings, the majority aimed at commercial targets considered "the artificial economy". The bombing campaign accounted for the deaths of scores of civilians, most notably on Bloody Friday, July 21, when 22 devices were detonated in the centre of Belfast, resulting in nine casualties. The Official IRA, in a complete reversal of their pacifistic policy, killed approximately 19 soldiers and wounded dozens in a series of gun attacks.

Loyalist paramilitaries, including the Ulster Volunteer Force and the Ulster Defence Association, responded to IRA attacks with the sectarian assassination of Nationalists, identified simply as Catholics. The Shankill Butchers, led by the sadistic Lenny Murphy, delighted in the savage torture of their victims before eventually granting them the mercy of death. Murphy had a fanatical hatred of Catholics. Martin Dillon, in his book *The Shankill Butchers: A Case Study Of Mass Murder*, suggests that Murphy's loathing may have stemmed from the suspicion that his own family had Catholic ancestry—the surname Murphy is more commonly found among Catholics in Northern Ireland. According to the late Irish politician, writer, and academic Conor Cruise O'Brien, the Butchers introduced a new and frightening level of violence to a country already hardened by death and destruction. Lord Justice O'Donnell, who oversaw their 1979 trial, described their crimes as an enduring monument to blind sectarian bigotry.

Another feature of the violence in this phase of the Troubles was the involuntary or forced displacement of both Catholics and Protestants from formerly mixed residential areas. In Belfast, Protestants were forced out of Lenadoon, and Catholics were driven out of the Rathcoole estate and the Westvale neighbourhood. In Derry, almost all Protestants fled to the mainly Loyalist Fountain Estate and Waterside areas.

The British government, believing the Northern Ireland administration incapable of containing the security situation, sought to assume control of law and order. The Northern Ireland government opposed this intervention, but the British government pushed on with emergency legislation: the Northern Ireland (Temporary Provisions) Act 1972, which suspended the Unionist-controlled Stormont parliament and implemented direct rule from London.

Talking to Irish journalist Shay Healy back then, Morrison said, "I'm definitely Irish. I don't think I want to go back to Belfast. I don't miss it with all that prejudice around. We're all the same and I think it's terrible what's happening."

In retrospect, Healy's reading of Morrison's profession of his Irishness was that "despite the brutal sectarianism and violence, Belfast has a wit that is suited to darkness and he buys into it. There's a northern way of looking at life, an almost permanently cynical point of view—the black humour of mistrust. It's part of Van's default defence mechanism."

As for Morrison's aversion to "all that prejudice", Healy felt he recognised the futility of violence "for the madness it was" very early on in the Northern Irish conflict. "He seems to have had no tribal affiliations, no sectarian political instincts, and throughout his career he has never made an overt political statement, even in his most autobiographical songs. He tells it like it is, or he paints you an allegorical picture. But I've never considered that he is foisting a rigid political judgement or opinion on me, the listener."

It's hardly surprising that Morrison didn't want to return home. The home he knew, the home he had idealised in 'Cyprus Avenue', 'Madame George', and 'And It Stoned Me', no longer existed.

In *Celtic Crossroads*, Brian Hinton compares Morrison to James Joyce or Samuel Beckett, declaring him to be an Irish artist who had "chosen exile, cunning, and silence. Nevertheless, the psychic death of his native land darkly shadowed his work, and made evocations of a paradise glimpsed in childhood unbearably poignant".

Morrison's friends and acquaintances in the city "had either moved on, given up, or found themselves straitjacketed in a moribund, culturally impoverished wasteland". Donal Corvin was roughed up by reserve police force the Ulster Special Constabulary (also known as the B-Specials), and shortly afterwards relocated to Dublin. Former R&B rebel Gil Irvine was playing light pop, country, and ballads to audiences of considerably advanced age at the Harland & Wolff social club. And Roy Kane blamed the Troubles for the demise of the music scene. Clubs closed, people didn't travel outside their own areas, and the creativity in bands was ruined.

"People not only ghettoised themselves, they ghettoised music,"

Kane told Johnny Rogan. "Even people like myself, who were cross-community, we were afraid. We could play a Proddy club and knew we'd be safe. But we didn't know for certain that someone might not come around the corner and throw a bomb into the place because it was a Proddy club, and we'd get blown up."

O

Whatever Morrison's reservations about going back to Belfast, there's a sense of yearning for the city—for home, the place that made him—on the title track of his next album, *Saint Dominic's Preview*. He cuts a desolate figure on the cover, sitting in the doorway of a church in San Anselmo, Marin County, strumming his acoustic guitar, staring plaintively off into the middle distance, clothed in gypsy attire, the scuffed boots suggesting roads well travelled, hard roads, rootlessness. He is a wandering troubadour, a spiritual seeker, an Irish immigrant in America. Exiled. Listen to the ache in his voice as he sings 'Saint Dominic's Preview'. "It's a long way to Belfast city too."

A longer way still to his Belfast, with its innocent images of cleaning windows, the Safeway supermarket, James Joyce, his father's Hank Williams records. It's hard not to hear this as the hymn of the dispossessed. Morrison's journey back to Ireland begins here.

The song was, he said, definitely influenced by his childhood.

"I'd been working on this song about the scene going down in Belfast," he told John Grissim. "And I wasn't sure what I was writing but the central image seemed to be this church called St Dominic's, where people were gathering to pray or hear a mass for peace in Northern Ireland."

Several weeks later, while having dinner before a gig in Reno, Nevada, it got spooky. Morrison picked up a newspaper, "and there in front of me was an announcement about a mass for peace in Belfast to be said the next day at St Dominic's Church in San Francisco. Totally blew me out. Like I'd never even heard of a St Dominic's Church".

It wasn't a coincidence, he told Donal Corvin. "I worked out in my head that 'Saint Dominic's Preview' was me seeing that before I looked at the paper. That's what I thought it meant."

St Dominic, for the record, was the founder of the (Catholic) Dominican Order, and is the patron saint of astronomers.

The extraordinary 'Listen To The Lion' finds Morrison sailing to Caledonia—the Latin name given by the Romans to Scotland, the land of his father. He is going back to his roots, "looking for a brand new start". For Johnny Rogan, the song "embraced Celtic mythology, using selected symbols, most notably the English national emblem, the lion". Caledonia is something of a Morrison motif. In 1970, he recorded a couple of tracks under the title 'Caledonia Soul Music'. In 1973, he had a 16-track studio built in his home, and called it Caledonia Studios. And arguably his finest ever ensemble of musicians was The Caledonia Soul Orchestra, later downsized as The Caledonia Soul Express.

Asked by Ritchie Yorke in 1977 to explain what and where Caledonia was, Morrison said, "It used to be Scotland. This funny thing happened a long time ago—a lot of people from Northern Ireland went over to Scotland to settle, and vice versa. They changed spaces or something. So a lot of people from Northern Ireland are of Scottish descent. And my name suggests that I am. My grandmother was Scottish, so I'd guess I'm of Irish and Scottish descent. I'm Irish and a British subject."

Years later, he insisted that Caledonia was "just a tag I came up with. I'm not sure how relevant it was or for how long".

'Listen To The Lion' is not just a cry from the heart but a veritable howl, an imploration articulated in a language that's got no words; a language of primitive sounds. This is the rawest of blues, a bastardised reinvention of the Sean-nós form of traditional Irish singing, a highly ornamented style of unaccompanied delivery. Morrison's voice is accompanied here, of course, but the musicians are in thrall to its presence, responding to rather than co-existing with its vagaries. 'Listen To The Lion' is a song of the beast that wants to be calmed, the man that wants to be loved, the traveller that wants to lay down his weary bones someplace where he belongs.

It is also a song that, perhaps more than any other in Morrison's catalogue, encapsulates the primal essence of his voice, particularly in the coda. One way of understanding this voice, according to Micheal O'Suilleabhain—pianist, composer, and professor of music at the University of Limerick's Irish World Academy of Music and Dance—in an unpublished paper, is to regard him as "a Francis Bacon equivalent in the realms of singing". Bacon, the Dublin-born figurative artist renowned for his bold, graphic, and emotionally raw imagery, created a series of so-called screaming pope paintings, "where a bellowing figure enclosed in what might be a glass frame can fixate the viewer with its intensity".

If the scream is a catalyst for Bacon, Morrison possesses "a primal roar", O'Suilleabhain writes. "We can feel when we listen that this roar is linked to something existential. There is a sonic overlap between the words he chooses, how he sings them, and the pitch levels he uses. His vocal accent is what links him to his first place. The thing that gives cohesion to the whole sound he makes is the timbre of his voice. That timbre is made up of breath, vocal cords, words, the pronunciation of words, the formation of melody—but it is a wind that blows through it all that catches our attention and holds us while he performs.

He bellows when he sings, his body becoming "a blast bag, a blowing bag, a wind bag. He sings from the belly. Morrison is singing from a gut feeling—a visceral emotional reaction to something. The word 'visceral' comes from the Latin 'viscus', which means internal organ. The stomach is the seat of the emotions. Morrison is singing from the gut".

Crude oil is drilled from the ground before it is eventually refined; Morrison, O'Suilleabhain writes, "is an oil well belching up crude oil. When he sings, he digs for oil, and when the conditions are just right, he strikes oil". But he is not just belching up crude oil—he is also "an inkwell through the lyrics he writes. His ink is a mixture of oil and

97

blood". If Seamus Heaney "digs with his pen" and Bacon "screams through his paint", Morrison "strikes oil through his roar".

For Greil Marcus, 'Listen To The Lion' consolidates the recurring themes in Morrison's work as an attempt to get a handle on his existence as an Irishman whose homeland is in flames, and who lives safely in America, and a will to discover or recapture Caledonia, the mythical place of his ancestry—"an attempt to shape and communicate a sense of freedom".

Marcus sees Morrison as the inheritor to a tradition of mysteries, a Celt and "a spiritual descendant of the Irish prelate, St Brendan", who, according to legend, set out from Ireland 1,500 years ago, eventually reaching America and perhaps founding a colony that subsequently disappeared. Furthermore, Marcus suggests that Morrison perhaps understands that he was always American, that his place in America was pre-destined: "even if it is unsettled, as he stretches out toward that mythical Caledonia, even believing, sometimes, that in a long and intricate manner, the blues came not from Africa, but from Scotland".

In other words, according to Lauren Onkey in her essay 'Ray Charles On Hyndford Street', "the Irish American relationship in Morrison's work is a site of creative hybridity where the idea of authentic or pure cultural identity becomes ludicrous, impossible to trace, a hall of mirrors".

Such indistinct cultural identity may be in large part the source of Morrison's torment. He has always seemed to me like a man weighed down by an unnameable suffering. It's more than the burden of the sensitive artist. It's not just melancholy. And depression is too unspecific, too catchall in its diagnosis of innumerable psychological ills. He really is the "stranger in this world" of 'Astral Weeks', someone who finds it difficult to engage, to adjust in the ways that we are required to adjust to the demands of our changing environments, to the extent that he can function consistently. He just doesn't lie as well as the rest of us. He doesn't do pretence.

This unnameable suffering is punctuated by periodic salvation. It has to be, if he is to avoid the inevitable denouement of constant suffering. That salvation is found in the music, but the music, too, is possibly responsible for the suffering. For as it raised him up, so did it bring him low. The music isn't real. It is metaphysical. The boy who got lost in his father's records, who listened to and sang with his mother, who occupied a prominent position in this familial trinity, and who was connected to the local community of Hyndford Street and the wider community of East Belfast was, in fact, the boy in the bubble. Outside the bubble, things became—and have continued to be—problematic. That's why he keeps repairing to the bubble. It's known to him. It's where he feels most affiliated. It lights him up, makes him whole. Some call it nostalgia. I call it refuge.

Morrison seeks out that refuge out again on *Hard Nose The Highway*, on songs like 'Wild Children', 'Green', and 'Purple Heather'. The last two are covers. 'Green' was written by Joe Raposo of *Sesame Street* for Kermit The Frog. Morrison appropriates it as a badge of his Irishness. Sure, he sings, "it's not easy, bein' green", but "I am green, and it'll do fine, it's beautiful / And I think it's what I want to be". Admittedly, such a hypothesis challenges credulity somewhat, but set within the context of what can only be described as Morrison's homesickness at the time, it stacks up.

'Purple Heather' is an old song from the repertoire of The McPeake Family. (Remember them?) Also known as 'Wild Mountain Thyme' and 'Will You Go Lassie, Go', it is a variant of 'The Braes Of Balquhidder', written by Scottish poet Robert Tannahill, a contemporary of Robert Burns. Morrison would have heard it sung by Francis McPeake, probably on the BBC programme *As I Roved Out*. His singularly soulful reworking of the song on *Hard Nose The Highway*—his first foray proper into folk music, albeit 19th century Scottish folk music percolated through 20th century Irish folk music—prefaces a similarly radical overhaul of traditional standards on *Irish Heartbeat*, his 1988 album with The Chieftains.

Talking about the song on RTE, Morrison said he'd "tried to get it on an album for a long time. I heard this song for years, but I never heard it done like the McPeakes. I was at a party, a phoney record company party, and the McPeakes were at it. They were the only real thing happening there, they just stood in the middle of the floor and sang this song. I don't sing it the way they sing it, but that's what inspired me. It's what turned me on to the song".

He told Donal Corvin in *Hot Press* of hearing the McPeakes perform the song "at a party in Belfast a long, long time ago. I'd probably heard it first from my mother, but the McPeakes sold me on it. I just thought it was one of the greatest things I'd ever heard. Period. On record or off record. And I had an album of Dolly McMahon's with the uileann pipes and all that stuff. I liked it too". (Galwegian singer McMahon was also the wife of the late Ciaran MacMathuna, venerated Irish broadcaster and folk song collector.)

As Peter Mills points out in *Hymns To The Silence*, the McPeakes are now regarded as the first family of Northern Irish folk music. Yet at the time of *Hard Nose The Highway*, "Irish music was 'nowhere', most unfashionable and almost invisible commercially."

'Wild Children' should apparently have been called 'War Children'. It was "written for all the kids born around that time," Morrison said, "because there was a heavier trip to conform"—which is why, presumably, the song includes a roll call of nonconformists: Rod Steiger, Marlon Brando, James Dean, and Tennessee Williams.

Hard Nose The Highway is arguably as notable for the songs it doesn't feature as those it does—songs that were omitted for reasons only Morrison can explain. 'Contemplation Rose', 'Not Supposed To Break Down', 'Drumshanbo Hustle', and 'Madame Joy' did appear on *The Philosopher's Stone*, the 1998 compilation of previously unreleased tracks from 1969 to 1988, but they could easily have augmented what was a rather slight set of eight songs on *Hard Nose The Highway*. 'Drumshanbo Hustle' was inspired by a contentious gig Morrison played with The Manhattan Showband in County Leitrim, on the west coast of Ireland, in 1964, though it could serve as a blueprint for his regular rants against the music industry that became tiresome on later albums. 'Madame Joy' was something of a sequel to 'Madame George'. That it took him 25 years to release "suggests an almost wilful perversity" on his part, according to Clinton Heylin.

Morrison crossed the Atlantic the same year of *Hard Nose The Highway*'s release, Caledonia Soul Orchestra in tow, for a brace of concerts at London's Rainbow Theatre. This was the best band he's ever played with, bar none—John Platania on guitar, David Hayes on bass, Jeff Labes on piano and organ, Dahaud Shaar on drums, Bill Atwood on trumpet, Jack Schroer on alto, tenor and baritone saxophones, and a string section of Terry Adams on cello, Nancy Ellis on viola, and Tom Halpin, Tim Kovatch, and Nathan Rubin on violins. The Rainbow gig, along with an earlier one at the Troubadour in Los Angeles on the same tour, is captured for posterity on the must-have live double album *It's Too Late To Stop Now*. As well as his own songs, including 'Warm Love' and 'Wild Children' from *Hard Nose The Highway*, 'Saint Dominic's Preview' and 'Listen To The Lion' (reciprocating the intensity of the recorded version, and then some) from *Saint Dominic's Preview*, and 'Cyprus Avenue' from *Astral Weeks*, Morrison acknowledges the influence of Ray Charles, John Lee Hooker, Sonny Boy Williamson, Sam Cooke, and Bobby Bland. As Chris Jones of the BBC enthused, "In a live setting all the hyperbole about Morrison's blend of genres into one Celtic, mystic vision makes perfect sense." And it does.

"The Caledonia Soul Orchestra was so different from everything else that was going on," said Paul Charles, who managed Morrison's business affairs from 1979 to 1988. "But if you want to take references, Van knows the showband sound, and knows how to use the magic of the showband sound, and he had found a way of setting it inside contemporary music."

His apprenticeship on the showband circuit had served him well.

CHAPTER 7
GOD'S GREEN LAND

Less than three months after the Rainbow concert, on October 20 1973, Van Morrison finally returned to Ireland—though not to his native Belfast. His parents no longer lived there, having moved to their son's US home earlier that year. Instead, accompanied by then-girlfriend Carol Guida and manager Stephen Pillster, he travelled through the south, visiting Cork, Cashel, Killarney, and Arklow. He even saw the Blarney Stone, a block of bluestone built into the battlements of Blarney Castle, which, according to legend, endows those who kiss it with what is known colloquially as the gift of the gab—namely, great eloquence or a facility for flattery. You don't need to have been there to know that Van probably didn't follow this whimsical tradition.

Pillster, who today edits demo reels for actors and other artists, began working with Caledonia Productions in 1972. His first project was to complete the preparations for *It's Too Late To Stop Now*. "Van's focus," he said, "was on his recently estranged wife, Janet Planet, and their child, Shana."

Pillster only joined Morrison and Guida part way through their Irish holiday.

"I got a call from Van which sounded so clear I thought he was back in Marin, but he was still in Dublin, staying at the Jamison House, which has since burned down. He asked if I could come over. I told him it would take me 24 hours, but when I arrived, he and Carol had left on a drive-about for a week. I went to London to meet with his European agent, Paul [Charles] at Asgard. When he returned, I spent a week with him, and he was enjoying his reconnection with Ireland.

"In fact, I met a solicitor, at Van's direction, to discuss the possibility of Van claiming Irish citizenship. There were benefits for authors and songwriters, [but] the tax break was not retroactive, so Van's previously written songs would not qualify. He elected to pass on Irish citizenship."

In November, back in Dublin after his "drive-about", Morrison appeared on RTE's *Talk About Pop*, hosted by Tony Johnston.

"We were delighted that he should want to appear on *Talk About Pop*," producer Bill Keating recalled. "Recognising his position in popular music, we paid him the courtesy of giving him the 30 minutes to do exactly what he wanted. If Morrison wanted to sing, dance, stand on his head, anything at all, all he had to do was let us know, and we would arrange it."

Morrison turned up for the TV special with Donal Corvin and insisted that his friend—not the presenter—would interview him. What followed was car-crash television. Only five numbers from a 13-song set were broadcast—'Wild Children', 'Slim Slow Slider', 'Warm Love', 'Drumshanbo Hustle', and 'Autumn Song'—but it was Morrison's obnoxious behaviour that caused furious viewers to bombard the RTE switchboard with complaints.

"It was dreadful television and unforgivable rudeness on Morrison's part," said Keating. "Tony Johnston was made to look like an idiot, with Morrison strumming loudly and turning his back on him when he said anything. It wasn't even clever. It was just downright rudeness."

During what passed for an interview, Morrison hit back at claims that he had cancelled two concerts at Dublin's Carlton Theatre at short notice.

"Let me elaborate: there was never any concert at all. I mentioned it to some people that I was really interested in playing in Ireland. I told the agency over in London that if I could fit it in, I would do it. But I had something happening in California that I had to go back to. I told the people concerned not to book or put a gig out with my name on it until I called them. I looked them straight in the eyes and said, 'If you get a phone call from me, you know I'm going to do it; if you don't, I'm not.' Straight ahead, no paper, just one-to-one.

"Obviously they didn't wait on my call and they started printing and putting up advertising and stuff like that. They just went ahead and did it themselves. It didn't have anything to do with me. People have been asking me why I backed out of the gig. I didn't back out of anything. It wasn't happening to begin with."

Morrison did eventually play four concerts in Dublin the following spring, as part of a week-long festival that also featured The Chieftains, Tim Hardin, Humphrey Lyttleton, and Ronnie Scott, with Elmer Bernstein conducting the RTE Symphony Orchestra. Morrison did supposedly speak to promoter Noel Pearson about playing Belfast around the same time, but was advised against it, according to Pillster.

"The reason he gave was that they couldn't guarantee Van's security and that there had been death threats, or some death threats against him," he told me. "I always thought that Pearson exaggerated them [the death threats] because he didn't want to promote in Belfast."

Whether this was true or not, Morrison's decision not to go back to Belfast provoked criticism from his compatriots, among them journalist Colin McClelland, who asked, in print, "How can you stand up an entire nation?" Another piece by Chris Moore was so loaded with invective that it provoked a furious reply from an outraged Violet Morrison in California, in which she claimed that she and George had begged their son not to risk his safety by performing a concert in his home city.

According to Steve Turner, Morrison had become interested in his Celtic origins "after spending most of his life looking toward America as the source of all good music, and then realising that blues, gospel, and country each owed a great debt to Scotland and Ireland".

Speaking to Donal Corvin for *Hot Press* in 1977, Morrison expounded on his theory that soul music originated in Scotland and Ireland, noting the strong structural similarities between traditional Irish and Scottish music and American R&B.

"Take 'Purple Heather'," he said. "There's a theme running through that which is pretty similar to the standard rhythm & blues trip, and there's a lot of connections like that. Bert Berns had the theory that this was where it originated. Bobby Scott, who wrote 'Taste Of Honey', has that theory too. Later on, I got one of Bobby Scott's records where he sings and plays piano, and his piano playing is very similar to my guitar playing. The way he thinks on the piano and the way he writes is very similar to the way I think and write. And he's into that soul thing too."

Author Rhetta Akamatsu came across the Irish role in the history of the blues while researching her book, *Irish Slaves*. "I tell in detail of the enslavement of Irish political prisoners, as well as other men, women and children, on the sugar plantations in the West Indies and Barbados in the 1600s and 1700s," she explained. "Some Irish slaves were shipped to the colonies as well, but most of the Irish in North America came in the 1700s and 1800s as indentured servants, agreeing to be sold to any employer who chose to buy them for a period of time in return for passage to America. These indentured servants were often treated exactly as slaves were. After the abolishment of slavery, Irish immigrants often worked at the most dangerous and least desirable jobs, along with African Americans and Asian immigrants."

Akamatsu's research on the subject is largely culled from Miachaelin Daugherty's article 'Irish Blue', in which he points out that while many people believe the blues originated in the Mississippi Delta in the early 1900s, "others acknowledge that the music actually had its roots in the blend of African and Celtic music produced by Irish and African slaves in the West Indies".

"Certainly, Irish folk music and African folk music have common traits, using music to express deep emotion and often using minor keys to evoke a sense of melancholy," Akamatsu added. "Both African and Celtic folklore was oral and not written, told with strong inflections and sometimes accompanied by music. One can see this reflected most directly in the 'talking blues'. The 'field holler' of the slaves and servants working in the sugar cane fields of the West Indies and the cotton fields of the [American] South evolved into the work songs of the 1900s labour camps, on the levees and on the railroads and in the fields, and this led directly to the early Delta blues."

Akamatsu concluded that the blues "is the gift of those slaves and virtual slaves, Irish and African, who worked the plantations of the West Indies and the south, and of the later virtual slaves who built the infrastructure of America, the roads and railroads, bridges and levees, and expressed their emotions through their music". The Smithsonian Institute traces American folk music to the blending of English and Scots-Irish traditions with those of enslaved Africans.

Meanwhile, during Morrison's stay in Dublin he expressed what amounted to his most political opinion yet. Three members of the Provisional IRA had escaped from Dublin's Mountjoy Jail with the aid of a helicopter that had landed in the yard. Hardcore Republican sympathisers The Wolfe Tones rush-released a single, 'The Helicopter Song', to mark the daring rescue. It topped the charts.

"I think a musician who gets involved in politics is way out of his depth," said Morrison. "Unless it's someone like Pete Seeger, who really knows what he's talking about. Guys like Pete Seeger have been through all that and that's why they can talk about it. I think it's terrible for musicians to use their position to influence people like that. They don't have any right. Music is universal. It's not for one side or the other. Black. White. Music is for people. There's no sides."

Commenting specifically on the Troubles up north, Morrison emphasised that he wasn't part of "the hatred thing … I don't have a specific country to be patriotic about. As for dying for my country, I wouldn't do it. I don't know what that means. What difference does it make where you were born? It's just a piece of land. All I can say is that I'm neutral".

In many respects Morrison's view—his stated neutrality— reflected the prevailing mood in the Republic of Ireland, although equivocation is perhaps a more apposite description of majority opinion down south. It certainly wouldn't have pleased the denizens of Protestant East Belfast.

So was Morrison's three-week Irish odyssey the beginning of his search for his Irishness? Stephen Pillster believed it was, if not the beginning, certainly the continuation of a search, but a search beyond nationality.

"His folks were not Catholic," Pillster said. "Was the Irish culture denied to him as a boy? I don't have a clue. My assessment is that he is a genius and a channel. He listened to his dad's records and blossomed from there.

"Van was always a sponge for what interested him. I suppose there was an influence due to his time in Ireland. He is a tortured Irish poet. He read a lot of Irish writers. He is a seeker of an ineffable state. That, by definition, is hard to write about.

"I think Van has always depicted himself as an Irish-born citizen of the world. He is a seeker of what resonates for everyone—the magic chord accompanying the most glorious lyric. In my opinion, he is reluctant to take author's pride in his compositions. I believe he thinks of himself more as a channel for a greater intelligence."

Guitarist John Platania believed Morrison "reached a tipping point sometime around then where he wanted to go beyond America and its music influences on him, and get back to his roots, or at least begin to acknowledge them more in his music. Van's repertoire since has become rife with songs relevant to his Irishness".

The trip certainly got Morrison's creative juices flowing. He wrote eight new songs on it—songs that would comprise the bulk of his next album, *Veedon Fleece*.

As Brian Hinton remarks in *Celtic Crossroads*, "Van was finding fresh inspiration in the landscape of his youth, as the beautiful and mysterious *Veedon Fleece* would signify. The years of self-imposed exile were over. As years went on, Morrison was to pay increasing attention to his own Irish heartbeat."

Let's return to Pillster's characterisation of Morrison as "a tortured Irish poet". Time to debunk this particular myth, among the more absurd to emerge from evaluations of The Man's work, and one which arguably has its origins in the early American years, when he was deified as "LA's mad Irish poet in residence"—a (misplaced) stereotype "based partly on ignorance and misunderstanding". As Johnny Rogan points out, comparisons were made between Morrison and W.B. Yeats on the spurious grounds that the aforementioned bard had an interest in mysticism.

"It reveals much about this simplistic media shorthand that nobody ever chose to mention Morrison in connection with any of the Northern Ireland poets of his own time. In such company, his lyrics would certainly have looked embarrassingly like trite poetry, but at least this would have been a saner comparison than any attempt to place him alongside one of the greatest poets of the 20th century."

The application of such good sense on Rogan's part certainly finds favour in this parish, for it's patently ridiculous to label Morrison a poet, Irish or otherwise. Even Van has bought into the myth, claiming, in 1974, that he was "a poet and a musician". In 2006, he would allay himself with the poetry of the Romantics, which he said "comes from a different place of being in touch with nature, so that's where I'm coming from. If there's any sort of lineage in this, it's people like that. Or in Ireland—Patrick Kavanagh, or Joseph Campbell, these kind of lyricists". Mind you, in the same 2006 interview with Paul Sexton, he did display a more astute awareness of his method in describing it as "an instinctual thing ... rather than sitting down and thinking more intellectually, like Seamus Heaney. He's a very intellectual poet. I'm coming from the other place".

Shall we cut through the bullshit? Morrison is a songwriter who derives inspiration, consciously or not, from the vast reservoir of poetry. As a consequence of which, his songs, on occasion, possess profoundly poetic elements that flow from feeling rather than any intentional manipulation of language. Couched another way, he's always been more about sensation than words. Like any soul man, blues man, or jazz man worth listening to. What sets him apart is that he brings a distinct Irish sensibility to the table, suffusing the songs with uniquely Irish cultural nuances. A sensory elegist, if you will.

The Northern Irish poet Tom Paulin placed Morrison in the "age-old oral and place name tradition known in Irish as the dindsenchas", which translates as "lore of places". I'll go with that. In another perspicacious call, Paulin equated Morrison with American action painter Jackson Pollock, another descendent of the same Scotch-Irish roots. Theirs, he said, is an imagination "that owes a lot to Calvinism. Jackson Pollock said, 'I don't paint nature, I am nature.' And I feel with listening to Van, you're inside a natural process. So it's something that's not composed from the outside, not formed and shaped, but it shapes itself from the inside."

O

So what exactly is the Veedon Fleece, mentioned in 'You Don't Pull No Punches But You Don't Push The River'? Steve Turner reckons it's Morrison's "Irish equivalent of the Holy Grail, a religious relic that would answer his questions if he could track it down on his quest around the west coast of Ireland".

In his book *Van Morrison: Too Late To Stop Now*, Turner quotes former Monarch Billy McAllen's waggish anecdote about a friend—a Van The Man devotee—who asked a professor of Irish history at Queen's University in Belfast to trace the origins of the Veedon Fleece.

"I told him that he could actually meet Van if he came round to my place one night, and then he could ask him face to face," said McAllen. "So I introduced this guy to Van, but Van wasn't on good form that night. The guy got him to sign the cover of an album he had and then he said, 'By the way Van, what is the Veedon Fleece?' Van just looked at him and said, 'It doesn't mean anything. I made it up myself.' He said it as quick as that. He didn't want to elaborate."

At the time of its release, Morrison did elaborate a little. "I haven't a clue about what the title means," he said. "It's actually a person's name. I have a whole set of characters in my head that I'm trying to fit into things. Veedon Fleece is one of them, and I just suddenly started singing it in one of these songs. It's like a streams of consciousness thing."

Whoever or whatever Veedon Fleece is, doesn't really matter. What does matter is that *Veedon Fleece*, the album, finds Van Morrison, the East Belfast Protestant, the Northern Irishman, making a connection with that other Ireland: the south, the Free State, the Republic, yes, but in a way that goes far beyond these mere constructs. He taps into the poetry of the place, the myths and legends.

Stephen Pillster described Morrison as "a mad Irish poet", an appellation given ballast by the cut of his jib on the sleeve, soberly suited with wild, flaming hair, prostrated between two magnificent Irish wolfhounds in the grounds of a country house—what the local peasantry would have referred to as 'the big house' in days of yore, when such properties were annexed by the Anglo-Irish ascendancy. It is an historical structure that has been frequently employed by Irish literary figures such as Maria Edgeworth, Elizabeth Bowen, and William Trevor, to represent "in a very concrete way the comparative wealth and power of the Anglo-Irish ascendancy as a class, as they straddled the chasm between the colonised, impoverished and predominantly Catholic, Gaelic Irish, and their coloniser, the imperialistic English".

Yet according to Peter Mills, *Veedon Fleece* "draws from Ireland from an outside perspective". Morrison, he writes, is "a visitor, a guest in his own country. It is an album of exile".

Exile is certainly an apparent theme in songs like 'Linden Arden Stole The Highlights', 'Who Was That Masked Man', and 'Streets Of Arklow'. The latter draws a line between "God's green land" and gypsies destined to roam. The protagonist of 'Who Was That Masked Man' is cast out in some sort of self-imposed exile, a loner "livin' with a gun" who can't trust anyone. You can't but think of the Troubles, the balaclava-clad Republican terrorists—and, maybe to a lesser extent, those on the Loyalist side—who felt disenfranchised in their own country.

At the time, Morrison described 'Linden Arden Stole The Highlights' as being "about an image of an Irish-American living in San Francisco. It's really a hard man type of thing". Yet in 2012, he professed to not know what it was about.

"It was a house I was staying in at the time. It was another way of writing songs. I just seemed to be picking stuff up, different ideas from this house. But I don't actually know what it's about. In fact, I don't have a clue what most of that album is about. I think I was picking those songs out of the air. Psychic air, whatever you want to call it. They were fictional characters. Sometimes a place will inspire something and you get ideas without knowing what they mean."

For Johnny Rogan, Linden Arden emerges as "a cross between Desperate Dan and John L. Sullivan". He identifies a subtext in "the extremely violent imagery, particularly the gruesome allusion to decapitation ('Cleaved their heads off with a hatchet'), a method of execution that was attempted by extremists within the UVF"—Lenny Murphy's bloodthirsty, Catholic-hating Shankill Butchers".

Speaking to RTE radio presenter Dave Fanning in 1997, Sinead O'Connor seemed in no doubt that 'Who Was That Masked Man' and 'Linden Arden Stole The Highlights' were Morrison's response to what was happening in Northern Ireland.

"'Who Was That Masked Man' does deal with a lot of the political situation," she said. "Politically, he's never approached Ireland, except for me in this one song which I think is an incredible insight into what was going on in those times in his country. Linden Arden is a gangster-type character, and the song is a very subtle comment on what was going on between Ireland and America in terms of assisting what was going on."

O'Connor was obviously alluding to Noraid—the Irish Northern

111

Aid Committee, an Irish-American fundraising organisation founded in 1969, whose mission statement declared its support through peaceful means for the establishment of a democratic 32-country Ireland. Membership was open to anyone who shared the values of the 1916 Proclamation by the Provisional Government of the Irish Republic. In Easter Week of that year, a group of insurrectionists from the Irish Republican Brotherhood seized several strategic locations in Dublin on the premise that it was "the right of the people of Ireland to the ownership of Ireland, and to the unfettered control of Irish destinies". After seven days of fighting, the rebellion was suppressed, and its leaders were executed. One of them, James Connolly, was transported by military ambulance to Kilmainham Jail, brought into the courtyard on a stretcher, tied to a chair, and shot. His body, and those of his comrades, were interred in a mass grave without a coffin and covered over with lime.

The contemporary Irish references on *Veedon Fleece* aren't all so doom-laden. 'Fair Play' is a phrase that Morrison heard everywhere he went in southern Ireland. It's synonymous with 'well done' or 'good on you'—a platitude, in other words. The same song name-checks Killarney's blue lakes and Oscar Wilde. The son of Dublin intellectuals, Wilde wrote drama, poetry, and fiction. *The Importance Of Being Earnest*, *The Picture Of Dorian Gray*, and *The Ballad Of Reading Gaol* are three of the most celebrated literary works of the 19th century, yet he is possibly—and bizarrely—just as well known for his capacity to coin a memorable epigram, as well as his trial and subsequent imprisonment on grounds of gross indecency with other men. Another exiled Irishman, he spent the last three years of his life penniless in Paris, eventually dying in 1900 from cerebral meningitis at the age of 41.

'You Don't Pull No Punches But You Don't Push The River' has, said Morrison, "flashes of Ireland"—he sings exultantly about going into the country "to get down to the real soul". The radio-friendly 'Bulbs' has a girl either leaving for America or for an American (because of Van's intonation it's hard to tell which) "with a suitcase in her hand"; her brothers and sisters are "all on Atlantic sand". This is the familiar Irish narrative of emigration, though judging by the uplift of the melody and the verve in Van's delivery, not—as with so many Irishmen and Irishwomen through the ages—enforced emigration, but emigration by choice.

The closing 'Country Fair' is another of Morrison's childhood reflections "about things that you remember happening to you ... You could say it's a bit like 'And It Stoned Me'. It has the same kind of feeling anyway, but it's not about fishing". In *The Isle Of Noises*, Mark J. Prendergast, describes the track as "an Irish mystical appreciation, a loosening of images remembered, a regeneration of experience past, a slow exorcism, a cyclical perception—a musical metamorphosis from human state to spirit".

Indeed, "an Irish mystical appreciation" might just capture the essence of *Veedon Fleece* as a whole. It is undeniably Irish in both inspiration and content—and arguably the most Irish thing Morrison has ever done as a writer. (*Irish Heartbeat* doesn't count because, with the exception of 'Celtic Ray' and the title song, it is made up of traditional compositions.)

It is also, as Peter Mills suggests, allied "to the body of work made by Irish artists in exile—Joyce's Dublin, reinvented in Zurich, Paris, and Trieste, Sean O'Casey's Ireland, coined in London and rural Devon, the Irish landscape felt as much as seen by Samuel Beckett in Paris".

Recalling his 1971 interview with Morrison for this book, Shay Healy didn't accept the exiled Irish writer theory.

"To me, the difference between Van leaving Ireland and Joyce leaving Ireland is that Van was choosing to leave Ireland without ever thinking of himself as an exile. He was seeking out new platforms. He didn't feel under-appreciated and unwanted. I reckon he felt Jackie Wilson tug at his soul very early on, and he began to make his way toward the light even while still in a showband in Ireland."

Put simply, Morrison's modus operandi as an artist seems to be rooted in going wherever his muse instinctively leads him. And like any artist worthy of the label, he is, after all, a seeker—someone untrammelled by extraneous restrictions. The muse took him as a young man across the Atlantic to the United States, the sounds of which he had absorbed back in Hyndford Street. But he had absorbed other sounds on that street too, and therefore it was only ever a matter of when he would follow the muse back home to the hearth of his Irish soul.

"Van has a jaundiced eye, but it has helped him as a songwriter," said Healy. "His Irishness has informed his songs from the beginning. His narrative style is a continuum of The Clancy Brothers and Tommy Makem's repertoire of historic ballads and street songs. In that way, Van's songs are identifiably Irish. They are like folk ballads conveying his perceptions and emotions as the news of the day. When he recorded with The Chieftains, his simpatico with the traditional Irish music was proof positive of his Irish sensibility. He has what in Ireland we call the 'neaaah', the authentic sound of an unaccompanied traditional Irish singer.

"There is a piece of Ireland that will be forever Van. His songs have influenced countless Irish musicians and thrilled the world with a voice that is truly a gift from the gods. He has used his voice like a painter, like a poet, as an actor and as a model of egalitarianism, and though he can be exasperating and churlish at times, he can also be incredibly tender. As rock icon, when he sings, we forgive him all his faults and peccadilloes. And on both sides of the border, in the Republic of Ireland and Northern Ireland, we each proudly claim him as 'one of our own'."

O

After *Veedon Fleece*, Morrison split the scene for a couple of years. In a Warner Brothers press release at the time, he talked of wanting "to get a new perspective. I wanted to change the way I was working. I wanted to open up new areas of creativity, so I had to let go of everything for a while". To Robin Denselow of *The Guardian*, he said, "I got to the point where music just wasn't doing it for me anymore. Something was telling me to knock it off a bit. I caught up with years of sleep."

Van had, as he told Ritchie Yorke, "been performing in bands since I was 12, which represented, at that point, about 16 years of playing music". There was the occasional live appearance, most notably with jazz guitarist George Benson on a reworking of the standard 'Misty', and as part of a fantasy line-up—including Bob Dylan, Joni Mitchell, Eric Clapton, Muddy Waters, Neil Young, and Dr John—at The Band's farewell concert in San Francisco, immortalised in director Martin Scorsese's film *The Last Waltz*. Van, plagued with nerves beforehand, had to be coaxed from his hotel by then manager Harvey Goldsmith and whisked to the venue with less than an hour to spare. You would never have guessed it from his high-octane, high-kicking 'Caravan', as memorable for the tight-fitting sequinned lilac-cum-burgundy number he wore as for the rapturous reception that accompanied his performance.

"He went out there and really stormed the place," Goldsmith recalled. "All the artists like Clapton, Dylan, and Joni were standing in a little area on the side, and everybody came out to watch him. To a person they all stood up and roared with the audience."

Unfortunately, the first of his two numbers, 'Tura Lura Lura (That's An Irish Lullaby)', didn't make Scorsese's final cut, though it can be heard on the accompanying album. It was a duet with Richard Manuel, The Band's tragic pianist, who committed suicide in 1986. An old friend from back in Woodstock, Manuel affectionately bestowed the sobriquet 'The Belfast Cowboy' on Morrison.

Seeing Morrison in *The Last Waltz* was something of a pivotal moment for Glenn Pattterson, not only because of Van's performance but because of what his presence on that stage with those artists in the United States illustrated.

"I went with some friends to the Avenue Picture House in Belfast city centre to see it, and all of us were astonished by Van's performance, because we had never seen him live," he said. "It was an extraordinary performance, but at the same time he looked like your dad, high-kicking across the stage. Or maybe that should be the other way around—he looked like your dad, and it was an extraordinary performance, the high point of the film.

"I don't think I realised how significant he was to people outside of Northern Ireland, or even just Belfast, until much later. *The Last Waltz* was maybe a starting point. I moved to England in the early 80s, and became friendly with a guy who had grown up in Corby who told me *Astral Weeks* had saved his life in his teenage years. If I'm honest, I had never listened to it myself up until then."

During this period, Morrison also engaged in a process of self-education: the seeking out of an Irish heritage denied him as a schoolboy in Belfast. He read the novels of Belfast compatriot Brian Moore and of J.P. Donleavy, an American writer who has lived in Ireland since the end of the Second World War. In 1946, Donleavy began studying at Trinity College, Dublin, but quit before completing his degree. His debut work of fiction, *The Ginger Man*, is listed by the Modern Library in the United States as one of the best 100 novels of the 20th century.

"He's written books that I can definitely connect with," said Morrison. "He has amazing insights which other people missed out on. Even with his descriptions of Northern Ireland. I haven't read anybody from Northern Ireland with equivalent insight. And Donleavy's not even from Ireland—he's from Brooklyn or somewhere."

Morrison studied that period of Irish history variously known as the Irish Literary Revival, the Irish Literary Renaissance, or the Celtic Twilight. This was essentially a rebirth of national consciousness in the late 19th and early 20th centuries through a renewed interest in the indigenous language of Gaelic and in ancient Irish legend and folklore, spearheaded by poet William Butler Yeats, scholar Douglas Hyde (later to become Ireland's first President from 1938 to 1945), and dramatist and folklorist Lady Gregory (alias Augusta Gregory). It formed an integral part of a wider movement that "began to uncover more and more of what slowly came to be seen as the evidence of a rich and splendid history". Hyde blazed the trail when he published a volume of folk stories, in Irish, in 1889. He followed this a year later with a second instalment, and then in 1893, in Irish with an English translation, his *Lovesongs Of Connacht* were hailed by Yeats as "the coming of a new power into literature".

Yeats himself, while less intimate with Irish peasant life than Hyde, nonetheless published his own collections in 1888 and 1892. He recognised a depth and passion in Irish and Celtic myth that European contemporaries found in the mythology of ancient Greece. However, it wasn't until he met Lady Gregory in 1896, and began to spend time in her home at Coole Park, Galway, "that he learned at first hand what a wealth of experience lay waiting to be transmuted into poetry and drama". Together, they established the Irish Literary Theatre in 1989, a precursor of the Abbey Theatre Company or Irish National Theatre Society.

"We propose to have performed in Dublin in the spring of every year, certain Celtic and Irish plays, which, whatever be their degree of excellence, will be written with a high ambition, and so build up a Celtic and Irish school of dramatic literature," its manifesto stated. "We hope to find in Ireland an uncorrupted and imaginative audience trained to listen by its passion for oratory, and believe that our desire to bring upon the stage the deeper thoughts and emotions of Ireland, will ensure for us a tolerant welcome, and that freedom to experiment which is not found in theatres of England, and without which no new movement in art or literature can succeed. We will show that Ireland is not the home of buffoonery and of easy sentiment as it has been represented, but the home of an ancient idealism. We are confident of the support of the Irish people, who are weary of misrepresentation, in carrying out a work that is outside all the political questions that divide us."

Yeats's writing for the stage, often in verse, was not to everyone's taste. It was sometimes too literarily allusive and solemn. Lady Gregory, who had almost 40 plays produced by the Abbey, compensated for his lack of the common touch with a series of immensely popular comedies of rural life and patriotic tragedies, among them *Spreading The News* and *The Rising Of The Moon*.

Another playwright who effectively made his name at the Abbey was John Millington Synge. His *The Playboy Of The Western World*, which pivoted around a story of apparent patricide, provoked riots in the theatre when it premiered in 1907. *The Freeman's Journal* slammed it as "an unmitigated, protracted libel upon Irish peasant men, and, worse still, upon Irish girlhood". Nationalist stalwart Arthur Griffith, who felt the theatre was not politically active enough, derided Synge's masterpiece as "a vile and inhuman story told in the foulest language we have ever listened to from a public platform". Yeats returned from Scotland to address the crowd on the second night in defence of *Playboy*, but was eventually forced to call in the police. Press opinion soon turned against the rioters, and the protests petered out.

The legacy created by Yeats, Synge, Hyde, and Lady Gregory was an enduring one. As historian F.S.L. Lyons writes in *Ireland Since The Famine*, "In little more than ten years they had enriched the experience of their fellow countrymen by the extraordinary variety and abundance of their talent. The results have passed into literary history, and have become part of the European inheritance. The poems of Yeats himself, the plays of Synge and Lady Gregory ... all this (which is by no means the whole canon) represents a staggering achievement reached in an almost incredibly short span of time."

CHAPTER 8
BELONGING TO ULSTER

Morrison may have spent much of his sabbatical from the music industry, if not the music itself, mining his Irish soul. But listening to the album that eventually broke the silence, you'd never think it. *A Period Of Transition*, co-produced by Mac Rebbenack, aka Dr John, is bereft of the Irish allusions that permeated *Veedon Fleece*. It's hard to argue against Johnny Rogan's assessment that, while the faithful were "hoping for a work of primeval vocal aggression that would challenge the emerging elite of Morrison pretenders, whose ranks included Bruce Springsteen, Bob Seger, Phil Lynott, Graham Parker, and Elvis Costello", what they got was "a master class in mediocrity". And this despite the involvement of The Anita Kerr Singers, whose choral backing can be heard on records by Roy Orbison, Webb Pierce, Willie Nelson, Jim Reeves, and countless others. A transitional period indeed.

The album's release did provide some classic Van confrontations with his nemesis—the media—especially Vivien Goldman of *Sounds*, to whom, in reference to that year's Royal Jubilee, he pithily remarked, "It's good to see the Queen and the Duke of Edinburgh waving." To the hapless Nicky Horne on Capital Radio, he said, "What I'm doing right now is I'm doing an interview for promotional purposes, no more, no less than that. There's an album, so I'm available for talking."

"I have never done an interview that bad," Horne recalled. "I was really upset that a man I had admired for so long could blow it so totally. He really did destroy my feelings for him as a man."

The most fascinating interview, however, came with Ritchie Yorke, author of the first ever Morrison biography, *Into The Music*. Here, Morrison vented his anger at reviewers who presumed to know what his songs were about, a diatribe that concomitantly afforded a glimpse into his own ideas on the creative process.

'Saint Dominic's Preview', for example, had nothing to do with James Joyce, regardless of what some critics might have claimed. As far Morrison was concerned, these critics were imposing their own intellectual readings on his work and misinterpreting or overanalysing what, for him, was "simple stream-of-consciousness stuff" that he himself had very little control over.

"You're like an instrument for what's coming through," he said. "It's the same thing as primitive Africans, Indians, nomads, or whatever—when they start getting up and doing their ritual and doing the dance, it's just what's coming through. It's the spirit."

Rock'n'roll, he said, was still as primitive as ever. "We might think that we're really intellectual and we're going to check out the library to research the meaning every time somebody puts out a new record … [but] it's the same now as it was at the beginning. Rock'n'roll is just spirit music—it's just coming through people. When you start to analyse it, it's only because you don't understand it."

Yorke, it seemed, was unafraid to tread on sacred personal ground as he disarmingly steered the conversation toward Morrison's relationship with the booze—the Irish Achilles heel.

"It's no secret that you were, some years back, rather fond of the juice?" Yorke asked.

"I was into it heavily," Morrison recalled. "But I was like one of those newspapers, those periodicals. There's all kinds of different alcoholics. There's the everyday kind—that's the consistent one. That's what people think an alcoholic is. But an alcoholic is basically just someone who's allergic to alcohol. That's all it means. It's just an allergy."

When Morrison first started drinking, he continued, it "worked" for him. Everybody was drinking back then, in the late 50s and early

60s, he said. But did you then reach a point, Yorke wondered, where you wanted to pack it in completely?

"Basically I got an insight into what it really was through Alcoholics Anonymous," Morrison replied. "One day the switchboard lit up and I saw where it was all going. I saw what alcohol could do to people and I saw that it wasn't a good thing anymore. I realised I was growing up or something like that. You have responsibilities; you've got to think about getting your act together. I didn't even know what it had been doing to me. I didn't realise how dangerous it was. People talked in terms of drugs and I used to think in terms of ... well, in Ireland, everybody drinks. Nobody gives it a second thought. You're Irish, number one, and you're a drinker, number two. That's the first two things about us Irish. And that's cool if you're not allergic to it. If you are allergic to it, that's another story altogether. And I happened to be allergic to it."

Morrison's depiction of the drinking Irish may read now like a cultural stereotype—as it no doubt did then—but the incontrovertible fact is that, several decades later, alcohol abuse remains a huge problem in the country. Statistical data gathered in 2003 found that Ireland had the second highest per capita alcohol consumption in the world. The Rutland Centre in Dublin, a private addiction clinic, estimates that one in ten people in Ireland are dealing with alcoholism, and that alcohol is the third most common reason why people are admitted to psychiatric wards. In 2012, a report by the Steering Group On National Substance Misuse Strategy found that Irish adults drink in a more dangerous way than those in nearly any other country.

○

A year after *A Period Of Transition*, Morrison's next album, *Wavelength*, was the sound of someone aiming squarely at the marketplace—or running low on ideas. 'Kingdom Hall' is an explicit reference to the place of worship of Jehovah's Witnesses—his mother, don't forget, was a disciple. And the title track pays homage to radio, the altar at which Morrison worshipped as a child. He hears the voice of America calling to him—not, as he told Jonathan Cott of *Rolling Stone*, the country.

"When I was growing up in Belfast," he said, "I used to listen to Radio Luxembourg and the Voice of America, which broadcast from Germany. Those lines are about returning to Europe and getting back to my roots."

In 1979, Morrison did finally return to his Belfast roots, playing the city for the first time in a dozen years. The venue was the Whitla Hall. Tickets sold out in under 30 minutes.

"People expected him to walk on water—the expectation was amazing," promoter Paul Charles recalled. "I'm sure to him it was just another opportunity for him to go onstage and sing his music. He came onstage and he just dug in. He didn't play to that 'I'm back again' thing."

By his own admission, Morrison didn't feel "one way or the other. I don't feel emotional or unemotional. I just feel like I'm doing the job. My job is to play music and deliver the show. It's more emotional for the audience, I think".

Still, he did return to his old haunts. *Van Morrison In Ireland*, a concert movie interspersed with documentary footage and directed by Mike Radford (who went on to make *Nineteen Eighty-Four*, *White Mischief*, and *Il Postino*) shows him strolling through Sandy Row, Cyprus Avenue, Stormont, and the Beersbridge Road. And after the opening gig he jammed with Phil Coulter and Herbie Armstrong, a contemporary from Belfast in the 60s, who, bizarrely, tried his hand on barrel-scraping reality TV show *Britain's Got Talent* in 2011. There were even rumours of him buying a property in Ireland—rumours he was quick to dispel in typically gruff fashion to Tony Stewart of the *NME*.

"How the hell can I live in Ireland? What am I going to do—move to Ireland and open a grocery store? I'm in the music business. I'm not going to sit up on a hill somewhere writing songs that are going to sell 10 or 20 albums. I'm not a 17-year-old rock'n'roll star."

After the tour, Morrison hung out with old friend Armstrong in the village of Epwell, Oxfordshire, where he wrote the majority of his next album, *Into The Music*. According to Steve Turner, 'Rolling Hills'—described by Brian Hinton as "the missing link between *Veedon Fleece* and Van's work with The Chieftains"—was written about the Cotswold countryside. To these ears, though, it sounds like a rapture to a higher power, as Van vows to life his life "in Him" and read his bible "among the rolling hills". The Supreme Being makes an appearance too in 'Full Force Gale' (featuring Ry Cooder on slide), as he is both lifted up by the Lord and will find his sanctuary in the Lord.

Morrison dismissed any suggestion that, like Bob Dylan, he had undergone a conversion, a born again experience. He saw himself as a Christian mystic. "I was born in a Christian environment in a Christian country," he added bluntly, "and I was born after the Christ event, so that makes me a Christian."

Into The Music remains one of Morrison's most bewitching releases, not least because of the final three songs, 'Angelou', 'And The Healing Has Begun', and 'It's All In The Game / You Know What They're Writing About'. On 'And The Healing Has Begun' he's back down the avenue again—Cyprus Avenue?—while on 'You Know What They're Writing About', which bleeds seamlessly into an erotically charged 'It's All In The Game' (a 1958 hit for Tommy Edwards, later covered by Nat 'King' Cole, Andy Williams, George Benson, and others) he commands the object of his feverish desire to meet him "down by the pylons", a landmark of his East Belfast childhood.

When he returned to the road in support of the album, Van shared a stage with The Chieftains at an outdoor festival in Edinburgh, the somewhat eclectic bill of which also included Derry punks The Undertones, Birmingham reggae outfit Steel Pulse, New York new wavers Talking Heads, and Scottish folkie Dick Gaughan. Ireland north and south came together on the faux jig 'Rolling Hills' and

'Goodnight Irene'. Allan Jones, then writing for *Melody Maker*, was far from impressed. The Chieftains, he wrote, "plucked, plonked, and squawked, Toni Marcus [on viola] scraped and screeched, Van bellowed and howled. He invited the audience to sing. They, at least, had the distinction of being in tune".

The seed had been planted, even if it would be nearly a decade before that seed germinated in the form of *Irish Heartbeat*. In the meantime, Morrison made a new friend in The Chieftains' eccentric multi-instrumentalist, Derek Bell, another Belfast local. Bell was a child prodigy, composing his first concerto at the age of 12, and later several other classical works, including *Three Images Of Ireland In Druid Times* for harp, *Nocturne On An Icelandic Melody* for oboe d'amore and piano, and *Three Transcendental Concert Studies* for oboe and piano. He was, at different times, manager of the Belfast Symphony Orchestra, oboist and harpist with the BBC Northern Ireland Orchestra, and Professor of Harp at the Academy of Music in his home city. Bell wore socks with novelty designs and scruffy suits with trousers that were often too short, and he told filthy jokes. Indeed, his lewd sense of humour was evident in his work—he titled his 1981 solo album *Derek Bell Plays With Himself*. On a tour with The Chieftains in Moscow, when the Cold War was below freezing, he stuck his alarm clock in his pocket in a rush to catch a plane, only to be stopped by Soviet police on suspicion of carrying a concealed weapon. Small wonder that The Chieftains' mouthpiece, Paddy Moloney, nicknamed him 'Ding Dong' Bell.

Bell's friendship with Morrison was cemented by a mutual fondness for ice cream and a mutual interest in the pursuit of self-awareness. "In the days when I first met him, he was really looking for some sort of spiritual answer to things," he said. "At the time ... he wanted to discuss mysticism, and he wanted to know did I think there was anything he should be studying. I suggested various things, but it was very difficult because he had already read something like 3,000 books on mysticism."

Van's spiritual search was in part motivated by the threatened suicide of a friend. It's likely this was Donal Corvin, who did actually gas himself in his Dublin home on September 6 1979. Despite a closeness dating back to Belfast in the 60s, Morrison didn't attend the funeral.

Sam Smyth, another mover in that hip Belfast scene, remembered Corvin affectionately in a published appreciation shortly after his death. "In the mid 60s, Belfast was a switched-on town, or at least that's what the most of us who lived there thought," he wrote. "Corvin's speciality was writing about rock music and he adopted the requisite lifestyle."

"For a while he managed Van Morrison," Smyth later joked. "I think this professional collaboration lasted about three days." Corvin, he said, was "one of the smartest people I've ever met. If I had followed all the advice he gave me, or if he had followed it himself, we would both be millionaires by now, living on easy street. Still, we would both have been that much poorer".

○

Morrison's spiritual quest was very much in evidence on *Common One*, which according to Steve Turner "demonstrated that he had an appetite for the whole New Age smorgasbord, from earth energy and Arthurian legend to Blakeian reverie and Yeatsian trance-states". It's an album that polarised opinion then and continues to divide Vanoraks to this day. On its release, Dave McCullough of *Sounds* wrote that it was "where Van Morrison leaves rock … where economy and self-measurement go to the dogs and a self-obsessive notion of pastoral harmony assumes unflattering, epic status". For Greil Marcus, it was Van "with nothing to say and a limitless interest in getting it across—to himself", while *NME*'s Graham Lock called it "colossally smug and cosmically dull; an interminable, vacuous, and drearily egotistical stab at spirituality". I'm with Lester Bangs, who said that Van "was making holy music … and us rock critics made the mistake of paying too much attention to the lyrics".

Let's face it, the lyrics are occasionally on the silly side—especially the mighty 'Summertime In England', where Van effectively informs us how well read he is (Wordsworth, Coleridge, Yeats, Blake, Yeats, Joyce, and T.S. Eliot all get a mention) while romping about Avalon chasing a bit of skirt. But as Bangs so accurately put it, this is holy music, and we are hopelessly hypnotised by its incantatory persuasiveness. It's best heard live, of course, Morrison doing the call and response thing with one of the band—a role fulfilled at various times over the years by Pee Wee Ellis, Brian Kennedy, and Richie Buckley. In performance, he also introduces new literary references into the song, be it W.H. Auden, D.H. Lawrence, Christopher Isherwood, Samuel Beckett, or Seamus Heaney.

The latter was awarded the Nobel Prize for Literature in 1995 for "works of lyrical beauty and ethical depth, which exalt everyday miracles and the living past". The Nobel committee's citation stated that, for Heaney, "poetry, like the soil, is evidently something to be ploughed and turner over. The poet has little time for the Emerald Isle of the tourist brochures. For him, Ireland is first and foremost The Bogland". Heaney had never allowed the Troubles in Northern Ireland to overshadow his verse, nor had he ever reduced "reality to a matter of political slogans. He writes about the fates of individuals, of personal friends who have been afflicted by the heedless violence— in the background somewhere there is Dante, who could yoke the political to the transcendental".

The son of a small Catholic farmer from County Derry, Heaney published his first collection, *Death Of A Naturalist*, in 1966. As well as being hugely popular—no small feat for any poet—it marked him out as a successor to Yeats. His entire canon reflects a modern temperament that is influenced by currents of contemporary Anglo-American poetry "in which can still be detected echoes of the older languages in Ireland, not only Gaelic, of course, but also the particular speech patterns of his own place, over the small fields of which several cultures in history have contended for mastery".

Van connected with Heaney "on a level where he talks about the weather reports ... 'cos I did the same thing when I was a kid. He found that to be very poetic and so did I. Rockhall, Faroes—where they used to give the weather report on the radio".

When Morrison invokes Heaney's name in the live 'Summertime In England', he cites *Preoccupations*, a collection of essays written between 1968 and 1978 and published in 1981. "Mr Heaney," Van hollers, "I read your book ... *Preoccupations* ... among the regions." The "regions" line relates to how Heaney, like his English counterpart Ted Hughes, "read the landscape as a kind of manuscript, seeing and decoding a meaning and a life within the land that was obscure or opaque to the casual glance"—precisely what Morrison does on 'Summertime In England'.

Common One as a whole is, in the opinion of Peter Mills, "that relatively rare thing: a consideration of England by an Irish artist". Yet in songs like 'Satisfied' and 'Wild Honey', the light and the darkness, the land and the sea, the mountain and the city, connect it "to a specifically Northern Irish song tradition" where the imagery of opposites co-exists.

Whether by design or intuition, this perceived correlation between Morrison's songs and the traditional songs of Northern Ireland could be understood as a yen for home—home not only in the context of Belfast and Northern Ireland, but of Ireland and Britain, and of Europe. He was still in California, though his parents had returned to Belfast. When Phil Coulter visited him there, the Morrison he encountered was "very mellow" and increasingly drawn toward his Irish heritage.

"He's discovered an Irish bar in San Francisco, where they played traditional Irish music," Coulter said. "There was a time in Van Morrison's career where there was no way you'd have got him into a pub, let alone an Irish bar where they played very average traditional music. He has got a thing about the evolution of the Celtic culture and he's very aware that he's a Celt. One evening he produced an album of chants in Scottish Gaelic from the Shetland Islands. It was very primeval and he was fascinated by that."

Morrison, in a couple of interviews at the time, talked about the importance of musical education, of what music is, "where it's going, and the force that's behind it. I'm a traditionalist. I believe in tracing things back to the source and finding out what the real thing was, how it became what it is today. I also think it's important for people to get into the music of their own culture. I think it can be dangerous not to validate the music of where you're from."

He acknowledged that, growing up in Belfast, he had failed to nurture his own roots. "Irish music was going on all around me, but that was nowhere," he said. "I was looking for something different. I was listening to black American music."

True, Morrison may have been plugged in to a different wavelength back then –a hipper New World wavelength—but he did at least assimilate some Irish music: John McCormack, The McPeakes, and Dolly McMahon, as outlined earlier. A seed had been planted in boyhood, and while it may have been a long time coming, that seed was beginning to flourish in the heightened self-awareness of manhood. *Beautiful Vision* continued the process, albeit somewhat esoterically. All right, it doesn't particularly sound Irish, but it catches the Irish and more broadly the Celtic spirit.

As Lauren Onkey emphasises, a significant characteristic of Morrison's Celticism "is that he embraces a Celtic vision across the British Isles. He is interested in English Romantic poets as he is in things specifically Irish; he has also repeatedly evoked Avalon, the burial ground of King Arthur and the site of Jesus' mythical visit to England". There is a unity of Ireland, Scotland, England, and Wales on 'Celtic Ray'—not a socio-political unity, but a spiritual unity of Celts. What Bill Flanagan calls "a vision of one place, one people", and what Morrison himself calls "a Celtic invocation". ("There's nothing political about it," he added.)

Peter Mills identifies "a complex set of relations between the term

Celtic and the term Irish" in Morrison's thinking, "though they may sometimes ostensibly be referring to the same emotion or idea". When Morrison uses the word Celtic, "he is referring to fixed, deep-rooted identity, one of place as well as people".

In esoteric teachings, each planet is associated with a particular 'Ray' or type of consciousness. The Celtic or Green Ray is, according to Dion Fortune in *Applied Magic*, the Ray of beauty and of the artist, symbolised by the planet Venus. "The Greeks with their art and the Celts with their music and dance were the true initiates of the Green Ray," Fortune writes, "and the influence of the astral contacts can be clearly seen to this day in the temperament of the Celtic races."

The Ray of which Morrison sings could have its origin in Alice Bailey's book *Glamour: A World Problem*, which she wrote in the 40s. It describes the pull of home and details seven factors: "soul, personality, mind, emotional, nature, physical vehicle, the energy of the sun sign, and the influence of the rising sun".

That pull of home was strong enough for Morrison to cross the Atlantic for good. It wasn't back to Belfast that he went, however, but to Oxfordshire and then London, where he eventually settled down in Holland Park. He told Bill Flanagan in 1984 that, although he was "a citizen of Europe and America", he belonged to Ulster. A year later, chatting to Al Jones on Danish radio, he reasoned that being in London meant he was "much closer to Belfast. It's not very far away. So it means I can go home more than I could when I was in America. It was too far away. So I can get back there more frequently, and I'd say that has had a big effect on my songs and music".

Oddly enough, in the same conversation, he declared himself to be British.

CHAPTER 9
HOLLYWOOD GLOCKAMORRA

Garbhan Downey is a novelist from Derry, a product of St Columb's College, the Catholic grammar school whose past pupils also include John Hume, co-recipient of the 1998 Nobel Peace Prize (with David Trimble, for helping to broker the Northern Ireland peace process), Nobel Laureate Seamus Heaney, dramatist Brian Friel, poet Seamus Deane, political commentator Eamonn McCann, and singer-songwriter Paul Brady. Illustrious alumni indeed.

In 2011, Downey took part in a debate hosted by Derry City Library to find Ireland's Greatest Writer. Rather controversially, he made the case for Van Morrison, while three other authors—Carlo Gebler, Brian McGilloway, and Anita Robinson—proposed Francis Stuart, Seamus Heaney, and Brian Friel respectively.

"Some people were genuinely horrified," Downey recalled. "I learned afterwards that a senior Irish literary figure, due to take part in the debate, withdrew because, apparently, I wasn't taking the thing seriously. I couldn't have been more serious if I'd carved my 2,000 words onto granite. Why should a world-acclaimed writer be disqualified because he also has the ability to perform his work through song? I remember once at a hotel pool in Italy, when my then four-year-old daughter asked me to sing her a song about swimming. Without thinking, I launched into 'And we looked at the swim, and we jumped right in, not to mention fishing poles' (from 'And It Stoned Me'). Across the pool, a German man laughed over and chipped in, 'Oh, the water, oh, the water / Oh, the water / Let it run all over me.' You'll not get that with Louis MacNeice [the 30s Irish poet and contemporary of W.H. Auden, Stephen Spender, and Cecil Day-

Lewis]. Morrison is part of the universal fabric. After the debate, all three of the other panelists told me they would have voted for Morrison on the basis of the case I put."

As it happened, Robinson's tribute to Friel, often labelled the Irish Anton Chekhov for his plays *Dancing At Lughnasa* and *Philadelphia, Here I Come!*, swung the house vote. The main planks of Downey's argument cited Morrison's "quality, productivity, awards and trophies, longevity, consistency, his permanence, his sense of place, his continued improvement, and his wisdom". John Keats and Arthur Rimbaud were burnt out by the age at which Van The Man "truly started to get going … with *Astral Weeks*". He wrote of "childhood, love, philosophy, his Celtic soul, Caledonia, Avalon, enlightenment, and sometimes just the sheer drudge of day-to-day living". He established connections "on so many levels, from the mundane to the ethereal".

"He is a great writer, full stop," Downey told me. "In saying that, he writes so lovingly and atmospherically about Ireland, he will be forever associated with the place. He took an unremarkable industrial city like Belfast and gave it a soul. *Hymns To The Silence* and *Astral Weeks* do for Belfast what George Gershwin's *Rhapsody In Blue* did for New York.

"It's his abiding sense of place and continual reference to—but not reliance on—his roots that make him an Irish writer. Morrison's writing journey has been classically Irish, featuring at times Ulster-Scots, Celtic, and Anglo-Saxon influences. But importantly, he has also taken his Irish experience into exile, to the US and elsewhere, and so reflected the changing nature of the Irish identity and its now global reach. For me, Morrison sees Ireland as part of the broader Celtic family, which stretches from Caledonia to Shenandoah."

Ultimately, Downey plumped for Morrison as Ireland's Greatest Writer "because he has got into my head, and stayed in my head, like no other writer, from Ireland or beyond". He began to realise his genius while a student at University College Galway in the late 80s.

"He had the ability to take incredibly complex philosophical arguments and reduce them to one line of beautiful, simple lyric:

'Rave on John Donne ... Rave on, you left us words on printed page / Rave on, you left us infinity.' You could write a doctoral thesis on that song, but thanks to Morrison, you don't have to."

'Rave On, John Donne', his panegyric to the English metaphysical poet, was a focal point of Morrison's *Inarticulate Speech Of The Heart*, released in 1983. The song filled two reels of 24-track tape in the recording studio before being edited down to the five minute-version that appears on the album. To get an idea of how it maybe should have been, check out the version on 1984's *Live At The Grand Opera House, Belfast*. It comes from the same place as 'Summertime In England'—again, what Lester Bangs pronounced as "holy music". We are less concerned with what Van's singing about—empiricism, theosophy, the Industrial Revolution, Walt Whitman, Omar Khayyam, Kahlil Gibran, Mr Yeats—than we are rapt by the reverie of the sound and the prayer-like invocation of the words. You don't so much shut up and listen as shut up and submit to the eloquent intensity of the experience, the mystifying capacity that song possesses to transport us, to give us wings and make us transcend.

All of which journalist Sean O'Hagan would probably say is a load of old bollocks, given his perception of Morrison as "a very Protestant artiste with a very Protestant voice", whose "flights of fantasy" sometimes contain "a lot of the lunacy of [Reverend Ian] Paisley". 'Rave On, John Donne' is, according to O'Hagan, one of those occasions when Van's "off on this mad testifying".

Inarticulate Speech Of The Heart is predominantly New Age music, the sonic fulcrums of which are Mark Isham's ebbing, flowing synthesisers and Davy Spillane's uilleann pipes and low flute. Spillane was a member of the groundbreaking Moving Hearts, an Irish folk-rock collective formed in 1981 by Christy Moore and Donal Lunny and featuring established players like Keith Donald on saxophone and Eoghan O'Neill on bass. The entire Hearts line-up would appear on Morrison's next album, *A Sense Of Wonder*. John Connell and Chris Gibson, in their book *Sound Tracks*, relate New Age music to a primitive Irish identity, suggesting, "Irish ambient music often incorporated uilleann pipes, and Scottish music the bagpipes. Natural sounds (an explicit conjunction of indigenous peoples as 'natural') contributed to the primitivist fantasies of tranquility, timelessness and human interactions with nature. Relaxation and spiritual healing were the anticipated consequences." Much of Morrison's music in the early-to-mid 80s "perpetuated the belief in Ireland's natural spirituality".

But alongside its cogitative agenda, *Inarticulate Speech Of The Heart* is also an album that embodies a theme of homecoming, palpable not just in 'Irish Heartbeat' and 'Cry For Home' but in the instrumentals 'Celtic Swing' and 'Connswater' (named after a Belfast canal). On 'Irish Heartbeat'—re-imagined by Morrison with The Chieftains as the title track of their collaboration in 1988—he dispels the notion that far away hills are always greener by urging the 'you' addressed in the song—which may well be Morrison himself—to linger a while with your own ones, to never wander. The world, he sings, cares nothing for your soul—the soul that you share "with your own ones". He has left the land, like so many of his compatriots, but now he's going back to his "own ones", back to Ireland where his heart beats with a rhythm of belonging.

On 'Cry For Home', he's the immigrant "waiting on that shore"— America?—for the call to bring him home, a spirit call, a call he will answer without hesitation. The home where he's bound is the childhood home preserved in his memory on 'The Street Only Knew Your Name'—Hyndford Street, East Belfast. His street—rich or poor, it doesn't matter—is where he was always "sure", and away from this street, away from this little enclave of Belfast that will be forever Van Morrison's, he is incomplete.

Morrison may have had an epiphany, he may have found his way back home—"I belong to, specifically, Ulster," he declared—but many in Belfast were unmoved. They couldn't have cared less. To them, he was a man out of time, a man removed from what defined contemporary Belfast. Principally, the Troubles. *The Belfast Review*'s Gillian Russell, in a scathing piece, wrote that he had "little direct relevance; he belongs—with George Best, another Belfast cowboy—to the 60s, before the Fall. His own concept of his Irishness seems to have been lost somewhere, and the image of Ireland conveyed by *Veedon Fleece* and some of his more recent LPs, seems to have greater affinities with a Hollywood Glockamorra than with political and social realities." Ouch!

Gavin Martin, a Belfast writer for the *NME*, seemed to concur with Russell's contention that Morrison was peripheral to what was going on in his city. In his less than flattering review of *Inarticulate Speech Of The Heart*, Martin derided "the latest incarnation of The Van Morrison Band" as one being "enjoyed by an audience that is predominantly middle class and middle aged"—a constituency so acutely parodied (with the rest of charlatanry) by Bob Dylan in 'Ballad Of A Thin Man'. In other words, something was happening in Belfast, and Morrison didn't have the first fucking clue what it was.

This was probably because the search for meaning, something of an esoteric pursuit, superseded everything else. It was a search that, according to Steve Turner, "rendered his new material almost inaccessible to anyone who was not a fellow seeker". Not strictly true. With Morrison, it's always been more about the sensual than the cerebral. The feeling elicited by the coming together of voice and music and, every now and then, a sagely perception. Much of what he was spouting at this point of his pilgrimage was recapitulated anyway, usually from primary sources. William Blake, for example, makes an appearance on *A Sense Of Wonder*, which, contrary to Turner's evaluation, is very accessible. Standard Morrison for the time, no better or worse than what went before. His recitation of Blake's 'The Price Of Experience' on 'Let The Slave' is a wee bit bumptious (a similar charge could be levelled at the Zorro garb he dons on the sleeve), but it actually succeeds. And while there is plenty of shining lights, the odd fiery vision and some piss poor nature poetry, Van's still on his Irish kick. 'A Sense Of Wonder' itself reincarnates wee Alfie on the Castlereagh Road and Johnny Mack Brown's horse. This track, and the stirring trad Irish instrumental 'Boffyflow And Spike', features Moving Hearts, "who had been drafted in for a session in London to see what might transpire if they were given no advance preparation and zero chance to learn the tunes".

Keith Donald's version of the Hearts' involvement differed slightly. "Van contacted me," he said. "Myself and my German actress girlfriend went to Belfast and Van put two chairs for us at the side of the stage at his gig in the Opera House. Afterwards we went to the Culloden Hotel with him and chatted. I visited him in London. He stayed with me in Dublin when he came over to rehearse with us at our soundman Norman Verso's house in County Meath. He invited us to record with him in Odyssey Studios."

What Donal Lunny remembered most of the session was Morrison's brusqueness. "He very consciously tried to destabilise us, and it worked," he recalled. "He made us uncomfortable and removed any air of predictability from what was about to happen. From a music point of view, that's a brilliant thing to do. But he didn't stop to explain what he was doing. It just felt as if someone was putting the squeeze on us. It wasn't very pleasant!"

Donald insisted that "Lunny's opinions are his own". He refused to elaborate other than to say that he "never had any problems at all with Van. It was a co-operative effort and good fun too".

The liner notes to the vinyl version of *A Sense Of Wonder* includes a piece penned by Morrison about two characters named Boffyflow and Spike. It could be read as either a short story excerpt from an aspirational Flann O'Brien, Samuel Beckett, or James Joyce; some kind of metaphorical memoir; or a doff of the cap to *The Goon Show*, the British radio comedy broadcast on the BBC from 1951 to 1960 that was dubbed surrealist, avant-garde, abstract, four-dimensional, and sound cartooning. The Goons were Peter Sellers, Harry Secombe, Michael Bentine, and Spike Milligan. The latter, though born in

British India at the end of the First World War, became an Irish national in 1962 after the British government declared him stateless. In 1997, he and Morrison met for a *Q* magazine feature, with Paul Du Noyer acting as the middleman.

"He was always just there," Van said of the comic's influence on him. "Sunday mornings, if I remember, was The Goons, then *Round The Horne*, Jimmy Clitherhoe—they all seemed to be on Sunday. The Goons were huge in Ireland. Kids I grew up with talked like that all the time."

Moving Hearts also played on 'Crazy Jane On God', which quotes a passage from W.B. Yeats's poem of the same name, but it didn't make *A Sense Of Wonder* because of a dispute with the poet's estate. Apparently they were averse to his words being used in any musical context but classical—since when they've obviously had a change of heart, as Morrison went on to record 'Before The World Was Made' for *Too Long In Exile*, the song later forming part of *Now And In Time To Be*, a Yeats tribute album. Meanwhile in 2011, The Waterboys released *An Appointment With Mr Yeats*, a selection of Yeats' verse in music.

Van's response to the embargo by the Yeats estate was typically combative. "We were told by the Yeats estate that they wouldn't give us permission to put this song on the album, right? So I thought about it for a couple of days, and I thought, OK, fine. I figured I was doing them a favour, you know? But they said that Yeats only intended the lines to be put in so-called classical music. So I thought, fine. I mean, my songs are better than Yeats, so we'll see you. I don't need that."

"My songs are better than Yeats"? Self-evidently this is a preposterous statement. To issue any kind of riposte would be to afford it credence. William Butler, a man not easily given to mirth in his lifetime, can still be heard laughing riotously in the sweet by and by.

○

Later the same year, Morrison played sax on Irish composer Bill Whelan's score for the movie *Lamb*, based on Northern Irish writer

Bernard McLaverty's novel of the same name, starring Liam Neeson. The Ballymena screen star had a vague recollection of Morrison's contribution.

"It was a lazy sax. I do remember thinking—now I might get in trouble when I say this—but I remember thinking, that was Van having a bath and thinking, fuck it, I have to deliver this by tomorrow morning. I'll just do a few notes and that'll do them. That's what it seemed to me. I didn't come out of the movie whistling the tune! But like those great jazz performers, it's the notes he doesn't play."

Yeats was still on Morrison's mind when he went to record his next album, *No Guru, No Method, No Teacher*. The song 'Here Comes The Knight'—an excruciating pun on Them's 'Here Comes The Night'—includes the line "Cast a cold eye on life, on death"—a straight lift from Yeats's 'Under Ben Bulben', and also the epitaph on the poet's gravestone. As the latter is considered public property, its usage didn't require the permission of the Yeats estate. There's a sense of Van getting his own back, in his own obtuse way, for the 'Crazy Jane On God' snub.

He premiered this and two other songs from the album in May 1986 at *Self Aid*, a benefit concert organised by RTE heads Tony Boland and Niall Matthews in Dublin's RDS, to highlight Ireland's chronic unemployment problem. The 14-hour event, based on the previous year's *Live Aid*, supposedly raised millions of pounds for a job creation trust fund, along with some 1,000 job pledges. Christy Moore, Rory Gallagher, Paul Brady, Clannad, The Chieftains, and Gary Moore were among the line-up. U2 headlined, Bono revelling in his new messiah status by berating the banks for not lending a hand to Irish business—yep, the same Bono who, with the rest of U2, has been accused of abusing the tax emption scheme for artists in Ireland, and who allegedly avoiding paying tax at home by moving commercial activities to Holland. Notwithstanding the spurious nature of said dealings, they showed why they were just about the best rock'n'roll band on the planet at that moment, infusing their own material with

Eddie Cochran's 'C'mon Everybody', Bob Dylan's 'Maggie's Farm', Lou Reed's 'Walk On The Wild Side', and John Lennon's 'Cold Turkey', during which Bono, like a sixth form drama student, wrapped the microphone cord round his arm to mimic shooting up.

Van's appearance had been eagerly awaited by the crowd through the long day. It's a fair assumption that the majority of them, myself included, wouldn't have seen him before. If we were expecting a familiar setlist—and given the shouts for 'Gloria', 'Moondance', and 'Brown Eyed Girl' that punctuated the chill Dublin night, many were—he was wilfully determined to disappoint. Shuffling on in a sports jacket, jumper, shirt and tie, and slacks combo—part-school science teacher, part-travelling salesman—and with an unctuous Arthur Scargill comb-over, he let us know the score straight off the bat. "This is all new material from the forthcoming album," he announced. What we got were perfunctory readings of 'Town Called Paradise'—prefaced by the warning, "If Van Morrison was a gunslinger, there'd be a lot of dead copycats" (were you listening, Paul Brady?)—'Here Comes The Knight', and 'Thanks For The Information'.

No Guru, No Method, No Teacher followed in July of that year. The quest for enlightenment continues here, but it's not as disparate this time, not as grab bag as on *Beautiful Vision, Inarticulate Speech Of The Heart*, and *A Sense Of Wonder*. Rather it's more concentrated on the idea that to find enlightenment, and some kind of concomitant healing if you like, it's necessary to almost regress, to re-envision those mystical adventures on Hyndford Street and correspond once again with the formative sensations of boyhood. This is keenly evinced on 'Got To Go Back', Van staring out of his Orangefield classroom window, dreaming, and then rushing home to hear Ray Charles, feeling "that love that was within me"—a love that brought him through whatever anguish assailed him, a love that raised him up and filled him with "meditation" and "contemplation". Kate St John's oboe—making like a snake charmer's pungi—is entrancing, easing the singer, the song, and the song receiver (the listener) through a portal into the past. We are all in the ghost world of memory, both real and fanciful. This is a place where magic happens, a place where the very elemental function of breathing gets you giddy. In the final verse, Morrison reveals as much about his identity—how he perceives himself—as he's ever done. He's living in "another country", one operating "along entirely different lines"—a difference toward which he feels indifferent, a difference he can't quite grasp. This other country is where he's made his home, yet it will never be home. The actual home he longs for—with a longing so exquisite he wants to be kept away from porter and whiskey lest they render him hopelessly sentimental—is undeniably Ireland. For he is, as he sings later, 'One Irish Rover'. Mind you, according to Chris Michie, lead guitarist on *No Guru, No Method, No Teacher*, 'One Irish Rover' was originally known as 'One Roman Soldier'.

"I never asked him why the change was made," said Michie. "I feel that the importance of expression is so personal, it shouldn't be discussed, it should just be experienced."

'Oh, The Warm Feeling' again juxtaposes childhood imagery with awareness and a sense of the restorative. He is "filled with devotion" for the object of his affection, and such devotion enables him to "plainly see", healing "all my emotions" and filling him "with religion".

Understanding also underpins 'In The Garden', a masterpiece to rank alongside those other opuses 'Cypress Avenue', 'Madame George', 'Listen To The Lion', 'Summertime In England', 'Haunts Of Ancient Peace', and 'And The Healing Has Begun'. There is going away and coming back—this time it's not the 'I' but the 'You' who possesses "the key to your soul", with that self-knowledge subsequently bestowed upon Van, igniting him "in daylight and nature in the garden". Spine-tingling eroticism ("And we touched each other lightly"), phantasmagoria ("You went into a trance / Your childlike vision became so fine"), and reverence for the sacred ("We heard the bells in the church / We loved so much", "And we felt the presence of the Christ")—it's all here, all of it recognisable to those of us who have listened to Morrison intently from the first. He told Mick Brown that 'In The Garden' "takes you through the meditation programme, from about halfway thought the song until the end. I take you through a definitive meditation process, which is a form of transcendental mediation. If you listen to the thing carefully, you should have gotten yourself some sort of tranquillity by the time you get to the end".

And if you haven't, to paraphrase another of Morrison's songs, got yourself healed by the end of this enchanting hymn to everything that's pure in this world and all of the other worlds that abound, then you are quite simply beyond the beneficence of redemption. To give yourself over completely to what he describes as "a definitive meditation process" is to rejoice in what can only be the nearness of the divine.

Steve Turner reckons that 'In The Garden' was Van looking back "at the young Van in Hyndford Street. The mentions of 'childlike vision' and going 'into a trance' allude to 'Madame George'". Brian Hinton, who admits to shivering with emotion whenever he heard it, went further than just Hyndford Street. The song, he argues, "takes us ... to the world of *Astral Weeks* and on to Eden", where Morrison "recreates the trances of his youth, going into a meditation in which he meets the Holy Trinity in a suburban garden, while sitting at ease with his own family. Forget the critics, this is great poetry". And, you know, he's right. It is great poetry because it reads like something that, rather than being contrived, rather than being grafted or worked at from the raw material of inspirational sources, fell from the conjunction of heart and mind and that hazy concept we call the soul.

'Tir Na Nog', soaked in Jef Labes's sumptuous string arrangement, is Morrison getting in touch with Irish legend. Translated from the Gaelic as 'Land of the Young', Tir Na Nog was a place beyond the margins of any map, located on an island far to the west of Ireland. The setting for popular tales during the Middle Ages, neither sickness nor death existed in this otherworld, a place of eternal youth and beauty where all pleasurable pursuits converged. When out hunting with Na Fianna, his group of warriors, Oisin was brought to Tir Na Nog by Niamh Of The Golden Hair, "a beautiful young woman with long red hair, riding on a spirited white mare". They built a life together "in this magical land", 300 years passing as though it was but a single day. Yet Oisin, whose "soul knew loneliness", pined for Ireland—for his family and for Na Fianna.

"Return to Ireland on the back of the white mare," Niamh told him. "But, my dear, your foot must not touch the soil of Ireland."

When Oisin returned to the mainland, he "realised how much the land had changed", and that "family and friends had long passed away". With nothing there to hold him, he rode the white mare toward the sea and Tir Na Nog:

"Approaching the sea, he came upon a group of men working in a field. As the mare reached the group, her fatigue caused her to stumble. Her hoof hit a stone. Oisin bent down to pick up the rock, planning to take it to Tir Na Nog. He was sure that it would ease his sadness to carry a piece of Ireland back with him. But as his hand grasped the stone, Oisin lost his balance and fell to the ground. Within moments, Oisin aged 300 years. Without her rider, the mare reared up and rushed into the ocean, returning to Tir Na Nog and her beloved Niamh."

It has been suggested that Oisin fell from the horse somewhere near Elphin in the landlocked County Roscommon. Fishermen and lighthouse keepers still speak of foggy nights when the moon is full and a shimmering white horse can be seen dancing atop the waves of the Atlantic Ocean off the coast of Ireland's western coast. Some say that a red-haired maiden who rides the horse is Niamh, forever seeking her Oisin.

'Tir Na Nog', the song, is a jumble of recognisable Morrison themes—a golden autumn day, in a garden wet with rain, by the "clear, cool, crystal streams", seated in contemplation—scattered throughout what is in effect an epic declaration of love posing as some sort of pseudo-philosophical tract about immortality. Of course, you could—if you had a mind to—link Van's refashioning of ancient fable to the already mooted idea of regression, the idea that you have to dig deep into personal history and cultural myth to find the answers you're looking for.

Morrison shared some of that personal history with saxophonist Richie Buckley, a Dubliner, on a brief visit to Belfast in November 1986. A guided tour around some of his old haunts in the east of the city sounded like a good idea, and Buckley too was all for it. Who wouldn't want to walk the streets and the avenues commemorated in song, those landmarks of a Utopian idyll dreamed up out of subjective, sepia-toned remembrances of times past? No matter that the mood in those same streets was now charged with malignity, that the sectarian conflict, festering for almost two decades by then, was being stoked up savagely once more by Reverend Ian Paisley and his flock of disenfranchised Protestants, Unionists, and Loyalists in fierce opposition to the Anglo-Irish Agreement, the latest attempt at hatching a peace.

This treaty, signed by British Prime Minister Margaret Thatcher and Irish Taoiseach Garret Fitzgerald, gave the Irish government in the south an advisory role in Northern Ireland's government, while affirming that there would be no change in Northern Ireland's constitutional position unless a majority of its citizens agreed to join the Republic. It also set out conditions for the establishment of a devolved consensus government in Northern Ireland, which did, of course, happen in the aftermath of the Good Friday Agreement. Paisley and his ilk rejected the Anglo-Irish Agreement because of the Republic's involvement in the governance of Northern Ireland, and because they had been excluded from negotiations. Paisley's Democratic Unionist Party, along with the Ulster Unionist Party, led a concerted campaign in opposition to the agreement, including mass rallies, strikes, civil disobedience, and wholesale resignation of Unionist MPs from the House of Commons. One of the pivotal events of the campaign was a demonstration outside Belfast City Hall on

142

November 23, of which one Northern Irish historian said that nothing like it had been seen since 1912, the year of the Ulster Covenant. Paisley, in a typically bellicose address to an audience whose number was variously estimated at either 35,000, 100,000, 200,000, or 500,000, retorted, "Where do the terrorists operate from? From the Irish Republic! That's where they come from! Where do the terrorists return to for sanctuary? To the Irish Republic! And yet Mrs Thatcher tells us that the Republic must have some say in our province. We say never, never, never, never!" Pretty unequivocal, then.

Such was the fetid atmosphere that prevailed when Morrison—out of naivety or ignorance—dragged Buckley into a former drinking den of his. "It was a Loyalist pub," Buckley told Clinton Heylin. "I didn't know it at the time. It was lunchtime and it was real dark, but we went in. Van ordered a coffee and he asked me what I wanted. I said, 'Oh, I'll have a pint of Guinness' at the top of my voice. Suddenly all these guys just stopped and looked around. The barman came over and said to Van, 'You better leave fairly soon.' So the two of us made a quick exit for the door."

East Belfast watering holes whose clientele had a bloodthirsty aversion to southern Irish Catholics weren't the kind of places usually frequented by Morrison whenever he was back on the burning ground of Northern Ireland in those days. He much preferred the rather more grand surroundings of the Crawfordsburn Inn, near Bangor in the north of County Down, a region known as the 'Gold Coast' because of the vast Protestant wealth on display there. Local wags still say it's socially divided between "the haves and the have-yachts". Johnny Rogan, in *Van Morrison: No Surrender*, writes, "A number of judges, spies, and police officers also called the area home, happy in the knowledge that there was only one main road in and out of the village, a feature that acted as a deterrent to the IRA. Morrison loved the place and was known to throw a Christmas party for his mother at the Inn, an establishment where he felt relaxed, confident and free to express himself."

The Inn has stood in its present form since 1614. During the 17th and 18th centuries, many famous writers stayed there, including Jonathan Swift, William Thackery, Charles Dickens, Anthony Trollope, and Lord Alfred Tennyson. It also provided something of a sanctuary for smugglers—secret hiding places for contraband were discovered well into the 20th century—and other nefarious characters, among them highwayman Dick Turpin.

Bangor itself boasts a marina and a health club with a pool whose waters are identical to those of the Dead Sea. Yet the town isn't all moneyed, as Susan McKay illustrated in *Northern Protestants: An Unsettled People*. Some of its estates are "as deprived as any in inner city Belfast. In Bangor West the contrast is particularly sharp, with mansions on one side of the road, and, on the other, an estate in which drug wars between paramilitary factions have led to several murders in recent years. Out along the coast beyond the town lie big caravan parks known witheringly to the local wealthy as Shankill-sur-Mer, where inner city Protestants from Belfast holiday, bringing their flags with them". A little further along the coast, between Bangor and Belfast, lies Holywood, the birthplace of golfer Rory McIlroy, whose worldwide renown is probably on a par with Morrison's.

If he went to Crawfordsburn to take a load off—to just be George Ivan Morrison, the Belfast boy made good—in his Holland Park base, Van got down to some serious reading. According to his then drummer, Roy Jones, "You couldn't sit down. There were books everywhere."

Mick Brown, a journalist Morrison befriended in the 80s, described it as "a completely enclosed universe" where Van would be up into the small hours listening to Irish folk music and reading Alice Bailey. Brown, eager to feed the singer's hunger for knowledge, introduced him to The Wrekin Trust, an educational charity formed in 1971 by Sir George Trevelyan for spiritual education of a non-sectarian bent. Its main aim is "to advance education and learning across different faith and spiritual communities by creating safe meeting spaces for connections, dialogue, learning, and social action". For the past six years, the Trust—whose symbol is based on the Celtic cross of resurrection—has developed The Wrekin Forum, "with the purpose of awakening and revitalising a spiritual dimension within society by empowering and supporting a deeper connection between visionary organisations and individuals whose approach is based on holistic, spiritual, and ecological principles".

In 1987, when Morrison made the group's acquaintance, he became involved in a conference entitled The Sacred Heart of Music, "an exploration into the power of music to change consciousness", whose objective was "to help restore music to a central place in our culture as a unifying and transcendent force". It took place over three days at Loughborough University in the East Midlands and featured lectures on 'Music, Magic, and Mysticism', 'The Effect of Music on Hormonal Secretions in the Endocrine Glands', and 'Music As a Force in Spiritual Development'.

"His passion for music and his bemusement with the contradictions inherent in being famous have led him to deeply question many of the underlying attitudes of our age," Morrison's biographical notes stated in the conference programme. "In particular, he has investigated the esoteric influences on music with a view to discovering more about its effects on the body-mind relationship. His own work is now increasingly intended as a means for inducing contemplation and for healing and uplifting the soul.

"His struggle to reconcile the mythic, almost otherworldly vision of the Celts, and his own search for spiritual satisfaction, with the apparent hedonism of blues and soul music, has produced many inspired and visionary performances."

Organiser Malcolm Lazarus, the chairman of the Trust, opened the event by welcoming Morrison and then reading from his song 'The Mystery', from the as-yet-unreleased new album *Poetic Champions Compose*. Afterwards, there was an informal set in which fellow seekers Clive Culbertson, Derek Bell, and Robin Williamson of The Incredible String Band joined Morrison on 'Tir Na Nog', 'And The Healing Has

Begun', 'Celtic Ray', 'In The Garden', and 'Mr Thomas'. These performances were interspersed with passages from Irish folk tales.

Lazarus felt that Van was "engaged in a sort of battle between not being able to grasp the intellectual dynamics and nevertheless wanting to, and between not being willing to grasp the experiential side and yet, at the same time, wanting to incorporate it into his music. I think that, like a lot of artists, he was afraid to do anything to the creative process".

Maybe Van couldn't get a handle on the highbrow discourse, but so what? While the scholastic minds mull over ideas, he goes about assimilating those ideas into his art. In the same month the Loughborough conference cogitated on music's healing faculties, one of the form's foremost healers released *Poetic Champions Compose*. Drogheda-born and Dublin-based Fiachra Trench's elevating string and woodwind arrangements suffuse Morrison's songs—particularly the instrumentals 'Spanish Steps' (described by Stephen Pillster as "the closest ever got to his dreams"), 'Celtic Excavation', and 'Allow Me', and the Celtic harp-helmed 'Queen Of The Slipstream'—with a kind of soothing dynamic—an emollient for the soul, if you will. When he asks, 'Did You Get Healed?', there can only be a singular affirmative response.

Talking to Bill Morrison around this time—a rare and insightful interview that you can find on YouTube—he laid down a marker for a project that would finally bring it all back home for him.

"A lot of serious musicians are either in the folk field or are headed in that direction, because that's really where the truth lies at this point," Morrison said. "The truth now lies in the traditional forms of music. I'm working in a traditional structure. The tendency is for people to explore their own traditions—musical traditions, genetic traditions. That's the key. There's no mileage for me in what's called rock. It's non-existent for me. It's not even my reality."

CHAPTER 10
FROM BACKWARD TO COOL

There's an old black-and-white photograph of a statuesque man in a suit—replete with handkerchief in the top left pocket, dark tie, and pullover—standing alongside a slightly plump and pretty woman in a bright summer dress. She's seated by a piano, one hand on the sheet music, the other resting on the lip of the keyboard. He's holding a fiddle and bow and smiling easily at the camera, the wind (they are posing outside) sculpting the hair on his crown into a quiff. It's like looking at a long ago version of myself, of what I might have looked like if I'd been born into another time, specifically the early years of the Irish Republic.

The resemblance between myself and this charismatic character is hardly coincidental. He is, after all, my grandfather, and the woman my grandmother. William and Marion Burke were their names, husband and wife, father and mother—traditional Irish musicians. This last appellation was always articulated with a certain pride by my father when I was a young lad—a pride, indeed, that has never waned, and why should it? It conferred upon them an identity that was separate from their domestic and community identities. It set them apart, made them seem exotic. I too was filled with a sense of pride in this other identity of theirs—less so, perhaps, because they were traditional Irish players than just because they were musicians and, therefore, invested with an element of cool. Truth be told, the music itself—our music—left me cold while growing up in the 70s and 80s. In common with many of my peers, I associated it with an insular, backward Ireland—an Ireland in which a tyrannical church, abetted by a cowed and crooked political class, exerted almost Orwellian

147

control over every aspect of supposedly independent citizens' lives. These toxic twins of church and state wouldn't countenance anything that didn't dovetail with their manifesto for an extremist Catholic and fervently Nationalist Ireland. Sex was solely for the purpose of procreation—God forbid that some pleasure should be derived from it. The English were hated unconditionally. And that lot up north could never be trusted. But we belonged to the generation that, with the advent of the BBC and Ulster Television—piped into our homes free of charge—saw the world beyond our own tiny island and wanted it. All of it. They could keep their Ireland. It bore no relevance to what we were becoming.

I emigrated from Mullingar to London in 1990, a time when it was still tricky being Irish there. The Troubles hadn't gone away. It didn't matter if you weren't from Northern Ireland. Johnny Englishman had little awareness of the lay of his neighbour's land. Irish was Irish to him, and that meant you were either thick or troublesome, a toper or a potential terrorist. Paul Brady's 'Nothing But The Same Old Story' succinctly captured the vibe even then—the song was written more than ten years earlier and appeared on his 1981 album *Hard Station*. In one verse, he sings of what was the Irish stereotype in Britain: the men who built houses, pulled pints of beer, and lived under suspicion, all the while enduring the hatred and fear in the eyes of their hosts. In another, the Irish incomer is a curio adopted by a hip crowd that takes him from one party to another like "some dressed up monkey in a cage".

Not long after moving to London, I secured a position on the now-defunct *Irish In Britain News*. Within months I was sitting opposite Brady in the offices of his management company, discussing—among other topics—'Nothing But The Same Old Story'.

"That took me back to the period between 1969 and 1972, when the shit first hit the fan in Belfast, and Paddies were very much Paddies in Ireland, and there wasn't anything like Puppies, the nice Paddy yuppies that are coming over now," he said. "I lived in

Willesden, Hammersmith, Shepherd's Bush, in dingy little flats with other Irish guys. We went to Irish pubs on Saturday night—the White Hart in Fulham, the King's Head—and it was just like you saw all these people and I just felt they were never, ever going to get out of this situation.

"I think everybody could have seen what that song said. There were only two kinds of Irish people in London—you were either a navvy or an artistic genius. If you were an artistic genius, you'd still get patronised. A lot of the whole Irish experience here is the way you approach the thing too. I approached it with a desperate inferiority complex, so you project your own insecurity on the situation, you bring your own self to the discriminatory process, I feel. So the song is made up of that two-way process of the fear of being rejected, and also the fact that you were being discriminated against. The person concerned in the song is not me, it's every Irish person."

That "every Irish person" is important. As I've already indicated, Johnny Englishman didn't discriminate—whether you were a Catholic from Carrick-on-Suir or a Protestant from Portadown, it made no difference to him. When Them were based in London in the 60s, they were, according to former drummer John Wilson, treated "like idiots from Ireland".

In a 1993 interview with Victoria Clarke, Morrison recalled how, in the 60s, "to be from Ireland was a disadvantage. For instance, to be in London and be Irish, you were fucked. Now it's cool, it's hip. So what happened? I was in London in the 60s and it was like, 'Fuck you, we don't want to know.' We were ostracised. Even if you were a rock star! You were just a Paddy".

When he relocated to London from the United States, Morrison encountered an aversion to Irish music from within the industry. He wanted to work with Moving Hearts, but his label wanted something else. "There was a barrier there, a definite fucking barrier," he said. "In the early 80s, they didn't even know what I was talking about. It took me until The Chieftains to convince them. They didn't want to know."

The antipathy Morrison outlined above explains why the Irish in London, and in other English outposts, became ghettoised. They stayed close to their own, worked with them, got drunk with them, and on occasion—no doubt once the drink had taken hold—scrapped with them over some vaguely defined regional dispute exhumed from history. I resolved to avoid a similar outcome to my particular narrative. But however integrated I became in London life, whatever the cultural diversity of my social group, I was helpless to prevent myself from being overcome by regular bouts of homesickness. This is a condition every bit as intense as that of unrequited love, except that there is at least a cure for homesickness, in theory anyway—go back home. Mind you, this was not an option exercised by a large proportion of Irish emigrants who came over to England in the 1950s, 60s, and 70s, nor indeed was it for many of the bright young things who made the short hop across the Irish Sea before the brief advent of the Celtic Tiger—return was seen as being commensurate with failure.

Louise Ryan, whom I spoke to in 2007 when she was deputy head of the Social Policy Research Centre at Middlesex University and I was researching an article on Irish people's invisibility within the UK mental health system, told me, "As an Irish emigrant here, you almost have to justify why you don't go back. That's a question that gets asked of people all the time. For lots of people that's an impossibility, for all sorts of reasons. And for people with mental health issues it's even more of a taboo. Shame is a huge part of it. To go back now to where they're just dripping in material assets, to a very ostentatious society, from your little bedsit somewhere in Archway, with your tail between your legs, some people just don't think about that. In an ironic way the Celtic Tiger has shut out a particular type of person from going back."

For my part, I didn't go back because I didn't want to be there in the first place. I couldn't wait to get away. And while there's hardly been a day in the twenty-something years I've been an Irish exile (by choice) in England—a place I could never consider home, incidentally—that I haven't longed to hear the familiar flat, reassuring rhythm of the Mullingar accent, I realise that my Ireland, not unlike that forged by Van, is a mythical one. I remember things that never happened, stake a claim to traditions that were never mine, discard those Irish idiosyncrasies that I find incompatible with my own persona, and emphasise the richness of my ethnic heritage— including the music to which I turned a deaf ear once upon a time. The music, its ebullience and its melancholy, says so much about a people—my people—and says it more eloquently than those people could ever say about themselves. It is the Irish soul made flesh and made beautiful. It is what I see and what I hear when I look upon that old black-and-white photograph of my grandparents. It fills me up with joy and with sadness, but above all, with gratification—and, if I'm being brutally honest, no little ignominy for rejecting it so arrogantly in my youth.

Not that I was alone in refusing to acknowledge the magic in the music. Philip King, founding member of Irish folk outfit Scullion, now a filmmaker and broadcaster, recalled that while the traditional sound "was part and parcel of the ethos of music in my environment, it was sometimes taken for granted, and sometimes slated by people who though it was very uncool and backward, and that you had to go away, you needed to travel and preach philosophy in someone else's land and then come back famous, as The Clancy Brothers proved when they came back, singing a genre of music that didn't exist in this country at all".

Hard to believe, given the global popularity of traditional Irish music in the here and now, that 60 years ago it was largely unloved in Ireland itself and virtually unheard of outside the country. Back then, despite the Irish government's best efforts to purge Ireland of its British influences—the indigenous language and music formed the cultural framework of this objective, while the Catholic Church was entrusted with the cultivating the rectitude of the new republic—there was great scepticism among the majority of the populace. The late

Peter Lennon, the journalist and film director whose social documentary *The Rocky Road To Dublin* (1967) was a devastating critique of post-colonial Ireland, made his view clear in the BBC Four television documentary *Folk Hibernia*. "They thought people would feel proud of their culture, but we had just no time for it," he said. "We were more interested in Frank Sinatra and Bing Crosby, who was Irish enough for us." The Chieftains' Paddy Moloney conceded that in the mid 20th century, the Irish "had a complex with their own music". The simplest explanation for such mistrust of their own heritage was the suppression of that heritage throughout several hundred years of British rule. In which context it seems harsh to excoriate former Taoiseach and President of Ireland, Eamon de Valera, for outlining his vision of a Gaelic Utopia in a radio speech made on St Patrick's Day in 1943:

"The ideal Ireland that we would have, the Ireland that we dreamed of, would be the home of the people who valued material wealth only as a basis for right living, of a people who, satisfied with frugal comfort, devoted their leisure to the things of the spirit. A land whose countryside would be bright with cosy homesteads, whose fields and villages would be joyous with the sounds of industry, with the romping of sturdy children, the contest of athletic youths and the laughter of happy maidens, whose firesides would be forums for the wisdom of serene old age."

Admittedly, these images of "sturdy children", "athletic youths", and "happy maidens" smack somewhat of the National Socialist German Workers Party agenda, with its emphasis on optimum health—and an implied exclusion of those with disabilities—and the subservient role of women. But what leader of a nation that had finally rid itself of an oppressive master wouldn't want to raise his people up, to inculcate them with a new boldness?

Comhaltas Ceoltoiri Eireann—meaning Society of the Musicians of Ireland—emerged in 1951 as an integral part of this Ireland reborn. Founded by a group of pipers in Mullingar, its aims included the promotion of the country's music and dancing, to restore the playing of the harp and the uileann pipes, to foster the language and to co-operate with all bodies working for the restoration of Irish culture. Comhaltas established an annual music competition, Fleadh Cheoil (Festival of Music), which is held at county, provincial, and national levels. Around 20,000 performers compete against each other in a range of categories from fiddle, two-row accordion, concertina, and mouth organ, to whistling, lilting, duets, trios, and ceili bands. North America has two regional qualifiers for Fleadh Cheoil—the Mid-Atlantic Fleadh, which covers the eastern seaboard, eastern Canada, and the Maritimes, and the Midwest Fleadh for entrants from Cleveland, Chicago, St Louis, Atlanta, Detroit, and San Francisco.

Then there was the composer Sean O'Riada, often cited as the single most important figure in the revival of the music in the 50s and 60s. He scored *Mise Eire* (*I Am Ireland*) for a documentary of the same name by George Morrison in 1959, re-imagining traditional Irish tunes with an orchestral arrangement—not dissimilar to what Ralph Vaughan Williams had done with English folk music. The national acclaim that followed enabled O'Riada to host a series of programmes on Irish radio under the title *Our Musical Heritage*. Between 1961 and 1969, he fronted the ensemble Ceoltoiri Chualann, which featured two founder members of The Chieftains, Paddy Moloney and Sean Potts. Their sober approach to the music, literally as well as metaphorically, brought it out of the pubs and the farmhouses and into the concert halls. They resurrected the bodhran as a percussion instrument and showcased the work of Turlough O'Carolan, the forgotten blind Irish harpist of the late 17th and early 18th century. Essentially O'Riada's attempt to create a traditional Irish music orchestra, Ceoltoiri Chualann found a receptive public in Ireland's emerging middle class.

"He took the orchestral concept and he taught traditional musicians to play things like harmony and syncopation and arrangements," said Liam Clancy.

Like O'Riada, Ciaran MacMathuna and Seamus Ennis also

introduced Irish audiences to their own musical history. MacMathuna was synonymous with Radio Eireann, hosting shows such as *Ceolta Tire*, *A Job Of Journeywork*, *Humours Of Donnybrook*, and *Mo Cheol Thu*. According to Dr Gearoid O' hAllmhurain in *The Pocket History Of Traditional Irish Music*, "He managed to tape traditional musicians in their own localities. His recording sessions, which were conducted in country kitchens, public houses and small halls, reflected the natural milieu of the musician in a manner which was far more authentic than studio or concert hall recordings."

A renowned authority on traditional Irish music, MacMathuna lectured extensively on the subject and, according to Sam Smyth, embarked "on a mission to collect songs and stories, music, poetry and dance, before they were buried under the coming tsunami of pop music". Upon his death in 2009, journalist Kevin Myers said his legacy would be "the rebirth of Irish music".

Meanwhile, Ennis—a contemporary of both MacMathuna and O'Riada—presented *As I Roved Out* on the BBC Home Service during the 50s, and was an uileann piper of near-legendary repute. Indeed Ken Hunt, in a retrospective piece about Ennis published in 2013, described him as "his generation's Jerry Garcia" on the instrument, "grounded in traditional forms and similarly open to new". His "idiomatic and improvisational talents, with their sly twists avoiding the sins of indulgence and predestination, set him apart". For Hunt, Ennis's work "was in the vanguard when it came to anticipating so much that has followed. That applies musically, linguistically, and culturally, whether through music, spoken word, or documenting folklore. Culturally, he looked both down and up, to the earth beneath his feet and to the skies, recognised and revelled in regional differences … and paved the way for a national pride in, and an equality of treatment for, Ireland's folkways."

Liam Clancy, the youngest of The Clancy Brothers, listened to Donagh MacDonagh on Radio Eireann. "I'd never miss *Donagh MacDonagh's Song Bag* on Thursday nights," he wrote in *Memoirs Of An*

Irish Troubadour. "He'd play an eclectic mix of music from whatever folk recordings came into Radio Eireann studios, mainly American."

MacDonagh was a poet, playwright, and barrister, the son of Thomas MacDonagh, one of the signatories of the Proclamation of Independence in 1916, and executed along with his fellow rebels. "On a more homespun level, there was another popular radio programme called *The Ballad Makers' Saturday Night*, which the whole country listened to."

But it was a couple of American women who were primarily responsible for Clancy's total immersion in his own culture, particularly the music, and arguably had a catalytic impact on his eventual decision to become a folk singer. He was just an innocent twenty-something with "one foot in the 20th century, the other in the Middle Ages" when song collectors Diane Hamilton and Catherine Wright called to the family home in Waterford looking for Clancy's mother, a human repository for tunes passed down in the oral tradition. He subsequently joined Hamilton and Wright as they travelled the country on their song crusade.

"I saw sights and heard music on that recording trip that I never knew existed on this island," he admitted. "It was to set the cornerstone, for me, of a life of involvement and fascination with the world of traditional music and song."

It was on this trip that Clancy met Tommy Makem, who would later join The Clancy Brothers and, after their demise, form a duo with Liam. Makem's matriarch, Sarah, possessed an even greater wealth of knowledge than Clancy's when it came to folk songs.

"Tommy's mother had worked in the linen mills with hundreds of other girls. There was no radio at the time, so while they worked all day, they would sing. She had a memory like a vice grip. So she remembered ancient songs, old versions of 'Barbara Allen', 'The Month Of January', some of the great Child ballads"—the latter collected by Francis James Child in the late 19th century and published, in 1882 and 1898, as *The English And Scottish Popular Ballads*.

155

The Clancy Brothers—like James Joyce, Samuel Beckett, and, yes, Van Morrison—had to go away from Ireland to find themselves and, in some fashion, to find their sense of Irishness. That they also found fame and no little fortune as part of the American folk revival—the hub of which was in New York's Greenwich Village—had a suggestion of the serendipitous.

"What stood to us was the fact that while the folk music boom was starting there, there was a limited American repertoire, and we had a whole new batch of songs that nobody had ever heard," said Clancy. "We were taking the old songs that had been slow and solo back in Ireland, and we picked up on the American rhythms and the attack of The Kingston Trio and The Weavers, and we'd put a bit of punch and drive into the songs.

"That was an eye-opener to people in Ireland, but also it was startling to Irish Americans that there was an authentic kind of music that wasn't 'Does Your Mother Come From Ireland?' or 'Mother McCree' and all that. It wasn't Bing Crosby and 'Tura Lura Lura'. All these songs were written in Tin Pan Alley. It was an American view of Ireland that bore no relation to the reality. So people couldn't believe it. We had no Irish people come to our first shows. For one thing, we had Pete Seeger playing with us, and he was a Communist, so that meant we were Communists. Then we were working with the great blues singer, Josh White, and his manager was our manager. So we became 'nigger lovers and Communists'! That was two big strikes against us. Then we appeared on *The Ed Sullivan Show* and it was like getting the blessing of the Pope—'These fellows are Irish, after all!' We got a whole new following."

It's easy to forget just how huge The Clancy Brothers and Tommy Makem were. We live in an ever-shrinking world. The remarkable technological advances of the past couple of decades especially mean that America is not as distant as it once was—you don't need to physically make the journey to make it there.

Migration from Ireland to America in the 19th and early 20th centuries had spawned new communities of ex-pat musicians in the major American urban centres like New York and Chicago. Michael Coleman, James Morrison, and John McKenna became mainstays of the New York recording scene during the 1920s, with its focus on ethnic music, and among the most influential Irish traditional musicians of the 20th century. In Chicago, Francis O'Neill collected and published traditional Irish melodies.

Philip King again: "Irish music travels. It found itself in the United States. Irish dance music—jigs, reels, and hornpipes—found itself being played in the largest industrial development in the world, in Chicago, Boston, Philadelphia, Washington. It was played in an industrial society that was loud and sweaty, full of machinery and noise. And because of that, it was played in a different way—louder, noisier and faster—and the arrangements were more in tune with an industrialised world. That is fundamental in the changes that took place in Irish music.

"The second and most important fundamental thing that happened to the music was that it changed from being an orally transmitted tradition to being one that was mechanically reproduced. In Ireland there were no means of reproducing music on tape. I had to learn a song from somebody else or I didn't learn it at all. What happened in America was that records were made and sent home to Ireland. They were played louder and faster in the United States, so that when they reached Ireland everybody tried to copy that sound. Music that was developed in America was to have the most fundamental effect on the way that our music subsequently developed. It is undoubtedly true to say that Irish music was there at the very beginning of the recording industry as we know it. You can see how it got sidetracked. Once Bing Crosby sang 'When Irish Eyes Are Smiling', that then became the music of the Irish who were after acceding to power. Everybody arrived in the shanty towns. People who moved out of the shanty towns became known as the lace-curtain Irish. They wanted to have something to do with Ireland, but they felt that the music was sort of tinged with a bit of backwardness. So once Bing started doing that kind of stuff, it became acceptable. It infiltrated what has now become American popular music, particularly country music."

The Irish, King enthused, are "storytellers, songwriters, and singers—our artistic baggage is our imagination. Our language is a very musical language, both in the vernacular and in Irish itself. We have a marvellous natural resource in our people, which we continue to export. I think it enriches other countries. And people like Pete Seeger, Emmylou Harris, and Ricky Skaggs acknowledge that— there's no way that their music would have existed today had it not interacted with the music which emanated from Ireland."

Before The Clancy Brothers, John McCormack was the only first generation Irish singer to succeed in the States. After The Clancys, it was Van Morrison. And you get the distinct feeling that he would have approved of the spin they put on tradition. The two parties share common ground in having recorded 'Purple Heather', though The Clancys did it as 'Will Ye Go Lassie, Go'. The Tipperary siblings and Armagh native Makem also covered 'The Dawning Of The Day', an Irish air composed by harpist Thomas Connellan in the 17th century, and expropriated by Patrick Kavanagh for his poem 'On Raglan Road' in 1946—the same Raglan Road that Morrison made his own on *Irish Heartbeat*.

Liam Clancy attributed The Clancy Brothers' conquering of America to the fact that they were "full of piss and vinegar. We didn't give a good goddamn about anyone or anything. And we didn't take it seriously. The concerts and the recordings were almost an instrumental part of what was going on. We'd interrupt our party briefly to go on and do two hours at Carnegie Hall. But that's the way the concert was—it was just a brief interruption of the party".

The Clancys embodied the kind of Ireland that Irish-Americans who had never set foot on the storied Emerald Isle, believed in. The kind of Ireland that the country's tourist board continues to flog to the same Irish-Americans even now—an Ireland of chunky Aran sweaters, creamy pints of Guinness, a benign rebellious spirit, devoted to the craic yet susceptible to sentiment. The Clancys were clever. Cultured men all, with a cheeky twinkle in their eyes, they knew what made the Irish-American heart beat.

As Philip Chevron of The Pogues put it, The Clancy Brothers' success was legitimised by virtue of the fact that "the great America had given their nod of approval. So this kind of downtrodden race in the early 60s was coming through, on the one hand living up to this prescribed culture, on the other hand recognising that there's something going on here that maybe we can take hold of".

They weren't the only Irish folk outfit showcased by Ed Sullivan in the 60s. The Dubliners—who had started out as The Ronnie Drew Ballad Group, named for their founding member—made an appearance on the show in 1968. The previous year, they had enjoyed a couple of hit singles in the UK charts with 'Seven Drunken Nights' and 'Black Velvet Band', and featured in a *Time* magazine piece that hailed them as "the undisputed leaders" of a folk music revolution in Ireland, although at home they were slated by the purists and unofficially banned by national broadcaster RTE. With their sinister beards and natty threads, The Dubs looked like the kind of renegades the townspeople would flee from in a spaghetti western—but they were so cool, and had a pair of mercurial touchstones in Drew and Luke Kelly. Not that the *Time* article gave this impression, comparing Drew's deep, rumbling baritone to "a bullfrog with a hangover (that) bestraddles the line with occasional forays a mile or so off pitch. Tenor Luke Kelly gives out what might be the mating call of a rusty file. Banjoist Barney McKenna, tin whistler Ciaran Bourke, and fiddler John Sheahan, round out the onslaught with a glorious disregard for niceties such as time or tune". They were The Rolling Stones to the Clancys' Beatles.

As Drew himself said in later years, "The Clancys were on a kind of different level than us. They were American ... well, they were

Irish, but there was kind of a certain American thing about them. But they did open it up [for us]."

Clancy admitted that The Dubliners were "far wilder. We had grown up with the theatrical tradition. But the lads are very different—the pub tradition!"

Ironically, Ireland's traditional music renaissance was given some impetus as well by the so-called second British folk music revival that happened between 1945 and 1969. Players like Willie Clancy (uileann pipes) and Michael Gorman (fiddle)—economic migrants who took the boat to England to labour on the building sites—discovered more enthusiasm for their music across the Irish Sea than they did at home. That began to change in the late 60s and early 70s, when a new kind of traditional music emerged in the old country. New in that its protagonists were the progeny of the rock'n'roll age—young, good looking, hirsute, and vibrant, with what we would say in Gaelic was a real gra for the music of their forebears, but with swagger enough to play it their way. Sweeney's Men and Planxty were at some considerable remove from leather-faced, straight-backed men with dead eyes and porter-filled bellies who channelled the music in previous generations.

The first line-up of Sweeney's Men featured Andy Irvine, Johnny Moynihan and Joe Dolan—not to be confused with showband star Joe Dolan. When Dolan left, he was replaced by multi-instrumentalist Terry Woods, later of Steeleye Span and The Pogues. Sweeney's Men listened hard to and learned well from the real music of Ireland they encountered in the trad heartland of places like Galway and Clare. For Moynihan, this was an epiphany.

"I was a middle class Dublin individual who hadn't been exposed to the wonders of this sort of culture," he said. At the same time, Moynihan insisted Sweeney's Men were not an Irish band but, first and foremost, "a string band", bringing together as they did influences and instruments—including the 12-string guitar, mandolin, and bouzouki—that were outside the traditional Irish music experience. We went out in a sociological context to mix styles. There were Eastern and African strains to our music. It was ethnic music with an innovative rock'n'roll backing."

Henry McCullough, drafted into the group following Andy Irvine's departure, "used to play acoustic and electric guitars, tin whistle, and even cider bottles. In effect, the polarisation between styles may have been reduced—American and Irish folk music pooled, with Henry putting funk into it. Henry would just pick up on traditional tunes and they would come out in his playing," Moynihan explained.

In 1972, Irvine hooked up with Christy Moore, Donal Lunny, and Liam O'Flynn to form Planxty, who had a "vision of a new folk music, rich with new textures and treatments". In achieving that objective, they became something of a phenomenon—they made it all right for the kids to dig this music.

"You could come out as being a fan of traditional music," said author and cultural commentator John Waters. "You were kind of secretly in love with the music but didn't want to admit it. There was a split between what it was and what it meant. What it was, was life-affirming, joyous, energetic. The meaning that had been attributed to it was reactionary, backward. Planxty, by just presenting it in a different way, it was OK to admit that you liked it."

Lunny, who went on to form The Bothy Band, a group of virtuosos that would take acoustic ensemble playing onto a whole other level, reckoned Planxty's popularity was down to an inherent rapport with their audiences and the earthiness of their sound.

"It was cool because people identified with people in the band and thought, they like rock'n'roll, too," he said. "The moment was right. It was a fresh picture. It gave the music a voice in its own way. There were no overlays to the music. That was happening in other areas. With folk rock bands, tunes invariably went down the tubes because they were given big boots. It didn't suit. Tunes were barefoot."

Big boots—and glitter—were what Horslips majored in.

According to Mark Prendergast, they formed "part of a younger generation who understood the communicative power of the electric medium and the potency of their Celtic ancestry". Horslips blended traditional Irish influences with rock, consequently inventing what was popularly tagged Celtic rock, a lazy categorisation equalled only by that of Celtic soul (of which genre Van was apparently the originator).

"We were doing what any normal rock'n'roll band was doing, getting dolled up," recalled guitarist Jim Lockhart. "Whenever we were in London, we'd get triple high platforms and major high heels and loads of glitter, playing 2,000-year-old melodies and singing about 2,000-year-old mythological stories. And it turned out to be a potent brew."

Van Morrison was certainly conscious of the developments taking place in traditional Irish music during this period. He had heard a couple of Horslips' records—though he declined to say what he thought of them—and was very aware of The Chieftains, of course. (In fact, there were tentative plans to record with them around 1978, but these plans never came together because of prior commitments.)

If Horslips were glam with a folk element, Thin Lizzy were at the heavier end of the rock spectrum, again with that traditional stimulus. Frontman Phil Lynott weaved Celtic mythology into the band's early albums—'The Friendly Ranger At Clontarf Castle' on *Thin Lizzy*, 'The Rise And Dear Demise Of The Funky Nomadic Tribes' on *Shades Of A Blue Orphanage*—but it was a reworked folk song, 'Whiskey In The Jar', that would bring them to prominence beyond Ireland. The tale of a highwayman or footpad who, after robbing a military or government official, is betrayed by a woman, its various versions are set in counties Kerry, Cork, Sligo, and other Irish locales. Musicologist Alan Lomax, in *The Folk Songs Of North America*, suggested it was written in the 17th century. The folk of 17th century Britain, he wrote, liked and admired their local highwaymen, and in Ireland (or Scotland), where gentlemen of the roads robbed English landlords, they were regarded as national patriots. Such were the feelings that inspired this rollicking ballad. Lomax also cites it as the inspiration for poet and playwright John Gay's 1728 work *The Beggar's Opera*. The composition was a particular favourite in colonial America because of its irreverence toward the British. It wasn't, however, a favourite of then Lizzy guitarist Eric Bell, a contemporary of Morrison's on the showband scene, who later played alongside him briefly in Van Morrison & Them Again. Bell disapproved of single releases, which he felt pandered to the establishment and compromised Thin Lizzy's principles, whatever they were. His resentment over the choice of a track that, to him, represented selling out simmered until they played the Ulster Hall in his native Belfast on New Year's Eve 1973. Bell spent the day boozing with family and friends. Come showtime, he was "in another place, a little voice in his head telling him that he had had enough of all this, the booze, drugs and star trip. So ... he threw his guitar in the air, kicked over his amps and fell off the stage, landing on cushions below". When the gig was over, Bell was no longer a member of Thin Lizzy, though he attributed it to being "burned out, in a real state".

Meanwhile, in the north west of the country, in Donegal—one of the three Ulster counties belonging to the Republic of Ireland—a family of Irish speakers were experimenting with tradition, concocting "a strange musical brew ... that would help shape the international perception of a brave new Celtic Ireland".

Clannad were raised in the Gaelic district of Gweedore and "touted a strong national element in their music, an element which went as far as singing most compositions in Irish and using Irish as much as possible in their work". Their largely ethereal sound was culled from the traditional Irish archetype, but it also incorporated jazz and classical strands. In this sense it was, as journalist Fiona Looney put it, "Celtic first and Irish second. It was more kind of northern European. It could have come from Breton. It could have come from lots of places". Which goes some way to explaining

Clannad's international appeal. The Ireland they espoused was an ancient and mystical land—not unlike facets of Van Morrison's Ireland—and arguably helped to form a romantic perception of the island in the 80s that was a boon for tourism chiefs until then mostly engaged in damage limitation as the conflict up north continued to generate the wrong kind of headlines. Indeed, as the excellent BBC television documentary *Folk Hibernia* suggested, "Music and culture eased the way for the Celtic Tiger, an economic explosion that would define modern Ireland."

Clannad's 'Theme From Harry's Game'—the title song of a British television drama—was one of those pivotal releases that heralded this new Ireland. Combining "the character of Irish folk with electronic wizardry", it sent the band global 12 years after they were formed. Clannad's triumph was equalled by that of another family member, Enya, sister of Moya, Paul, and Ciaran Brennan, though while Clannad's traditional roots showed, Enya's were barely discernible on the studio engineered 'Orinoco Flow' with its layered vocals and synthesised backdrop.

Elsewhere, The Pogues—a London-Irish combo—gave traditional Irish music a playful punk kick up the arse. But as the brutal and beautiful poetry of Shane MacGowan testified, they were no novelty act. The purists, of course, hated The Pogues; the young bucks, less Catholic in their tastes than their forerunners, loved them. This was a traditional Irish music with attitude—drinking and swearing and fighting—played with a rock'n'roll rebelliousness. It was also arguably more authentic—if less palatable to some—in its Irishness than either Clannad or Enya, or the traditional Irish dance spectacle *Riverdance*— the version of Ireland favoured by those tasked with flogging Ireland abroad, a version adulterated for mass appeal, the rough edges smoothed out, the innate Irish melancholy given an almost wistful makeover. Not everyone approved.

"The music has been used in quite a cynical way," said Paddy Glackin, formerly of The Bothy Band. "The Irishness being promoted is very kitsch. It doesn't have a lot of soul. It portrays happiness and a false sense, I think, of what we are."

Fiddler Martin Hayes thought it was about time to re-evaluate traditional Irish music. "Truth is, Ireland is somewhat diverse," he said. "Everybody doesn't march to the same drum. And everybody's notion of what Irish music could be and should be is not at all clear. We have wrapped our identity into this music in some way. And I think to understand the music fully we may have to undo that, too, because in a way, it's music. And it's music that's related to a wide world of music all around us."

CHAPTER 11
THE INNER PADDY REVEALED

They made for an unlikely pairing, the oddest of couples. There was Van, the irascible, monosyllabic East Belfast boyo, and Paddy, the leprechaunish Dubliner with the gift of the gab. Opposite sides of a divided land—remember, this was before Republican and Loyalist terrorist groups relinquished their arms, before the peace process, before devolution—the orange and the green, mixing their cultural blood, re-inventing the Irish folk song in a contemporary, cross-border accent.

It was inevitable that, sooner or later, Morrison would get round to truly revealing his inner Paddy. Ireland had been, he said, "an inspiration in terms of some of the songs, and some of the lyrics to some of the songs, and the poetry in some of the songs … but the fact that I was born there, and the inspiration is there, at times it comes, at times it goes, depending on what's happening". That he did so with The Chieftains, a group that represented the established order of traditional Irish music, rather than any of the new innovators—such as, for example, Moving Hearts, who had, after all, already featured on *Inarticulate Speech Of The Heart* and *A Sense Of Wonder*—was a curious decision, yet one wholly consistent with his contrariness.

Formed in 1962 by Paddy Moloney, with Martin Fay (fiddle and bones), Sean Potts (tin whistle), Micheal Tubridy (flute), and bodhran player David Fallon, The Chieftains released their eponymous debut album in 1963. They honed their craft in the early 60s with informal sessions in the back of O'Donoghue's in Dublin's Merrion Row—the same hostelry that was The Dubliners' proving ground—remaining semi-professional until the 70s, when their success at home was repeated in the United Kingdom and the United States. While Moloney came out of the groundbreaking Ceoltoiri Chualann, it was The Clancy Brothers and Tommy Makem who provided the thrust for The Chieftains' musical vision. They had effectively shone a spotlight on Irish songs, and now Moloney wanted to do the same thing with instrumentals.

"I felt if they can get away with it, why shouldn't Irish music?" he said. "I wanted to bring out the colours in the music. Not so many tunes all at the one time, maybe just a combination of one or two that blended."

The Chieftains became the first western group to perform a concert on the Great Wall of China in 1983, at the invitation of the Chinese government; won an Oscar for their work on director Stanley Kubrick's movie *Barry Lyndon*; played before 1.3 million people in Dublin's Phoenix Park as part of an open-air mass by Pope John Paul II; and have joined forces with a veritable 'who's who' of many genres, including Luciano Pavarotti, The Rolling Stones, Ry Cooder, Tom Jones, Ziggy Marley, Earl Scruggs, Willie Nelson, Bon Iver, and The Low Anthem.

Dr Gearoid O' hAllmhurain, in *The Pocket History Of Irish Traditional Music*, credits The Chieftans with helping "to place Irish traditional music on a par with other musical genres in the world of popular entertainment. By collaborating with pop and rock musicians, they have taken Irish music to a much wider audience".

For Brian Hinton, The Chieftains, prior to their work with Van Morrison on *Irish Heartbeat*, occupied "a comfortable niche somewhere between classical and traditional music. Following a top 40 album in 1986 with Irish pop flautist James Galway, some long-term fans accused them of emasculating their art, which was to miss the point entirely. The whole glory of The Chieftains was their stylistic inclusiveness. Indeed, it was through their flexibility of style and attitude that a synthesis of Celtic music and rock would reach an audience previously biased against one another".

In late 1987, Moloney received the call from Morrison that went along the lines of, "Paddy, Paddy, we've got to do an album together!" There wasn't, The Chieftains' amiable frontman recalled, very much talk about it.

"Van's not really a great one for discussions about music. He'll talk about everything else but music. I think at that time Van was searching for his Irish roots. It was this man of blues, of rock'n'roll, jazz, and—more importantly—soul coming home to his Irishness with The Chieftains and the music we'd been playing for so many years. Musically, we were going to meet each other halfway. It was a friendship and trust. Very important to him, I think, is trust. But I doubt it was the other way round."

Morrison's route back to traditional Irish music was a by-product of the meditation practice with which he'd been experimenting on *No Guru, No Method, No Teacher*.

"I started meditating and doing sounds, and seeing what I could do with my voice when I was meditating," he said. "That led me more into listening to Irish folk music and Scottish folk music—the drone, the pipes, and all this sort of stuff."

A more prosaic explanation for the venture was his affection for John McCormack and his many recordings of Irish folk songs.

"It was always part of the picture," he insisted. "And I always liked those sort of songs anyway. So whether I did it with The Chieftains or not, was neither here nor there. I always loved those songs. So basically, that's where I came in on that. I was coming from the John McCormack angle into The Chieftains angle. So it was like marrying the two things."

Guitarist Arty McGlynn tried to persuade Morrison to do an album of "soul Irish music ... a serious album of Irish music—meet older singers and learn the songs and then rehearse. That's the album I saw Van making. But it went another way. At that stage Van wanted to make an Irish-identity album. It was part of wanting to be Irish in some way. So that's what he did".

To Micheal O'Suilleabhain, the liaison between Morrison and The Chieftains made perfect sense. "The Chieftains represent a professional honing of the Sean O'Riada ensemble model of the 60s," he said. "All contemporary Irish traditional group playing can be traced back, one way or another, to that model. By linking with The Chieftains, Morrison was linking into an O'Riada vision. It is fascinating to imagine what might have happened if O'Riada had lived to interact personally with Morrison."

To road test the union, Morrison joined The Chieftains in late 1987 for the recording of a BBC TV special to be broadcast on St Patrick's Day the following year. He sat behind the drum kit for 'Raglan Road' and 'Celtic Ray', and went out front for 'Star Of The County Down' and 'My Lagan Love'—all of which would feature on *Irish Heartbeat*.

"The studio was decked out in Celtic emblems," writes Brian Hinton in *Celtic Crossroads: The Art Of Van Morrison*, "Van wears a green shirt for the occasion, and his performance is mesmeric but bizarre, meatily beating at a drum kit with brushes, or strumming his guitar. He hums, fills his lungs and roars, moans like an old bluesman, and whispers: it is all too much for one violinist, who cannot prevent a grin breaking out. Van's commitment to this music is certain: he sounds drunk with inspiration."

The trial run—which according to Bill Graham in *Hot Press* "made explicit what had been implicit in his (Morrison's) music"—had evidently pleased both parties. Morrison and Moloney got down to talking about songs.

"I said, 'Look, Van, I have a list of songs we could do.' And he said, 'So have I.' We met up and went for a walk around St Stephen's Green in Dublin, and eventually we settled on the songs that we'd do. I went away and got what Van calls 'the shapes'—the arrangements— together. Then I got a message on my answering machine, saying, 'Great shapes, Paddy.'"

When it came to recording at Dublin's Windmill Lane Studios, there was only one rehearsal, and the album was completed in five days.

"There's no fiddling around, trying things out," The Chieftains' Kevin Conneff recalled. "If it went past take three he would lose interest. He'd say, 'You're wasting your time. Go on to something else.' And I like that. OK, there may be a few skid marks, but what the hell."

Conneff found Morrison "a very curious person coming obviously from a Protestant background in Belfast but singing in such a broad scope of understanding"—a remark which, according to Peter Mills, itself illustrates "an aspect of the Irish conundrum: the perceived distances between next door neighbours, or fellow Irishmen. The man from up Sandy Row seems 'curious', even 'obviously' so, and Conneff attributed an 'otherness' to Morrison and how he worked, equating that with his background in Belfast and, by inference, a narrowness of scope".

The sessions weren't without their comedy moments—wholly unintentional on Van's part, of course.

"When we were doing *Irish Heartbeat*, Van was into these long cadenzas, very traditional west of Ireland keenings, long warbling endings," Moloney recalled. "So I said to him, 'Fine, but just before you're going into one of these cadenzas, can you give me the Billy?' That's Dublin slang for 'give me the nod'. So he says, 'Yeah, great. I'll give you the Billy, no problem.' The song is coming to an end, and we're about to crash into the last chorus, and Van starts shouting, 'Billy! Billy! Billy!' He didn't know what I meant. And he was dead serious."

O

The traditional songs that make up *Irish Heartbeat* are very much representative of Ireland as a whole, with Down, Derry, Cork, Dublin, and Galway—points north, south, east, and west of the compass—all mentioned. The opening track, 'Star Of The County Down', is an Irish ballad whose tune resembles that of several other works, including the almost identical English air 'Kingsfold', well known from the popular hymn 'Led By The Spirit' and adapted by Ralph Vaughan Williams for his 1939 symphony *Five Variants Of Dives And Lazarus*. The melody was also used in the Irish folk composition 'My Love Nell'. Cathal McGarvey from Ramelton, County Donegal, wrote the words of 'Star Of The County Down'. Van's regimented but rousing version is, he said, "straight off John McCormack. Even his arrangement, the piano with Derek Bell—that's the way John McCormack would have done it, but he did it with just piano and voice. That stuff comes from that tradition of those Scottish and Irish type of singers that just sang with piano accompaniment. I always liked that music, so it was just a matter of getting the right songs".

Van is restrained in the first verse, as The Chieftains' ensemble playing dominates. He locates the soul of the song on the chorus, transforming himself into a bar room chanter, hand clamped over one ear, eyes shut tight, unfurling—as Greil Marcus would have it— "the song as a thing in itself".

Peter Mills finds it intriguing that McCormack's reading of 'Star Of The County Down' is "unmistakably Irish, and Northern Irish at that, while sporting no recognisably codified 'Irish' musical signifiers at all—thus suggesting that the 'Irish' trad arrangement is in some senses a modern creation, after the manner of Yeats's adaptations of folk tales in *The Celtic Twilight*—a reinvention of tradition which stakes a claim to absolute authenticity, in the way that Derek Bell described ('the purists won't like it'), yet it in itself is a confection".

Morrison's own 'Irish Heartbeat' is up next, its tempo slightly quicker than the original on *Inarticulate Speech Of The Heart*. The vocal is shared with June Boyce, a Northern Irish singer who featured on 'Did You Get Healed?' from *Poetic Champions Compose*. Van lets go after the final verse, scatting along with The Chieftains as they turn the sentimental trad Irish arrangement up to ten, and despite the sometime stodginess of their performance, it works. Indeed, Peter Mills makes a salient point in identifying the difficulty of Morrison's songs on *Irish Heartbeat* as being that "The Chieftains don't know

171

them, in the intuitive or even visceral sense, as well as they do the trad material here". They're still feeling their way into the material, just as Van is feeling his way into the trad songs.

The summit meeting of these two Irish institutions, north and south, really gets into its stride on 'Ta Mo Chleamhnas Deanta (My Match It Is Made)', on which Morrison trades verses with Conneff. The latter sings in Gaelic, while Morrison replicates in English. Conneff's touch is light, Van's less so—despite the shadowing presence of Irish folk stalwart Mary Black—but the rendition is utterly charming for all that.

The last two tracks on side one are where the magic happens. 'Raglan Road' and 'She Moved Through The Fair', along with side two's 'My Lagan Love' and 'Carrickfergus', constitute the real gold here.

Raglan Road lies between Pembroke Road and Clyde Road in Dublin's well-to-do Ballsbridge area. Named for Lord Raglan, alias Fitzroy Somerset, the first Chief Commander in the Crimean War, it retains a kind of ragged grandeur, even if the Georgian houses that fall back from the steady tramp of pedestrian feet and insistent hum of vehicular traffic are now mostly sub-let into self-contained apartments.

This was the setting for 'On Raglan Road', arguably the most famous and best loved of Patrick Kavanagh's canon. Kavanagh was born in the rural town-land of Inniskeen, County Monaghan, one of the three Ulster counties under the jurisdiction of the Republic of Ireland, in 1904. He quit school at the age of 13, and, like his father, entered the shoemaking trade and toiled away on the family's small farm. For more than 20 years, Kavanagh gave himself over to the country life, buying and selling livestock at fairs and markets, attending Sunday mass, wakes, funerals, and weddings, playing 'pitch and toss' at the crossroads, cycling to dances, and turning out for the local Gaelic football team. But he had another life, a secret life in which he furthered his education by reading and composed verse of his own. By the late 1920s, his poems were appearing in *The Dundalk Democrat*, *The Irish Independent*, and several literary magazines.

Kavanagh became increasingly suffocated by the confines of his rural existence. He craved recognition as a poet and association with kindred spirits. Monaghan had, he wrote in the excoriating 'Stony Grey Soil', thieved the laugh from his love, took the gay child of his passion, and clogged the feet of his boyhood. In 1938, he finally quit Inniskeen and crossed the Irish Sea to London, remaining there for only five months until eventually settling in Dublin.

In the autumn of 1944, Kavanagh, a fervent disciple of the drink, a curmudgeon, a rake, a scrounger, was living in a boarding house at 19 Raglan Road and subsisting on hand-outs from, among others, John McQuaid, Archbishop of Dublin and Primate of All Ireland. He met and fell hard for a 22-year-old medical student, Hilda Moriarty. According to Kavanagh's biographer, Antoinette Quinn, "With her black wavy shoulder-length hair, creamy complexion, high cheekbones, and dark blue eyes, Hilda was ... considered one of the most beautiful women in the city." Kavanagh called her his Madonna. He came to know Hilda's haunts and effectively stalked her, often standing at the top of Grafton Street when he knew she would be passing through the gateway of St Stephen's Green so that he could watch her approach. Yet much as Kavanagh tried to woo her, even transforming his grubby appearance into a smarter image more befitting a gentleman suitor, Hilda wasn't interested. Quinn speculates that perhaps Kavanagh's own ardour was motivated more by Hilda's inspiration as a muse rather than any designs he may have had on ravishing her.

'On Raglan Road' was first published as a poem in *The Irish Press* on October 3 1946, under the title 'Dark Haired Miriam Ran Away'. The Miriam of the title was actually the name of the girlfriend of Kavanagh's brother, Peter, who said her name was used instead of Hilda to avoid embarrassment. Luke Kelly of The Dubliners set the words to the melody of 'The Dawning Of The Day'—written by Thomas Connellan in the 17th century, and a song Morrison would have known well from John McCormack's recording—after an encounter with the poet in the Bailey, one of Dublin's most celebrated literary pubs.

"On one occasion I dared to actually speak to the man, because … he was a rough sort of man," Kelly said many years later. "He was singing in his own peculiar manner, as was I, and he said, 'I've got a song for you!' And he said, 'You should sing "Raglan Road".' And I'm very proud that I got the impromata, as it were, from the man."

But back to *Irish Heartbeat*, and the reading of 'Raglan Road', the place where Kavanagh pined for romance with a young woman almost half his age, and the song on which Morrison's intentions come over altogether less honourable. There's a gruff machismo to his delivery that suggests he wants to do more than just hold hands and gaze gormlessly into her eyes. There's a quiet howl, too—a forlorn, desolate abjection—as he concedes defeat. She walks away from him, hurriedly, and he can't stand to see her go. The rejection is unendurable. Morrison has seldom been so vulnerable. If he wasn't such a grumpy bastard, you'd probably cradle his neck in the crook of our elbow and march him to the nearest watering hole for a consolatory few pints.

'She Moved Through The Fair' was first collected in Donegal by Longford poet Padraic Column and musicologist Herbert Hughes, and published by London's Boosey & Hawkes in 1909 as part of an anthology entitled *Irish Country Songs*. There is, apparently, a longer variant of the song, 'Our Wedding Day', and two related songs, 'Out Of The Window' and 'I Once Had A True Love', the last of which shares some of the lyrics of 'She Moved Through The Fair'. Hundreds of artists recorded it in the second half of the 20th century, among them Anne Briggs, Fairport Convention, Sinead O'Connor, Odetta, Art Garfunkel, Mike Oldfield, and even Boyzone. Simple Minds adapted the melody for 'Belfast Child', a UK number one single in 1989.

The melancholy grace of the lengthy instrumental introduction to 'She Moved Through The Fair' on *Irish Heartbeat* bears the movement of the swan moving over the lake in the second verse. It's more than a minute before Morrison intones, "My young love said to me / My mother won't mind", but really at this point in the track it's all about The Chieftains—until the third and final verse, when something almost preternatural happens. Van is subsumed by the plaintive sounds that surround him, he goes deep into both music and character, singing—whispering—in the tongue of a ghost girl, "It will not be long love / Till our wedding day."

'I'll Tell Me Ma' is a well-known children's song. Collected in different parts of England during the 19th century, it appears in compendia from shortly after the turn of the 20th century. In Ireland, the chorus usually makes reference to either Belfast or Dublin, and is known colloquially as 'The Belle Of Belfast City' or 'The Belle Of Dublin City'. Maurice Leyden, in *Belfast: City Of Song*, claimed that other variants of the song existed in Britain and America, denoting that children's street games were part of a universal folklore and a self-perpetuating oral tradition that has endured without adult intrusion.

Van and The Chieftains' interpretation is lively if elementary, a bit of light relief after the intensity of 'Raglan Road' and 'She Moved Through The Fair'. The fade-out includes a mischievous snatch of 'The Sash My Father Wore', a ballad commemorating the Williamites' triumph over the Jacobites in the 1690–91 war fought over who would be king of England, Scotland, and Ireland. Peter Mills hears the inclusion of 'The Sash' as "a wiping clean of the slate and a reclamation of folk culture, and a bold non-sectarian gesture: a southern Irish group playing with a Protestant northern artist, playing a Belfast song, matched with an anthem of militant Protestantism".

The origins of 'Carrickfergus' are vague, although it has been traced back to an Irish language song, 'Do Bhi Bean Uasal' ('There Was A Noblewoman'), written by poet Cathal Bui Mac Giolla Ghunna in 18th century County Clare, and has roots in the Irish ballad 'The Young Sick Lover', published in 1830. The Irish lyrics, concerning a cuckolded man, are bawdy and delightfully humorous—in marked contrast to the nostalgia of the English version. There is a suggestion that 'Carrickfergus' came from at least two separate songs, which would explain the inconsistency of the narrative. *The Ancient Music Of Ireland*, published by George Petrie in 1855, included a song by the name of 'The Young Lady', featuring many of the lyrics used in 'Carrickfergus'. 'Sweet Maggie Gordon', which can be found in the Music For The Nation section of the US Library Of Congress, was published by Pauline Lieder in 1880, and contains verses similar to those in 'Carrickfergus', yet the chorus is closer to another Irish/Scottish folk standard, 'Peggy Gordon'. In the mid 60s, Dominic Behan, brother of renegade Irish writer Brendan, learned it from the actor Peter O'Toole, wrote a new verse, and recorded it as 'The Kerry Boatman' for his 1963 album *The Irish Rover*.

As with 'Raglan Road', 'She Moved Through The Fair', and 'My Lagan Love'—songs that demand of the singer some serious emotional mining, an engagement with inner truth—Morrison makes 'Carrickfergus' his own. Perhaps, in this instance, because much of the narrative is so personally evocative for him—he sings of the exile's experience ("But the sea is wide and I can't swim over / And neither have I wings to fly"), the yearning for another time, another place ("My childhood days bring back sad reflections / Of happy days so long ago / My boyhood friends and my own relations / Have all passed on like the melting snow"), the restless spirit ("So I'll spend my days in endless roving / Soft is the grass and my bed is free"), and the Irish soak ("I'm drunk today and I'm rarely sober").

If Morrison's 'Carrickfergus' is the prototypical anthem for the dispossessed and doomed Paddy, 'Celtic Ray', the second Morrison original on *Irish Heartbeat*, is the complete opposite. When he shouts out that he wants to go home, that he's been "away from the Ray too long", you believe he might just make it—that we all might just make it home, wherever that is. And adding to the sense of exhilaration on this rendition, there's that (unintentional) thigh-slappingly funny exclamation of "Billy!" before The Chieftains' coda.

The words of 'My Lagan Love' have been credited to Joseph

Campbell, a Belfast man whose grandparents hailed from the Irish-speaking area of Flurrybridge in South Armagh, while Herbert Hughes adapted the music from a traditional air taught him by Prionseas Mac Suibhne in Donegal in 1904. Mac Suibhne had learned the tune from his father, Seaghan, who had picked it up some 50 years previously.

John McCormack loved to sing 'My Lagan Love'. He made a recording of it in 1929, and several times subsequently over the years. Lonnie Donegan too did a version. But it's unlikely either of theirs—or any other rendition—comes close to the heightened and horny take here—for evidence of the latter, just listen to Van's lustful delivery of the line "The song of heart's desire" against Paddy Moloney's dizzy improvisation on tin whistle, as traditional Irish music gets down to some dry humping.

'Marie's Wedding'—also called 'Mairi's Wedding', 'The Lewis Bridal Song', or 'Mairi Bhan'—is a Scottish song originally written in Scots Gaelic by John Roderick Bannerman for Mary C. MacNiven on the occasion of her winning the gold medal at the National Mod—the highest singing accolade in Scottish Gaeldom—in 1934. No matter that Mary didn't actually tie the knot until 1941. Van and The Chieftains, augmented by a trio of heavenly angels (Mary Black, June Boyce, and Maura O'Connell) give it socks, as they say in trad circles, serving "as a reminder of the unifying power of song, and of what this music is really for"—the craic.

O

A former colleague of mine, someone who belonged to old Ireland, with its faithful observance of impossible Catholic morality and its dedication to the preservation of culture in cobwebs, responded to a cursory inquiry about whether he'd heard *Irish Heartbeat*, with a diatribe against Van Morrison that carried the vehemence of a hate speech by Dr Ian Paisley in his pomp. The fact that he hadn't indeed heard the album only compounded my own suspicion that his aversion to it was predicated on something more sinister than a contemporary singer—a rock singer, I believe he called him—tampering with sacred tradition. Ancient religious animosity never dies, it only lies sleeping.

To those of us who grew up feeling a sense of mortification at our cultural inheritance, especially the music, *Irish Heartbeat* was an ear-opener. These songs belonged to our history, yes, and we were familiar with some or all of them. But they had never sounded like this. Morrison took 'Carrickfergus', 'My Lagan Love', and 'Raglan Road', and, whatever the spell he cast, he made them new again. The Chieftains played like The Chieftains—a mostly well-mannered company who knew when it was all right to get rowdy—but Morrison's performances were transcendent. They embodied the ghosts of his antecedents. He was onto something here. A connection had been established with his inner Paddy. He's even smiling on the sleeve.

"They're all Irish songs, basically, because that's where I'm from," he said on the album's release. "Going away and coming back are the themes of all Irish writers, myself included."

Critical response to the collection was, in the main, enthusiastic. Jon Wilde in *Melody Maker* described it as "a bloody considerable marvel". Morrison's alliance with The Chieftains had "awakened the roisterous spirit", and you had to return to "the giddy days of *Astral Weeks* to find him quite so let go".

Denis Campbell was just as excited in *NME*. "Awesome", he declared under the heading, 'Celtic Champions Compose'. The Chieftains' bonhomie had rubbed off on Morrison, "who has responded with a warmth worthy of the tunes". London's *Evening Standard* was slightly more measured in its critical appraisal—*Irish Heartbeat* was "a marriage of convenience which worked". In the United States, *Rolling Stone* applauded the record's "splendour and intense beauty".

Morrison, for once, yielded to the critics. "It [*Irish Heartbeat*] is a breakthrough, it's different," he said. "That's the consensus of every critic that's reviewed it. So I'm prepared to accept that. I don't need any more than that."

The consensus wasn't quite as overwhelmingly positive as Morrison liked to think. Not everyone heard *Irish Heartbeat* as a soulful reinvention of the traditional form—including The Chieftains' own Derek Bell.

"It's a classic, but from the purist's point of view, it's grotesque," he said. "I mean, no purist is going to sing things like 'She Moved Through The Fair', repeating 'our wedding day' three times. That's an element of soul music. The repetition and jazz-like style of words for the sake of emphasis—it has nothing to do with our tradition at all, and the folkies don't like it."

Yet even Bell would concede that "every single Irish song we've done, Van has done a completely different and new way. Many of the songs have been sung, and maybe they've been recorded rather too often by both good and bad artists, and to hear them done in a completely different way will make them live longer. And if you throw new light on a piece of music it will last longer, and people will study Van's performance as they won't have heard it done that way before".

Phil Coulter, composer, arranger, producer, and an ally of Morrison's from back in the day, described the coming together of two Irelands on *Irish Heartbeat* as a mismatch. Arty McGlynn believed Van was shafted musically on the album. "It was a very simple album—an album of songs that Van knew," he said. "But I don't think that he moved any further into Celtic music. I think Van sang those songs that he was enticed to sing by The Chieftains."

And *The Belfast Telegraph* reckoned Patrick Kavanagh should return from the grave to haunt Van The Man for desecrating 'On Raglan Road'—with a version, the reviewer added, that would prompt "trouble in the Dublin pubs"—while if Morrison sang 'My Lagan Love' at a party in Belfast, "people would leave early".

This kind of negative opinion to a project that dared the listener to hear outside the comfort zone of what the guardians of the music decided were the definitive versions of these songs, was predictable. Obviously the same guardians were unfamiliar with Morrison's reworking of The McPeake Family classic, 'Purple Heather', on 1973's *Hard Nose The Highway*.

The most scholarly evaluation of Morrison's work with The Chieftains came from Dublin poet Paul Durcan—who would later co-write and recite on 'In The Days Before Rock'n'Roll' from Van's *Enlightenment* album—in the Irish current affairs and cultural magazine *Magill*. 'Raglan Road' "brings together the two finest poets in Ireland in my lifetime. No other Irish poets—writing either in verse or in music—have come within a Honda's roar of Kavanagh and Morrison.

"Both northerners—solid ground boys. Both primarily jazzmen, bluesmen, sean-nós. Both concerned with the mystic—how to live with it, by it, in it; how to transform it; how to reveal it. Both troubadours. Both very ordinary blokes. Both drumlin [small hills] men—rolling hills men. Both loners. Both comedians. Both love poets. Both Kerouac freaks. Both storytellers. Both obsessed with the hegira [a term often used for an escape or flight]—from Monaghan to the Grand Canal, from East Belfast to Caledonia. Both originals, not imitators. Both first-time cats, not copycats. Both crazy. Both sane as can be. Both fascinated by at once their own Englishness and their own Irishness. Both obsessed with the audience and with the primacy of audience in any act or occasion of song or art. Both fascinated by the USA. Both Zen Buddhists. Both in love with names—place names as well as person names."

If Durcan were to become Ireland's Minister for Education, he declared, Kavanagh and Morrison would be foremost in a new poetry curriculum as part of the Leaving Certificate (the final examination in the Irish secondary school system, for which students have two years to prepare).

"All of Kavanagh and Morrison—not my selection or St Augustine's selection or Barry McGuigan's selection or Dean Martin's selection, but the entire oeuvre—and let the audience (students are a free audience, not a concentration camp of suitable victims) pick out what they like and what they don't like."

At the end of two years' listening to Morrison, Durcan would invite students to compose an essay from a choice of what he described as "the top 30 of Morrison's poems"—a choice that would include 'Summertime In England', 'In The Garden', 'Listen To The Lion', 'Rave On, John Donne', 'A Sense Of Wonder', 'Madame George', 'Cypress Avenue', and 'Tir Na Nog'.

"And I'd state in my Leaving Certificate essay that no Irish poet since Kavanagh had produced poetry of the calibre of those 30 compositions. Even the very titles are original. I'd state that in order to introduce William Blake to an audience, you don't necessarily have to give them poems by William Blake. You give them Morrison's 'Listen To The Lion'. I'd write a love letter to the examiners about my favourite Morrison poems. I'd tell them about 'Summertime In England', which to me is an Irishman's hymn to the Englishness that is in all of us if we care to look inside ourselves, which of course, so many of us don't, except when we are eating young English soldiers for lunch."

Like Kavanagh, Durcan posited, Morrison "is a maestro of the improvised line. In fact, the only new development in recent Irish poetry was Kavanagh's introduction of the jazz line and Morrison's continuation of it. Kavanagh was a great tenor sax who was content to blow his horn in the sunlit angles of Dublin street corners in the 50s. He was the king of anonymity".

Durcan would parallel "the spiritual adventure of Morrison's poems ... with Kavanagh's philosophy of 'not caring'". He would write about "Morrison's visit to the Church of Ireland in his 'Tir Na Nog' as if it was the only church in Ireland. There was just this one church in Ireland and one day, after thousands of years, a man stopped there, a man called Morrison, and he wrote a poem about it, about this strange place, this strange site, this strange building called the Church of Ireland. Maybe I'd tell them also that I like Morrison because I know that his work comes from the same level as my own poetry—the level of daydreaming. That he's out to annihilate ego, that he's after the same nothingness as Kavanagh was after. In this sense, he's really not a poet at all, no more than I am. He's after the musical technique of how to live."

Poetry, Durcan concluded, is essentially "part of an age-old oral and place name tradition (known in Irish as the dindsenchas), and Morrison is a modern Irish exemplar of that ancient tradition".

Declan Sinnott, former guitarist with Horslips and Moving Hearts (and now Christy Moore's right hand man onstage), wasn't surprised that Van gravitated toward The Chieftains when it came to recording an Irish album. But he dismissed the notion that *Irish Heartbeat* was a significant addition to the Irish folk pantheon, arguing that the songs were too obvious, and that Morrison's choice of collaborators reflected his status as a "sub-consciously Irish writer".

"I don't think The Chieftains represent Irish music," he said. "They're not popular in Ireland. They're more popular in America and Europe. Van wasn't doing anything new with these songs. I think he was scratching the surface of Irish music."

So would Moving Hearts have been a better fit?

"That wasn't what he wanted to do. Moving Hearts were as much a part of the world he came from as the traditional world. Maybe if he'd worked with Donal Lunny or Steve Cooney, people like that ..."

Sinnott compared *Irish Heartbeat* to *We Shall Overcome: The Seeger Sessions*, Bruce Springsteen's homage to Pete Seeger, in that "a lot of people who didn't know the music would go for it". The comparison was not meant in a flattering way.

Tommy Fleming, a singer from Sligo whose career was given a huge boost when he toured the United States in the 90s with Phil Coulter, has covered 'Raglan Road' and 'Carrickfergus'. His version of the former was, he insisted, wholly influenced by Luke Kelly, *Irish Heartbeat*, and in particular Van's reading of the song, making no impression on him whatsoever.

"It's a strange one," he said. "It wouldn't be one of my favourite albums. Maybe The Chieftains gave Van the Ireland he was after, the Ireland he wanted to be a part of, but I don't think they're representative of real trad music anymore. They've crossed so many boundaries, they've become almost a novelty act."

So what kind of Ireland was it that Morrison was after? And what kind of Ireland did he evoke through his own material?

"There's a bit of the land of saints and scholars coming out of his music—a bit of the far away hills are green. I don't think he puts modern Ireland into his songs. The Ireland he paints is very much an American version of Ireland."

Morrison's "literary background—that is, his Irishness as such" never interested John Platania, the New York guitarist who has featured on a slew of albums from *Astral Weeks* to *Keep It Simple*. As far as he was concerned, "it was all simply good music. That's all that interested in me. I never analysed things that way. It wasn't until after we toured behind the *Irish Heartbeat* album that Van as an Irish writer began to come into focus."

For Liam Neeson, *Irish Heartbeat* was "just fucking remarkable. Van's forays into different musical spheres was still very, very pleasing to me then. When I knew he had an album coming out, it was like waiting for a book. 'Raglan Road', on *Irish Heartbeat*, I just love it. It happened way before Van, but I just thought the power of the performance value of The Chieftains and Van just made it—I don't want to say palatable, more palatable, that's not true—but he just took it on to another level. It was like him going back and saying, 'This is where I'm from. Even though I'm a Northern Ireland Proddy, I love this Irish music and it's part of my soul, too.'"

Micheal O'Suilleabhain saw the intersection of Morrison and The Chieftains as "less a story of Morrison in the Irish trad world as one of Irish songs in English permeating his own repertoire. He holds steadfastly onto his own voice and singing style when singing 'She Moved Through The Fair' or 'Carrickfergus'. The result is something that can be viewed from a spectrum of perspectives ranging from travesty on the one hand to release on the other. The streetwise street singer side of Morrison comes through best in 'I'll Tell Me Ma', an urban children's street song from his native Belfast. Here the rough, gruff Morrison take on African American tradition allied to his Belfast accent, finds ground in a circle game song common in different versions across Ireland, Scotland, and England".

According to Glenn Patterson, Morrison 'Vanned' the traditional songs on *Irish Heartbeat*, in large part because of that voice.

"It's still recognisably a Belfast voice. It pulled them back, I think—and I realise this is quite a parochial response—into our orbit. Of course, a number of the songs on the album are traditional to this part of the world—'I'll Tell Me Ma' is the quintessential street Belfast song, and 'Star Of The County Down is one I recall from sing-alongs in my parents' front room. So perhaps what he achieved was a realignment. It's all song."

Noel McLaughlin and Martin McLoone, in *Rock And Popular Music In Ireland: Before And After U2*, cautioned against reading too much into the political implications of the album, although they did laud it as "an interesting example of cultural pluralism—Protestant Belfast meets Nationalist Ireland; one of the most distinctive voices in rock music meets the unmistakable rhythms of Irish music, setting up interesting tensions both musical and cultural". In other words, it was "a process of musical interchange rather than evidence of Morrison having discovered 'his essential Irishness'. Throughout his career, Morrison invokes too many cultural influences to warrant raising The Chieftains collaborations above all others, or to suppose that his sense of cultural identity is synonymous with a traditional Irish nationalist conception. The geography of this mental landscape is too complex and too idiosyncratic for this, taking in contemporary myths like Woodstock or California and the 'ancient roads' that lead to Caledonia, Avalon, Albion and the England of the Romantic poets".

Looking back on *Irish Heartbeat* in 2005, Morrison himself seemed to reject the notion that it was a conscious decision to reconnect with his Irish roots.

"I never think about music in terms of categories," he told Jon

Wilde. "When I was growing up, it was all just music. Categories meant nothing to me. As well as blues, jazz, and folk, I grew up listening to a lot of Irish singers. So the Irish thing was just another strand that found its way into my own stuff more and more because I'd absorbed that stuff a long way back."

O

Morrison lost his true mentor, father George, on 22 April 1988—just a week before the start of the *Irish Heartbeat* tour. George, who was 66, died after suffering a myocardial infarction resulting from ischaemic heart disease. The funeral was a private affair; nothing about it appeared in the media. For Morrison, according to Johnny Rogan, it was "a time to reflect on all that his father had contributed to his life. Exposure to the most arcane blues and jazz records of the pre-war era enabled the singer to find his own distinctive style and establish himself as one of the great white soul singers of his time".

Unusually, for someone not given to emotional concealment, Morrison masked his grief well on the live dates.

"He came out of himself a bit," said Paddy Moloney. "He only really gets that when he's onstage, and there's that music that comes out of improvising and interplay and reaching some kind of state. That's the only time he feels he can let loose. He's in a cage otherwise."

The good cheer that seemed to characterise Van's working relationship with The Chieftains was never going to last. Tensions first surfaced when Moloney vacillated over a contract that Morrison wanted him to sign.

"For a while, neither one of them would give way," Derek Bell recalled of the episode. "Bad feeling continued to brew. They didn't talk for a while. But you couldn't be with a personality like Van and not run the risk of something like that happening."

Arty McGlynn was part of Morrison's own band on that tour—they played their own set with Van before The Chieftains joined him onstage—and claimed the merging of north and south was, as Phil

185

Coulter had already charged, "a mismatch. We're all from Northern Ireland, and Van is very northern. So there was a lot of tension on that tour. It was the first time this had ever happened, these two extreme elements. There were huge frictions, no doubt about that".

The "bad feeling" to which Bell referred finally erupted in an acrimonious exchange after a London show, as Clive Culbertson recalled.

"We were all sitting about and Van goes, 'Let's do something important here. Let's talk some shit. Where do you want to be with your life? What do you want to be doing in 20 years' time? Let's get deep here, man. We're living on top of each other.'

"So we go all the way round, and Paddy refuses to tell. Van wasn't baring his soul himself, but he opened the cage a wee bit. 'Well, I want to look for the answer. I want to get free.' It wasn't from the soul, it was only from the head. But Paddy wouldn't give. So, of course, Van goes, 'Everybody else has told us. Where do you want to be, spiritually?' 'I just want to be playing with The Chieftains.' 'Look, hold on here. Everybody else has bared their soul. Now I want you to bare your soul like we have.' Finally Van says, 'Fuck you!' and he flings the glass of wine at him. So Paddy gets up, flings a glass of wine back."

At the end of a second tour with The Chieftains, Morrison even turned his ire on his Belfast mucker, Derek Bell, accusing him of being "too much under Moloney's apron strings". As the amiable multi-instrumentalist told it, Van taunted him that it was useless reading "all these books about these masters and then not living the life".

"Of course, for the sake of peace, I had to agree with him," Bell continued. "He said I just hadn't got the guts to break out, stand up on my own and do something. Then he says, 'Look, where do you think I am? I've got to the top of the tree here. Where do you think you are? You're down here.'"

Kevin Conneff found Van increasingly difficult to be around.

"There were times when he would get into a mood," he said. "Usually alcohol was involved, and I didn't want to be near him. He could be quite unpleasant. Everybody around him had to suffer."

Things reached a nadir in Helsinki, Morrison deciding "he'd had enough of The Chieftains at the exact same time they reached their own limit when it came to hearing his 'forthright' opinions, colourfully phrased". It was, said Clive Culbertson, the worst he'd ever seen Van. Under threat of expulsion from the tour, Culbertson was delegated to tell Paddy Moloney not to talk between songs.

"So I lean over to Paddy. I says, 'Paddy, forgive me, I know I should tell him to fuck himself, but he says would you do a wee bit less talking between the tracks and let's get this over as quickly as possible. He wants to go home.' Paddy just chats away. We do the song. And Paddy's now talking longer and longer—ever since he was told not to. So Van leans over to me, and goes, 'Right, you fucking tell him now. If he doesn't stop talking between songs, I'm going home. Now.' This is all onstage."

Things then became slapstick. Every time Moloney got near the microphone, Morrison placed himself in front of it. When Moloney walked to the microphone on the opposite side of the stage, Morrison followed to intercept him.

"He does this for the whole song. So he gets to the end of the song and he just turns around. 'You fucking Chieftains, I'm fed up carrying you fuckers', etc. The audience start throwing cans, bottles, once they see him shouting at The Chieftains. So he storms off. 'Fuck this. It's over.'"

Sean Keane squared up to Van as he made his exit. Matters could have turned uglier still had it not been for the intervention of the tour manager, who warned them in no uncertain terms that if they didn't get back out there and play, he would deal with them.

Despite these differences, the two parties did record together again, Morrison contributing 'Have I Told You Lately That I Love You?' and 'Shenandoah' to The Chieftains' albums *The Long Black Veil* and *The Long Journey Home* respectively, and Moloney doing his tin whistle thing on Van's *Magic Time*.

"We did try to do a second album, a follow-up to *Irish Heartbeat*," said Moloney. "We had two days in rehearsal and we ended up falling around the place laughing, just in stitches. It just never happened. But we did play together again on *The Long Journey Home*. I got him doing 'Shenandoah'. He said to me, 'Paddy, you fucker, you never came up with that song—that would have been a great one for the album [*Irish Heartbeat*].'"

○

In 2007, at a pre-Oscars party, Van was presented with an award by actor Al Pacino for the extensive use of his songs in films such as *Breakfast On Pluto*, *The Royal Tenenbaums*, *Wild At Heart*, and *The Departed*. He then played a brief set, during which his daughter Shana, late soul legend Solomon Burke, Irish folk chanteuse Maura O'Connell, and Moloney were invited to join him.

"He said to me, 'Paddy, have you got your whistle? Come on!'" Moloney recalled. "So I was up there playing something I'd never heard before. But you just go for it with Van."

Irish Heartbeat remains Van Morrison's most unequivocally Irish body of work. However, three years after this landmark recording with The Chieftains, he became involved in a project that explored further the depths of his Irishness. Cuchulainn, which translates as 'Culann's Hound', was an Irish mythological hero who featured in the stories of the Ulster Cycle, one of the four great cycles of Irish mythology, as well as in Scottish and Manx folklore. The son of Lugh and Deichtine, his childhood name was Setanta. He became Cuchulainn after slaying the smith Culann's fierce guard dog in self-defence, offering to take its place until a replacement could be reared. At the age of 17, Cuchulainn defended Ulster single-handedly against the armies of Queen Medb of Connacht in the epic Cattle Raid of Rooley. It was prophesied that his great deeds would give him everlasting renown, but that his life would be short.

In modern times, Cuchulainn is frequently referred to as the

Hound of Ulster, and his image has been invoked by both Irish Nationalists and Ulster Unionists. For Irish Nationalists, he is a Celtic Irish hero—a bronze sculpture of the dead Cuchulainn stands in Dublin's General Post Office, headquarters of the leaders of the Easter Rising in 1916. Ulster Unionists, meanwhile, regard him as an Ulsterman defending the province from enemies to the south.

In 1991, Morrison recorded *Cuchulainn*, a spoken word collection described in the accompanying liner notes as coming "from ancient Ireland, written out by monastic scribes in the Middle Ages, but dating from a much earlier pre-Christian Celtic culture. The central theme is the life and death of the hero, and the dispute over the sacred land of Ireland between the royal houses of Ulster and Connacht." The 42-minute recording, adapted and produced by R.J. Stewart—a Scottish-born composer, author, and teacher who has written books on occultism, ceremonial magic, and Celtic mythology—from his own tome, *Cuchulainn*, also features actress Fay Howard and percussionist Ben Norman. It was issued without fanfare or publicity, initially available only on cassette in esoteric bookshops, until indie label Mole Records released a limited edition pressing.

According to Morrison scholar Peter Mills, the singer's reading "is strongly performative", his delivery leaning "on the Northern Irish pronunciation which is his to use ... His delivery of the line 'Would ye make an eejit of me?' is pure East Belfast, and reminds us of the continuities between the ancient and the modern, and furthermore that these tales are built to be read in this voice".

Van, whose singing style is a composite of the many (mainly American) jazz, blues, and soul influences to which he was exposed as a youngster, was almost rediscovering his Belfast accent—and, in it, a sense of the poetic. Accent is an indicator of identity. And Morrison, by stressing that accent on *Cuchulainn*, is professing his Belfast—his Northern Irish—identity within the wider context of Irish identity through a renewal of its folkloric traditions.

CHAPTER 12
THE HILL OF SILENCE

Despite Van Morrison's legendary status, his hallowed place in the annals of contemporary music, his albums had sold moderately—if steadily—since the cult classic that became the compulsory addition to any collection, *Astral Weeks*, and its altogether more accessible successor, *Moondance*. He has reportedly never received a royalty cheque for 'Brown Eyed Girl', the song that launched him as a solo artist and one of the biggest earners ever, because of what he has consistently described as creative accounting on the part of Bang Records. But in 1989, Morrison finally hit pay dirt with *Avalon Sunset*, which spawned an unlikely hit single in collaboration with Cliff Richard.

The evergreen Richard, alias Harry Webb, was the acceptable face of British rock'n'roll in the 60s. A clean-cut, inoffensive, malleable kid—he is now in his seventies, but looks at least three decades younger—he has always possessed what the industry suits just love. Mass appeal. The x-factor, if you will. The polar opposite of Van The Man. And yet ...

Asked by Sean O'Hagan of *NME* if he was an admirer of Richard's work, Morrison retorted, "You're joking, aren't you? You're kidding? I grew up with Cliff. I was a teenager, so I listened to records, TV, radio, and all that just like any other teenager. He couldn't be around this long if he wasn't a great singer. I think he plays himself down though, underestimates himself. He's a good singer, very good."

In terms of temperament, it was a coming together of beauty and the beast—or, if you prefer another fairy-tale analogy, Peter Pan meets Captain Hook. But in spite of the disparity, the improbable duet is a triumph. 'Whenever God Shines His Light' would have been an engaging enough Van song without Cliff, but the latter's angel-boy chops against the former's gruff delivery makes for a compelling contrast. There's no doubt that Richard, a committed Christian since the 60s, is exulting about his God.

Quite what form Morrison's entity assumes, given that his search for spiritual enlightenment had led him down one creedal cul-de-sac after another, will forever remain a source of conjecture. Herbie Armstrong had found what he was looking for, having suddenly converted in 1988 through a Pentecostal church in London's Notting Hill Gate—though his attempts to bring Van into the flock came to nothing.

"I now play music for pure love and love of every day, and it's definitely through Jesus Christ and the Church that I've come back," he said. "He's put something back into me, and I'm praying that perhaps one day Van will find the Lord, because Van is checking it out, and he certainly knew about the Lord long before I did."

While *Avalon Sunset* is "shot through with contemplations about Christ", it also finds Morrison returning to old haunts, the places of his childhood—Orangefield and the seaside at Coney Island in County Down. The monologue 'Coney Island' revisits an enchanting day on which he treks from Downpatrick to Strangford Lough, through Shrigley and onto Killyleah, over the hill to Ardglass, always moving toward Coney Island. This was a route the BBC Radio 4 programme *Going Places* tried to follow in 1996, only to discover that it "zigzags from the coast of County Down up to Belfast", before concluding that Morrison's sense of direction, while perfectly agreeable in the realm of the imagination, would test the stamina, both mental and physical, of any traveller.

The thick Ulster brogue of Morrison's recitation over Fiachra Trench's exquisite string arrangement—not least on the line, "I look at the side of your face", which still sounds like, "I lick the side of your face"—is a sublime piece of performance poetry. For all of his poetic pretensions, on the whole his lyrics, when read from the page, don't really convince as poetry. Much of the time he has a workmanlike approach in the application of words to music. Images and ideas, often half-formed or merely posturing, are pulled from a range of inspirational sources and can sometimes smack of style without substance. But 'Coney Island', whether written down but especially when heard against the backdrop of that magnificent melody, certainly ranks as one of those occasions when such pretensions are warranted. The reflective closing line—"Wouldn't it be great if it was this all the time?"—says much about Morrison's inclination to escape in nature, away from the noise of the world, the endless analysis of what he does, the banal lines of inquiry pursued by journalists already equipped with their own preconceptions anyway, even the unconscious demands of his audiences. The impression conveyed is that he just wants to be. That he wants to be free, to rid himself of all the superfluous bullshit forced upon him by his occupation—he is, after all, as he has emphasised many times over the years to whoever will listen, a songwriter, nothing more.

The Coney Island that he conjures up in song is symbolic of a congenital need to commune with something other than what the modern world offers—to commune with something higher. It's about tuning out. As he told Don Was, head of Blue Note Records, the jazz label on which Morrison released his most recent album, *Born To Sing: No Plan B*, in 2012, "From a sociological point of view, if you went into the middle of town here, or any town, and you weren't tuning out all the stuff that was going on around you—audio—you'd die. So to exist in the modern world, we have to tune out all this audio stuff, because it would kill us, basically. So that happened over a long, long period of time, where people were tuning things out to exist. We're not really in touch with all these parts that used to be natural part of a human existence."

Liam Neeson covered 'Coney Island' on *No Prima Donna: The Songs Of Van Morrison*, a 1994 tribute album, releasing it as a single, complete with promo video.

"I was doing a film in Carolina with my wife [the late Natasha Richardson], God rest her, and Jodie Foster," he recalled. "I can't remember where it came from, but it was a case of, 'Would you be interested in directing a video on your day off?' I shot some stuff of me fishing, walking along the riverbank, and reminiscing about this place called Coney Island back home."

Coney Island itself, a densely wooded area of almost nine acres, is situated in the southwest corner of Lough Neagh, near Maghery, County Armagh, between the mouths of the River Blackwater and the River Bann. Now owned by the National Trust, it was once known as Innisclabhall, and later as Sydney's Island. Excavations carried out during the 60s indicated the existence of a settlement in Neolithic times, enduring to the Bronze Age. It was one of the most westerly outposts of the Normans when they occupied Ireland. A native population flourished there in the later Middle Ages. It bears a 16th century stone tower, used by Shane O'Neill—the Irish king of Ulster's O'Neill dynasty—as a lookout post and stronghold for his wealth. In the 17th and 18th centuries, the island was largely uninhabited. Eventually, in the 1890s, James Alfred Caulfield, the seventh Viscount Charlemont, bought the land for the sum of £150, building a summerhouse in 1895. His remains are entombed in a tower.

Coney Island was connected to the mainland by a causeway or submerged ridge—still visible in the summer when under less than two feet of water—known locally as St Patrick's Road, as Ireland's patron saint is said to have used the island as a place of retreat. This causeway was breached in the 19th century to enable the passage of barges from the Bann to the Blackwater.

According to *The Belfast Sunday Telegraph*, Morrison "fell in love" with the island as a schoolboy, making regular trips "to the seaside with his mother, passing through Shrigley near Downpatrick, on the way to the beach at Coney Island. Van spoke on his *Avalon Sunset* album of taking photographs in Shrigley on those school day visits".

Coney Island is, of course, also a resort on a peninsula at the southern tip of Brooklyn in New York, the subject of Lou Reed's 1975 album *Coney Island Baby* and Beat writer Lawrence Ferlinghetti's 1958 book *A Coney Island Of The Mind*. Peter Mills believes the young Van "may well have been intrigued by the unexpectedly specific connection between the world of the Beats and his own childhood haunts".

Coney Island Of The Mind was also the title of a half-hour British TV special in 1991, featuring Van in conversation with Irish poets Seamus Deane, Michael Longley, and John Montague. Filmed mainly in County Wicklow, at the home of Claddagh Records boss Garech De Brun, it included the revelation from Morrison he was "an Irish writer".

"I wanted to find out where I stood and what tradition I came from," he said. "Well, eventually, I found out that the tradition I belong to is actually my own tradition. It was like getting hit over the head with a baseball bat."

The quartet compared the way in which their writing was defined by their native landscape. The countryside gave Morrison the mental space "in which to receive"; for Deane, the terrain conceived in poetry, or, by extension, any art form, "might be a way out of belonging to something fractured, discontinuous. One can cross all the borders of time and place and find some imaginative locale in which one can say, 'Here we are in possession again—an Ireland that represents a healing unity'".

When you think about it, this is precisely what Morrison achieves in songs like 'Coney Island'. A simple childhood memory of a time and a place—of going to the beach with his ma—is transmuted into a virtual Eden. To reference Peter Mills again, "As with James Joyce's imaginative remapping of Dublin in *Ulysses* or *Exiles*, we have the spirit of place mapped out for us in 'Coney Island' as surely as we have the happily jumbled road map of one man's memories."

Mills also sees a correlation between the worlds created by Morrison when his sensors are at their most receptive—such as on 'Coney Island'—and somewhere like the fictional realm of Narnia in

C.S. Lewis's *The Lion, The Witch And The Wardrobe*, a realm which, he insists, can clearly be seen as deriving from the panoramas of Northern Ireland, "and particularly those of County Down, with its mountains and glens and stunning vistas over the hills".

Like Morrison, Lewis, another Belfast boy, developed a fascination for Irish mythology and literature. Yeats was an especial favourite because of how he absorbed Celtic heritage into his poetry. Once, in a letter to a friend, Lewis enthused, "I have here discovered an author exactly after my own heart, whom I am sure you would delight in, W.B. Yeats. He writes plays and poems of rare spirit and beauty about our old Irish mythology." That the English were somewhat indifferent to Yeats proved a source of enormous consternation to Lewis, although he conceded that "perhaps his appeal is purely Irish—if so, then thank the gods that I am Irish".

'I'm Tired Joey Boy' is the second of a triumvirate of Irish songs on *Avalon Sunset*. Here, the narrator is a rural expatriate in the city, his "life is so troubled". He hankers after the uncomplicated life on the farm, because he's too preoccupied to complain when there's work needs doing. In the second verse, this tormented soul expresses a wish to sit by the river, watching the stream flow, reviving long-gone dreams that he once used to know, things he'd forgotten that took the 'you' he addresses in the song—which again is most likely Van himself—to "pastures not greener but meaner".

There's a sense of been there, seen this, done that—now he just wants to return from whence he came. That locus may no longer exist as he remembers it, and it almost certainly carries little resemblance to the idealised version he has assembled from the unreliable articles of nostalgia, but then that's not what matters. What does matter is to feel connected. What matters is the affirmation of that ache to belong somewhere. This is the Irish exile's lament for home writ large—a belief in the curative qualities of the environment there (the mountains, the glens), where silence touches you, and heartache mends. It is one of the saddest things Morrison has ever written.

Then onto the familiar stomping ground of East Belfast. 'Orangefield' revives lost love when, "On the throne of an Ulster day", the object of the singer's desire made all his dreams come true. Again, whether she did or not—whether she even existed outside the domain of fantasy—is irrelevant. It's not about the girl, if indeed it is a girl. It's about Orangefield. It's about East Belfast. It's about Northern Ireland. It's about all of Ireland. It's about affinity. Pardon my reversion to cliché—you can take the man out of the country, but you can't take the country out of the man. Or, as Liam Neeson, put it, "That's where he's from. If it looks like a duck and quacks like a duck, it's a duck. He's an Irishman, and a Northern Irishman to be particular."

"Basically Irish writers, and I include myself here, are writing about the same things, energy and about when things felt better," Morrison himself told Sean O'Hagan upon the release of *Avalon Sunset*. "Either that, or sadness. And that's it."

Other Irish writers were keen to acknowledge Van's influence on their own work when, the week before he played Glastonbury in the summer of 1989, several of them spoke to the *NME*. Bono envied Cliff Richard for having duetted with him on 'Whenever God Shines His Light'. Morrison made "beneath the skin music", he said. Shane MacGowan hailed The Man as "brilliant and inspiring, a natural Irish soul singer—always uplifting", while Gavin Friday—formerly of avant-garde provocateurs The Virgin Prunes—recalled a concert featuring Van and The Chieftains being "as tight as a knot in a nun's knickers".

In the same piece, Scottish siblings Charlie and Craig Reid, alias The Proclaimers, defined him as "an Ulsterman who sings soul music without insulting black people by mimicking them"—a salient point. Unlike many white artists who have co-opted intrinsically black musical forms such as jazz, blues, and soul—even as I write this, it seems utterly ridiculous to divide sound along colour lines, but such boundaries appear to have become admissible (among certain black artists, too) within our sometimes simplistic culture—and made them more agreeable to white audiences, for Morrison, as Laura Onkey propounds, "blackness and Irishness are inseparable rather than comparable ... Because blackness and Irishness are sonically and thematically tangled at the root of his work, Morrison avoids the *Riverdance* problem of depicting the Irish as one successful ethnic group among man. Even when Morrison is consciously exploring Irishness, he does not—or cannot—separate his relationships with Irishness and black music as distinct experiences. When he returned to Irishness, he did not treat it like an 'ethnically pure folk culture', but as an identity understood through black music".

Examples to support Onkey's argument are plentiful throughout Morrison's oeuvre, not least in his reinvention of songs like 'She Moved Through The Fair' and 'My Lagan Love' from *Irish Heartbeat*— Irish songs but with a blues impulse. The gospel impulse too can be heard in so much of what he does, whether in the jubilant delivery of lines that glorify some kind of divinity or lover, or the call and response of his voice and other voices or instruments. Craig Werner, in *A Change Is Gonna Come: Music, Race And The Soul Of America*, attributes Morrison's "Irish version of the gospel impulse" to his pursuit of the truth. "*Astral Weeks, Moondance* and the underrated *A Period Of Transition* may not be washed in the blood, exactly, but they are awash in blues and gospel spirit," he writes.

O

The artist Cecil McCartney, a friend of Morrison's going back to the Belfast scene of the 60s, claimed his paintings helped to inspire the title of *Astral Weeks*. Whether or not there's any grain of truth to such a boast, it has become incorporated into the fabric of Van's biography during the intervening period. No doubt The Man himself would beg to differ. In 1989, McCartney, according to his account, did it again, contributing the appellation *Enlightenment* to Morrison's next album. In brief, McCartney hosted Morrison at his home in Bangor, County Down, regaling him with an anecdote about how, when mediating on a mountain in Lake Tahoe, he had received enlightenment.

"I felt a transformation come over me," he recounted. "I looked at the mountains around me and felt totally and utterly in perfect harmony with the entire universe—that's galaxies, stars, planets, quasars, the earth, the rocks, everything. I'd never felt like that in my whole life. It lasted about three minutes' Earth time, but it was an infinity. I said, 'Wow, this is what I've been waiting for my whole life. This is the enlightenment that Buddha received.'"

I've had numerous such epiphanies myself, usually while strung out on John Coltrane's *A Love Supreme* and smoking a small kingdom's supply of skunkweed. Van listened to McCartney's yarn, and shortly afterwards "made the album called *Enlightenment*, which was kind of related to the conversation we had". The two men eventually fell out the same year following an argument over—incredibly—whether Myra Hindley, Moors murder Ian Brady's accomplice, could be forgiven for her sins. During a heated debate inside the Crawfordsburn Inn, McCartney cast doubt on the sincerity of Hindley's conversion to Catholicism. This prompted Morrison—"a committed born-again Christian who believes in the cleaning power of the blood", as *The Guardian* newspaper had it in a 2006 article on McCartney—to fling his keys at the painter and storm out. In said article, McCartney talked about reconciliation. It was time, he said, for Van to "let bygones be bygones. All I was trying to do during that discussion was make it clear that asking for forgiveness doesn't erase a terrible crime. Sometimes pleading forgiveness is a cop out".

The fallout broke McCartney's heart. "I was like his big brother. When we met I was 24 and he was only 18. I can remember we used to chase girls in my mini-van." (An unfortunate turn of phrase, I'm sure you'll agree, that makes the innocent pursuit of the opposite sex sound decidedly unedifying.)

Enlightenment is Van-by-numbers, with the exception of 'In The Days Before Rock'n'Roll', co-written by and featuring poet Paul Durcan. A hymn to the transcendent qualities of radio—Durcan makes his way through the frequencies, investing names such as

Athlone, Luxembourg, Hilversum, Helvetia with a kind of strange allurement—it also cites Elvis Presley, Fats Domino, Sonny Boy Williamson, Lightning Hopkins, Muddy Waters, John Lee Hooker, Jerry Lee Lewis, Little Richard, Ray Charles, and jockey Lester Piggott, the chimerical cast of childhood on Hyndford Street. The coda has Durcan raving about some fella called Justin ("gentler than a man"), wondering where he could be and what he could be doing now. Never mind that—I want to know who he is!

Georgie Fame, who had become part of Morrison's band, was sufficiently stirred by Durcan's lyricism to mimic "a signal on the organ which is Morse code—three dots, three dashes, three dots, the SOS signal. You always used to get that Morse code interference on the radio when you'd be trying to tune it in. You'd pick up the ships. It was all completely out of time, but it fitted".

Elsewhere on the album, Micheal O'Suilleabhain plays some euphonious piano on 'So Quiet In Here'—staggering when you consider that it was a one-time-only take, and that O'Suilleabhain was totally unaware his extemporary contribution would wind up on the eventual release. His connection with Morrison came about following *Irish Heartbeat*, when The Chieftains were unavailable to do a concert with him in Dublin's College Green.

"Van wanted to do it with musicians from Comhaltas Ceoltoiri Eireann and he asked me to be music director," O'Suilleabhain recalled. "I quickly found myself holed up in Litton Lane rehearsal studios off the Dublin quays for the best part of a week with him. For several hours each day, I would take the four-piece band—drums, electric bass, guitar, and myself directing from the piano—through the six songs Van had selected. As is my style, I lost no time in creating the right gel to bring the band together as one voice, prompting a comment to me from Van that I still remember—'You're well able to crack the whip.' It was meant as a compliment!

"The whole scene was surrounded by strict privacy. A notable occurrence happened toward the end of the week, when a Guinness

PR lady, who had arranged for a photo shoot of Van in rehearsal, opened the door to a horde of manic news photographers. Suddenly the space was full of flashing cameras and whirring video machines. Van gave them short shrift and went into a very creative rant, shouting at them to get out as he pushed them back out the door. On the last day we headed for Comhaltas HQ in Monkstown, where a band of some 80 or so traditional musicians awaited us. We patched together the insertions of the trad band into some of the song choruses, and that was that.

"Next day, what looked like 40,000 people assembled in a light but constant rain at College Green in front of the specially-constructed stage. Van was in a caravan dressing room to the side. The trad band went onstage. Then I took to the stage with the Van band, at which point one of Van's assistants appeared at the side of the stage gesticulating to me to play something while Van got ready to appear. This was news to me, and with nothing prepared for such an eventuality, I struck up 'Raglan Road'. The crowd got stuck in, and Kavanagh's heady words wafted through the air to the traditional tune he selected, 'The Dawning Of The Day'—which was fine, except that Van seemed intent on making the crowd wait for at least 30 minutes in the rain for his appearance.

"As fevers mounted, he suddenly appeared, walked to the centre of the stage and looked across at me. My piano was situated quite a distance from him, and there is a photo of him that appeared in all the newspapers next day with his hand over his eyes as if to say, 'What are you doing over there in outer darkness when I need you over here within striking distance of me?' He then proceeded to sing the six songs in the wrong order, quite different from the one we'd been rehearsing all week! After we left the stage I sought him out backstage and found him leaning against the wall, murmuring that the audience hadn't cared enough for his performance—or words to that effect! I thought of the many thousands of fans who had stood patiently in the rain to hear him, and wondered at the disconnect between their loyalty and his disappointment. Observing this, and some other occasions where I was with him before he went onstage, I would conclude that he finds it difficult to seize that moment when the artist walks on stage to confront his audience for the first time. A certain shyness, reclusion, and personal apprehension and nervousness seem to combine to make the transition difficult for him."

Unfazed by the unpredictable nature of working with Morrison, O'Suilleabhain didn't hesitate when, some time later, he was asked to attend a session at a recording studio outside Bath.

"I said yes, but that only if it were for a rehearsal and that we would look at a recording afterwards if needs be. I arrived late at night by taxi to the studio, which was in a disused, slightly renovated small church. There I found Van with a three-piece band. I sat at the small upright piano, wondering what was to happen now, when Van turned and announced a song entitled 'So Quiet In Here'. One, two, three, four, and we were off. Never having heard it before, I knew neither what key it was or what tempo was involved. I quickly sensed the key of G major, and did the old trick of hitting an octave G in the bass and playing for time. I picked up the slow, steady 4/4 time from the drummer, and the general chord structure from the bass, and we were off! Which was just about fine until Van finished a verse, turned to me and shouted, 'Take it away!' Nice one! I was a cool cat adrift up a creek without a paddle, so I adopted a minimalist style never heard from me before or since. Every note was longingly caressed as if I knew what I was saying through these mysterious, understated tones. Van brought the train to a halt with a final verse and then called it a night. I looked up to find the poet, Paul Durcan, scribbling in a notebook while the music had been going on. We renewed an old acquaintance and ambled out into the night.

"Generally, the atmosphere around the session was somewhat demonic. I was uncomfortable. Next morning, at breakfast in the hotel, I sought out Van and told him gently but firmly that I was heading off and that we would talk again some other time. He was entirely respectful of my decision and we parted on a good note. That was until some months later, a new album appeared from Van and, yes, there it was—'So Quiet In Here', recorded at that Bath sessions, mixed and printed. I listened to the song for the second time in my life—remembering that the first time I had heard it, I was playing it— and smiled. If you join a circus, you had better be ready for the high-wire act. I still have the smell of the sawdust from the ring and the circus band in my ears. And yes, if he called me again for another set, I would say, 'Yes, yes, let's boogie. Yes!'"

O

After paying his dues for more than 30 years, Morrison was not only—in the parlance of the industry—shifting more units, but he was suddenly hip. A legend, no less, spoken of in the same hushed reverential tones as Bob Dylan. Fitting, then, that this recalcitrant pair of geniuses should be filmed together beneath the Acropolis in Athens, for the BBC *Arena* documentary about Van, *One Irish Rover*. Bob, like always, looks cool as fuck—even if it's obvious he doesn't quite know all of the words to 'One Irish Rover', one of two songs they duet on (the other being 'Crazy Love'), while Van resembles a cross between a pub darts player and an Irish farmer on holiday. Still, it manages to be pretty special. Also in the programme, Morrison shares a jetty in Mississippi with John Lee Hooker—a union that amused the watching Liam Neeson. "Van has on this fucking plastic suit—he has no sense of dress at all! He's sitting there sweating away, John Lee's singing and Van pulls out his harmonica. He just can't stop himself."

It was that kind of year. Apart from *One Irish Rover*, Morrison featured in the already-mentioned *Coney Island Of The Mind* and was honoured by the Belfast Blues Appreciation Society with a plaque at 125 Hyndford Street. You'd think being applauded by his own people in this manner would have pleased him. It didn't. He fired off a letter to *The Belfast Telegraph*, making it clear that the accolade had nothing to do with him. The society subsequently apologised for any embarrassment caused. The plaque was erected "in the best of faith". East Belfast DUP councillor Jim Walker, in a deft display of political opportunism, entered the debate. "He should remember that the people of Belfast admire him not just for his music, but as a man and one of their own," he said. "Belfast is part of Van Morrison and what he has done in his lifetime." Bluesman Buddy Guy was invited by the society to perform the unveiling.

A year later, Morrison was more gracious in accepting an honorary doctorate of letters from the University of Ulster in Coleraine. Professor Peter Roebuc, Dean of the Faculty of Humanities, eulogised about how "Belfast childhood and the city's atmosphere, streets, scenes and people were reflected throughout his work". There was, he added, "unremitting integrity" in the same work, "and a refusal to admit commercial compromise which, I suspect, has its roots—like his music—in the Ulster soil from which he springs. It has long been fashionable to accuse universities of remoteness from the communities which it is their duty to serve. In our case there could be no better answer to that charge, than our recognition of the excellence of one of our most celebrated local artists".

Obviously emboldened by such validation, Van expressed an ambition to develop a philosophy class at university. If he was offered a position, he said, he would "do it tomorrow". According to Johnny Rogan, within days a faculty member at the University of Ulster "was excitedly offering the singer the opportunity to fulfil his dreams"— conveniently disregarding his lack of academic qualifications, the fact that "he had never taught, had never written a book or even had a single article published in any journal, respected or otherwise. Indeed, there was no objective proof that he knew anything about philosophy".

And then there was *Hymns To The Silence*, a double collection with a split personality. There's Van the grouse, bitching about professional jealousy, how he's not feeling it anymore, yearning for an ordinary life and wondering why he must always explain himself.

Neurotic stuff. And then there's the other Van, the wide-eyed Van in thrall to the magic of memory, attuned to the nuances of nostalgia, a believer in the house of love. The Van that sends a shiver from your neck down to your spine on 'Take Me Back', 'Pagan Streams', an ardent reading of 'I Can't Stop Loving You' (with The Chieftains), the wonderfully evocative 'On Hyndford Street', and a title track that may have had its origins in *Coney Island Of The Mind*. There is a point in the programme when John Montague reads his poem, 'The Hill Of Silence', to Morrison, explaining, "In ancient Ireland there were four ways of achieving supreme knowledge, and one was the Way of Loneliness, and the second one was called the Hill of Silence. The Hill of Silence was a path followed by some of the old Gaelic poets, and it's a way of being healed by nature." Montague was speaking Morrison's language.

"When I started writing songs at a very early age, I didn't have a clue what I was doing," Morrison admitted at the outset of *Coney Island Of The Mind*. "Later on, I tried to connect what I was doing with my contemporaries. I discovered, however, that I was writing what some people call transcendental poetry, other people call it mysticism in poetry, other people call it nature poetry. Why was I was writing this kind of material when my contemporaries weren't? So I wanted to find out where I stood and which tradition I came from."

That tradition, as indicated earlier in this chapter, was Morrison's own Irish tradition. "You find out that what you've been searching for you already are," he said. "This writing comes from places I used to go—for example, when I was a kid, the area I was brought up in. The thread took me from there to research poets like Yeats, Keats, Wordsworth, and Coleridge, eventually to the Glen Poets of Northern Ireland."

This is the tradition he invokes when, on 'Hymns To The Silence', he sings of wanting to go out into the countryside, sit once more by those clear, cool, crystal waters, get his spirit, and find his way "back to the feeling" deep down in his soul.

There's no follow through on *Too Long In Exile*, which as well as being a reversion to his jazz and blues roots—John Lee Hooker features on a revamped and futile 'Gloria'—is an indicator of the direction he would pursue throughout the 90s and into the new millennium since when, disputably, Morrison has allowed us mere glimpses of his genius. Yes, the title track finds him singing once more about exile, but it could be social exile rather than exile from any specific homeland. The litany of Irish exiles—James Joyce, Samuel Beckett, Oscar Wilde, George Best, and Alex Higgins—listed at the end smacks of superficiality. They seem to be just names he throws out there for the express purpose of corresponding with the exile theme. In fact, the lyric, in part, could easily be interpreted as yet another rant against the suits, the wheelers and the dealers that, if you subscribe to Van's version, have repeatedly fucked him over. Peter Mills feels the song "asserts his sense of belonging and also his distance from the certainties and comforts that the idea of belonging should or could entail. He also connects himself to a non-user friendly element of Irish culture—in the early 90s, the Celtic Tiger was awakening and 'Irishness' was being marketed very heavily as a virtue and as an acceptable alternative to other versions of national identity. The idea was, as far as marketing and tourism went, to appeal to the Irish in all of us—so that somehow we all felt some connection to the place, and felt at home there".

This "appeal to the Irish in all of us" was the gist of 2013's The Gathering, a project ostensibly about bringing it all back home for the diaspora, those with even the most tenuous Irish links, but really about attempting to boost an economy that is at rock bottom. "Ireland is opening its arms to hundreds of thousands of friends and family from all over the world, calling them home to gatherings in villages, towns and cities," trumpets the official website in the sort of dew-eyed romantic spiel designed to seduce anyone with an Emerald Isle fixation. "Over 70 million people worldwide claim Irish ancestry. The Gathering Ireland 2013 provides the perfect excuse to reach out to those who have moved away, their relatives, friends, and descendants, and invite them home."

More like the perfect excuse to fleece them, "to shake them down for a few quid", as Irish actor Gabriel Byrne—a US resident who previously served as the culture ambassador for Ireland in the USA—saw it.

"The other day I was talking to a group of people. One of them was an illegal immigrant. His father died, he couldn't get home. He feels abandoned by the Irish government. He feels an alien. He can't go back.

"Then I talked to two kids, a girl and a boy, who were forced to emigrate because there are no jobs. And they blame the incompetence and the gangsterism of the government."

Mills is absolutely right when he makes the historical connection between Irishness and a "suspicion of creativity, leading to judgement and exile". It is in this respect that he suggests Morrison's mention of Joyce, Beckett, Wilde, Higgins, and Best is because he viewed them "as good examples of this, if not likeness to himself—the circumstances were different but the net result was the same".

Beckett, like Joyce and Wilde, spent most of his adult life in Paris. From a comfortable middle-class upbringing in Dublin, he graduated from Joyce's alma mater, Trinity College, after which he taught French in Belfast before moving to Paris to take up the position of lecturer at the Ecole Normale Superieure. Beckett befriended another Irish exile, poet and art critic Thomas McGreevy, and was introduced to Joyce's circle, eventually assisting him by reading and researching material for what became *Finnegans Wake*. During World War Two, he joined the French Resistance, and was later awarded the Croix de Guerre (Cross of War), a military decoration. Considered among the last of the modernists, and one of the first post-modernists, he was awarded the Noble Literature Prize in 1969 "for his writing, which—in new forms for the novel and drama—in the destitution of modern man, acquires its elevation". Joyce saw Ireland as "the old sow that eats her farrow", charging that "the economic and intellectual contradictions that prevail in his own country do not allow the development of individuality". For Beckett, it was "suicide to be abroad" but "a lingering dissolution" to be at home.

That the exiled Irish cited by Morrison on 'Too Long In Exile' placed footballer Best and snooker player Higgins alongside literary giants Joyce, Wilde, and Beckett is testament to his odd sense of humour, yes, but also affirms Colin Bateman's accentuation on the Northern Irish tendency to celebrate sporting heroes. Best, like Morrison, grew up in East Belfast, the son of working class Free Presbyterians. His father, Dickie, was a member of the Orange Order, and as a boy Best carried the strings of the banner in his local Cregagh lodge. At the age of 15, he was scouted for England's top football club, Manchester United, by Bob Bishop, who told the club's manager, Matt Busby, "I think I've found you a genius." And he had, as Best became one of the game's first superstars. A predilection for alcohol and beauty queens, in that order, meant he probably never fully realised his enormous potential. He died in 2005, at the age of 59, after suffering from a kidney infection caused by the side effects of immuno-suppressive drugs used to prevent his body from rejected a transplanted liver. Following his death, Belfast City Airport was renamed George Best Belfast City Airport in his honour.

A similar fate befell Alex Higgins, universally known by his sobriquet 'Hurricane'. Coming from Belfast's south side, he honed his snooker skills at the Jampot Club in his native Sandy Row from the age of 11. Higgins was a maverick of the sport, helping to popularise it in the 70s and 80s with his flamboyant style, winning a brace of world titles along the way. A hell-raiser away from the green baize, he drank and smoked heavily, had a gambling addiction, and dabbled in hard drugs. At the end of his life, Higgins, who had been diagnosed with throat cancer in 1998, weighed six stone and lived in sheltered housing on Belfast's Donegal Road. Despite having been worth around £4 million at the height of his career, he was bankrupt and surviving on disability allowance when found dead from a combination of malnutrition, pneumonia, a bronchial condition, and the aforementioned cancer at home in 2012.

If *Too Long In Exile* is Van repeating himself, and prefacing the repetition still to come, a notable exception is 'Before The World Was Made', his second adaptation of a W.B. Yeats poem, after 'Crazy Jane On God', which remained unreleased until 1996, when it was included on *The Philosopher's Stone*. According to Clinton Heylin, neither the melody nor the arrangement was Morrison's.

The late Kenny Craddock, musical director and keyboard player in his mid-80s band, recalled, "I read a lot of Yeats myself. I also wrote a few tunes to different Yeats things, one of which was 'Before The World Was Made', and I played it for Van at his house in Holland Park. There was no recording of it, or anything like that, I just played it a couple of times. I was down there with Arty McGlynn, just having a little acoustic rehearsal. It must have been a year, year and a half later, we're playing somewhere in Europe, and he said, 'I haven't forgotten about that song. I'll definitely do something with it one of these days.'"

And so he did, sharing the credit with Craddock, who died in a car accident in 2002.

CHAPTER 13
DUBLIN'S FAIR CITY

First it was the Brits—pardon my colloquialism—and then it was the God squad. They both subjugated us for centuries, through a combination of brute force and psychological torture—mostly through fear. They kept us in our place, kept us down. We were impoverished, materially and emotionally, and spiritually subservient. We were ashamed, and we didn't know why. There was a wildness in us, a predisposition toward drinking more than was decent, for smashing things and people up. We were big thickos. No better than animals.

Gerald of Wales, in *Topographica Hibernia* (1187), wrote, "They live on beasts only, and live like beasts. They have not progressed at all from the habits of pastoral living. This is a filthy people, wallowing in vice. Of all peoples, it is the least instructed in the rudiments of the faith. They do not yet pay tithes or first fruits or contract marriages. They do not avoid incest." Barnaby Rich, in *A New Description Of Ireland* (1610), said we "lived like Barbarians, in woods, in bogs and in desolate places, without politic law or civil government, neither embracing religion, law, or mutual love. That which is hateful to all the world besides, is only beloved and embraced by the Irish."

Charles Trevelyan, head of administration for famine relief in the 1840s, when over a million died in the country of starvation, said that the judgement of God had "sent the calamity to teach the Irish a lesson", that this calamity "must not be too much mitigated. The real evil with which we have to contend is not the physical evil of the famine, but the moral evil of the selfish, perverse and turbulent character of the people". The Cambridge historian Charles Kingsley, in a letter home to his wife form Ireland in 1860, told of how he was "haunted by the human chimpanzees I saw along that hundred miles of horrible country. To see white chimpanzees is dreadful. If they were black one would not see it so much, but their skins, except where tanned by exposure, are as white as ours." And the *Antropological Review And Journal* of 1866 described us as having "a bulging jaw and lower part of the face, retreating chin and forehead, large mouth and thick lips, great distance between nose and mouth, upturned nose, prominent cheekbones, sunken eyes, projecting eyebrows, narrow elongated skull and protruding ears"—which sounds like nobody you'd want to meet on a lonely road of a dark night.

When we finally got rid of the neighbours and recovered what was ours—well, most of it—the men in black assumed the real power behind this hard won sovereignty, publicly preaching the doctrine of unfeasible virtue while privately devouring the ripe flesh of our young. A pitiful people, we were, being traumatised all over again while already victims of inter-generational trauma, unknowingly suffering the effects of the horrors inflicted upon our forebears. Not unlike what US academic Dr Joy DeGruy Leary has theorised as post-traumatic slave syndrome. Although incomparable on so many levels—scale, for one—the Irish ordeal under British rule and that of African men, women, and children sold into slavery have caused untold damage to the descendants of both groups. "People begin to doubt themselves, their experiences and their worth in society because they have been so invalidated their whole lives in so many ways," DeGruy Leary said. We Irish didn't have the first clue about who we were, what we were worth, where we figured in the grand scheme of things—which partly explains why we left in droves, principally for Britain (the irony of it), the United States, and Australia.

Then everything changed. And the change was very sudden. We went from being pariahs to being feted, from penury to prosperity on an unprecedented scale. And we couldn't handle it. We fucked up.

The dramatic reversal of fortune in the 90s was brought about through a belief in economic openness to global markets, low tax rates, and investment in education. Ireland went from being one of the poorest countries in Western Europe to one of the wealthiest. Disposable income soared, enabling a huge rise in public spending. Unemployment fell from 18 percent in the late 80s to 4.5 percent by the end of 2007, and average industrial wages were among the best on the continent. Continued growth and development derived principally from the multinational sector—electronics, pharmaceuticals and chemicals. Where once upon a time we exported our people, immigrants from other countries—many from the former Eastern Bloc—flocked to the Republic to benefit from the Celtic Tiger. This significantly altered Ireland's demographic composition, with multiculturalism increasing in cities like Dublin, Cork, Limerick, and Galway. In 2007, it was estimated that 10 percent of all Irish residents were foreign-born. Happy days indeed.

Dublin in the 90s was, Johnny Rogan writes, "the most vibrant and exciting city in Europe". Comparisons were frequently made with London in the 60s or Paris at the turn of the 20th century. This new Ireland was "a strangely paradoxical statelet half in love with Europe but still immersed in its older Celtic traditions. It was personified for many in the form of the radical young president Mary Robinson, the first woman to hold the position". Then Taoiseach (or Prime Minister) Albert Reynolds—a former dancehall impresario during the showband years—set about brokering peace in Northern Ireland, meeting in secret with his British counterpart, John Major, as well as Sinn Fein's Gerry Adams and the SDLP's John Hume.

The famous too flocked to Dublin. Carole King, Elvis Costello, Maria McKee, Marianne Faithfull, and Jerry Lee Lewis all laid down roots there for a while. Killiney, a seaside resort about half an hour outside the city along the eastern coastline where King Bono has his mansion, was home to Hollywood high fliers, sporting icons, and a fair smattering of local notables such as Enya and film director Neil

211

Jordan. According to Rogan, "In hotel lounges and trendy diners, politicians mingled with pop musicians, flanked by playwrights, artists, actors, and journalists. It was a closed, insular world that embraced everybody from the horsey Curragh clique to the music-loving, late-night denizens of Temple Bar."

And into this exclusive society came Van Morrison. I don't know about you, but I've never had Van down as a party animal. For a while, he avoided the trendy haunts, the movie premieres, the book launches, and other such gatherings, preferring the haven of his townhouse in Dublin's affluent Ballsbridge. Then he accepted an invite to a fundraising party at Leixlip Castle, the home of Desmond Guinness, a part of the Guinness dynasty. It was there he met an attractive, tall brunette. Our boy was smitten, so he was.

The first time I heard Michelle Rocca's name was in relation to Arsenal, the English football club I'd supported since the age of seven. A winner of Miss Ireland in 1980, she married Arsenal's Irish defender John Devine the following year. Devine was part of a team helmed by Irish players, from both north and south, including Liam 'Chippy' Brady, Frank Stapleton, David O'Leary, Pat Rice, Sammy Nelson, and Pat Jennings. The second time Rocca registered in my consciousness was in 1987, when she co-hosted the Eurovision Song Contest with television presenter Pat Kenny. These were the days when the Irish entry could have put flatulence to musical accompaniment and the majority of our European cousins would still have given us the maximum score of 12 points. We couldn't stop winning the bloody thing.

Anyway, that was it for me and Rocca. She returned to modelling, with occasional presenting gigs—among them the 1990 Miss World— and I had counselling to cure my Eurovision fetish. Until she entered Morrison's orbit.

Rocca had a limited knowledge of what passed for popular music. So when someone pointed out Morrison to her at the Guinness soiree, she mistook him for Val Doonican, the innocuous Irish crooner and mannequin for comfortable, middle-aged knitwear, who hosted his own BBC television show for 21 years between 1965 and 1986.

The Dublin media was intrigued by the subsequent romance between Morrison and Rocca, even though the pair emphatically denied there was a romance, insisting they were just good friends. Sam Smyth, after seeing a photograph of them together, described it as "the most unlikely coupling in human history". Terry Keane, the late diarist at *The Sunday Independent,* wrote in June 1993 that Rocca was "having an intensely platonic relationship with Van Morrison". She wasn't buying the official line that there was nothing going on; that, in Rocca's words, the former footballer's wife and clothes horse merely looked after Van whenever he was in Dublin—which was, of course, all the time back then. And so Keane embarked on a crusade to out Morrison and Rocca as lovebirds, regularly featuring them in her column. In one particularly rib-tickling if pun-laden post, she declared, "When it comes to protesting too much, Michelle Rocca leaves Lady Macbeth in the ha'penny place! But despite denials of any romance as mere rumour, Van The Man and Michelle The Model continue to Rocca'n'roll their way around nightclubs ... Michelle says that their relationship is platonic (though in his case it looks more like gin 'n' platonic, he certainly looks a few horsepower short of a Van!). Clearly Michelle gives him a place to rest his weary head—a head which, I must say, makes a coot look positively hirsute! A picture paints a thousand words—and 'platonic' just doesn't make it to the list. It could be that Michelle is 'in denial' over this whole romance business—once bitten etc. Perhaps she should simply say, 'I Van to be alone.'"

Whatever the context of her personal relationship with Morrison, Rocca certainly became a more visible—and influential—presence in his career. He began inviting her on stage toward the end of concerts to recite Irish poetry, thus presenting the one-time anchor with the opportunity to transfer the skill of reading from prepared text to large audiences acquired at Eurovision. Nothing in life, no experience accrued along the way, is ever wasted. She worked on his wardrobe.

Suddenly the sartorially challenged Van went from variously looking like a barman, bookie, or fusty civil servant to a silver screen mobster or the lost Blues Brother. The denim was dispensed with, a dapper fedora was applied to his thinning pate, and he took to wearing the mandatory rock'n'roll accessory, shades. The whole ensemble was, Johnny Rogan claims, "designed to disguise. A hat covered his unfashionable comb-over hairstyle; dark glasses hid his porcine eyes; a black frockcoat suit drew attention from his frighteningly large girth." Rocca told *The Sunday Life* that she was also "trying to persuade him to relax more", adding, "He is pretty introverted except when he is in the company of good friends."

When she wasn't being a mystical beauty at his gigs, dressing him up or playing life coach, Rocca became Morrison's nemesis, the interviewer, for a series of promotional Q&As, one of which found its way into the now-defunct *Vox* magazine. The following exchange will give you a gist of Rocca's interrogative technique:

> Rocca: "The contemporary poet, Paul Durcan, called you the greatest Irish poet since Patrick Kavanagh. That must have been gratifying?"
> Morrison: "Yeah, sure it is. It is gratifying."
> Rocca: "When was the last time you read James Joyce?"
> Morrison: "I haven't read him for 25 to 35 years."
> Or how about this one?
> Rocca: "Do you believe that as people we persecute ourselves?"
> Morrison: "Oh, yeah. I think so, yeah."
> Rocca: "Do you think more so the Irish, or is it a universal thing?"
> Morrison: "Well, I think more Irish."

Hardly the stuff of penetrative journalism. Suffice to say, nothing was ever revealed by such banal inquiries. Van was just as reticent with his belle Michelle as with all of those other hapless individuals who had gone before, and indeed those others who have since followed in her wake.

Another of Rocca's functions—whether designated to her by The Man, or assumed by her own volition, we don't know—was to oversee *No Prima Donna: The Songs Of Van Morrison*, released complete with a black-and-white cover image of Rocca coming over in a pose redolent of Hollywood heyday glamour. It was an underwhelming homage to an artist who deserves better. Sinead O'Connor, Hothouse Flowers, Elvis Costello, Lisa Stansfield, and even Cassandra Wilson could have phoned in their perfunctory vocal performances, while Liam Neeson's 'Coney Island' sounds exactly like what it is—an actor overdoing the actorly thing on a monologue, the effect of which is only really heightened through being delivered by someone with Van's conflicted persona. Phil Coulter and his orchestra turn 'Tupelo Honey' into the kind of soundtrack that belongs in the elevator of a three-star hotel desperately vying for five-star status. The less said about Marianne Faithfull's 'Madame George', the better. Brian Kennedy gets two songs, one of them a duet on 'Irish Heartbeat' with Morrison's daughter, Shana. I've been more captivated listening to paint dry.

Kennedy was now part of Morrison's coterie. A fortuitous twist of fate for a West Belfast lad who once believed that Van, rather than an elder statesman of the city, was actually American. Such was the indifference the young Kennedy felt toward whatever his peers were listening to.

"I made a conscious decision not to embrace what everyone else was embracing at the time, which was Van Morrison, Bob Dylan, and Joni Mitchell. The first single I ever bought was 'Dancing Queen' by Abba!" he told me in 1991, the year after his debut album, *The Great War of Words*, elicited comparisons with Morrison in several reviews. For Kennedy, while these comparisons were perhaps understandable, given the two men's shared geography, they were way wide of the mark.

"Some people just assume that I'm from Northern Ireland and I play acoustic guitar, therefore my reference point must be Van Morrison. If people hear that it must be an element of preconception because we come from the same part of the world. I wouldn't for a moment assume that my talent is anywhere near his. It comes from a completely different place."

Fast forward a few years, and Kennedy was part of Morrison's Rhythm & Blues And Soul Revue, singing back-up on albums *Days Like This*, *The Healing Game*, and *Back On Top*, and performing with his mentor before then American President Bill Clinton.

"He plucked me from obscurity," he said, "and shared his global audience that he worked for, got them to check out this young fella from Belfast. He's just a one-off. They broke the mould when they made him. He's just extraordinarily generous to me, and continues to be so. Without being asked by him to sing, I would never have met Joni Mitchell, I would never have met or sung with Bob Dylan or Ray Charles or John Lee Hooker. I just wouldn't have had access to any of that music or those experiences.

"And also, the experience of watching somebody work as hard as he does onstage, seeing that as normal, taking risks even at that point in your life. He could just do the greatest hits, take the money and go home again. When you go see a gig of his you know you're going to go and see something that you're never going to see again. He doesn't repeat himself. He's like a saxophone. It's like singing with a saxophone—you'd think there was a reed in there."

According to Johnny Rogan, Kennedy, "Catholic, falsetto-voiced, and gay—in short the complete antithesis of Morrison", was drafted in to append "a pleasant sweetness to Morrison's darker vocal". For those critics who'd been waiting to give Morrison a good kicking in print, the boy wonder Kennedy's presence as a vocal foil gave them the perfect excuse. Of his 1995 appearance at the Fleadh in London's Finsbury Park, the *NME* bitched, "A rancid fog of blind reverence has cloaked Morrison for decades now, with nobody daring to peek beneath it … Van Morrison is an overrated old donkey who has churned out endless variations on the same limp pseudo-soul formula for too long. His influence on music, as the Fleadh proves, has been to inspire Mafia-style respect and lame imitation in equal measure, crippling generation after generation of potentially interesting Irish musicians." The same publication, once a Morrison loyalist, carried on its tirade in reporting back from that summer's Phoenix Festival, where Van's set featured "an annoyingly enthusiastic horn section, and a prancing gimp boy—the hopeless Brian Kennedy—to sing the notes he can't reach any more."

This scathing indictment of Kennedy was perhaps a tad harsh, though probably on the money in outlining his real job description. Morrison's voice was no longer a powerhouse. It didn't so much take flight as stay stubbornly grounded. Once a thing coated in wild honey, now it was largely a belligerent growl. You'd almost expect it to invite you outside. He gave the impression that he couldn't be arsed most of the time. Maybe his interminable protestations that he was just a working musician, that this thing was just a job, were true, after all. Certainly, during Kennedy's time in the organisation, it appeared that Morrison was punching the clock.

There is, of course, another perspective on this. A little naïve, admittedly, but one that merits mention. Could it be that Morrison, mindful of the imminent last days of the Troubles, was engaging in a kind of gesture politics? He had always maintained his distance from the sectarian minefield. His religion—the religion into which he was born—had never been a matter of importance to him. But to many in Northern Ireland, and many more down south, he would forever be associated with Protestantism. Yet here was Morrison, reaching across a torn city to a Catholic raised in the Falls Road, where it was "a really dangerous, illegal thing to be Irish and to flaunt your Irishness". The Belfast of Kennedy's youth pitched him and thousands of others into "a life and death situation every day".

"You had to really be on your toes and be aware, and be able to react in the right way when a difficult situation arises," he recalled.

"So, on the one hand, really sharply aware of it; on the other hand, like any young person who only has one life, it's all so inconvenient. You can't go into town, you can't go out after a certain time at night. It's scary. You want it all to stop. You want people to stop killing each other. Consumed by that kind of stuff, and seeing things that a child should never see—like people being shot dead and hearing about people that you knew that were shot or blown up. You have these adult concerns on childhood shoulders, and it should never happen.

"There's a thing I used to do that now, with hindsight, I see what I was up to. There would be an ambulance or a fire engine constantly coming down the road, because we didn't live too far from the hospital. My reaction was to think of a harmony to this siren. What notes would go well with this? On the one hand, it's a bit bonkers to be at that, and on the other hand it's perfectly rational. And it's a way of making it less frightening, because ultimately that's a very frightening sound. It's literally an alarm going on and they have to get to the hospital or the fire as quickly as they can. Like every little kid, you just try and make your environment less frightening, I suppose."

Kennedy's involvement with Morrison during this period wasn't simply a matter of kindness on the older man's part. Make no mistake, if Kennedy couldn't cut it, if he didn't possess some vocal attribute that could be assimilated within the music, it's likely he would have represented Ireland at the Eurovision Song Contest a lot sooner than he eventually did in 2006. Van not only made it possible for Kennedy to share stages with Bob Dylan or Ray Charles or John Lee Hooker, he gave him credibility. Whatever semblance of said credibility remained, Kennedy himself destroyed with an ignominious appearance on the Irish version of British TV's *Celebrity Come Dine With Me* in 2012, when, in a catfight with fellow contestant Paul Martin, he hurled a glass of red wine over the obnoxious showbiz journalist. Classy.

So mentoring is not really Morrison's thing. But there is a

beguiling yarn about how he gave one young Dublin singer-songwriter a glimpse of his genius at close quarters on the night of his 50th birthday. Beguiling yet at the same time revealing about Van's knotty personality—the ego, the emotional impotence, the cruelty, the sweetness, the eccentricity, yet principally, the sanctuary he finds in song, how, for him, music is the agency of communication where he feels most at ease. Glen Hansard, the carrot-topped Outspan Foster in Alan Parker's 1991 adaptation of Roddy Doyle's novel *The Commitments*, about a Dublin soul band, was a busker on the streets of his native city, paying his dues, honing his craft. His advocates included Marina Guinness, descendant of the brewery dynasty.

"She was a slightly older woman than me and she would give me money. She was very supportive. She said to me one day, 'Glen, if you want to come out to the house, Van is turning 50 and there's going to be a bit of a [party].' She knew I was a big fan. I used to busk his songs. She said, 'Bring a bottle of port,' because Van loves port. I was so grateful," recalled Hansard, who went on to win an Oscar in 2008 for 'Falling Slowly', from the movie *Once*, in which he played—guess what?—a struggling singer-songwriter.

Guests at the small and very exclusive gathering to which the affable Hansard was invited included Jerry Lee Lewis.

"I went in and Van and Jerry Lee were singing. I'm just sitting there, blown away, loving it, loving it, loving it, because I'm a huge fan. And he was singing old Hank Williams songs, Waylon Jennings—just great old country music. And at one point he said," and here Hansard affects a comically gruff Belfast accent, "'Does anyone want to hear a song? Any requests?' I was standing quite far back. I said, 'Van, "Hungry For Your Love".'

"And he just looked over and said, 'YOU don't know me.' And I was just like, fuck! I was crushed. I crumbled inside. So I went outside. I sat down on the step. I was totally freaked out, because I'm just a kid, and this was someone to me—he was like a Dylan to me. My heroes are Dylan, Van, and Leonard Cohen. They're my men. So anyway, I'm outside and I'm thinking, I'll just go home, I shouldn't have come here. Of course I'm blaming myself because I'm Catholic! Marina comes out and says, 'No, come back into the house. It's going to be cool. He's just a bit touchy sometimes. But trust me, come back in, it's all good.'"

Hansard, swallowing hard on his hurt, relented.

"Of course, I knew not to cross him in any way. Again at one point he held up the guitar and said, 'Anyone else want to sing a song?' And he was passing the guitar around. And so Marina said, 'Glen will sing a song—Glen, you'll sing a song.' And I was like, 'No, no, no!' And so Van looks down and sees me. And people are like, 'Come on, Glen, sing a song.' I went up to Van and he hands me the guitar, then stands up and walks out of the room. I'm standing there thinking, oh, God, the only guy I want to sing to is gone.' I was freaked out, because now I've had another interaction with him, and I don't want to be in his way at all."

Hansard performed a couple of songs. Morrison returned during the second one.

"He sat with his back to me at the table. I was just devastated. Again, I wanted so much—you want people to like you. You want him to have some time for you. I was having to deal with it. And so I finished my second song and people clapped. Van turned around and said, 'What did you want me to sing?' And I says, 'Hungry For Your Love', and I'm trying not to look him in the eye! And he says, 'Do you know it?' I says, 'Yeah.' He says, 'Well, sing it!'

"I had the guitar in my hand, and thank God I know the song. So I was able to start playing it. I'm singing the song, I was about two verses in and he was like, 'Yeah! Great, great. Yeah!' And I'm kind of saying to myself, I know that sound. I know on his records when that happens … I just felt he was into it. I was getting something now. And then he started kind of singing with me, like a kind of harmony. And I'm freaked out. And you can tell by everyone around the room that there's something going down here. It's almost like watching a boxing match.

Everyone's on my side! And I finished the song and he just says, 'Do you know any Bob Dylan?' And I was like, thank God, I know loads of Bob Dylan songs. I was like, 'Yeah, which one?' He said, 'It's All Over Now, Baby Blue'. 'You take the first verse, I'll take the second verse.'

"So I started playing, and Van sang the second verse. I'm blown away watching him. My God, I'm singing with Van Morrison! It's like jamming with a Beatle, it's the most amazing thing. It's better than jamming with a Beatle, what am I saying? It's Van Morrison! So we're singing back and forth and it's an amazing experience. And I put down guitar at the end of it and everyone clapped. He was like, come on. And I was like, 'Where are we going?' 'Come on.' I take the guitar and I follow him up the stairs in this beautiful old house. I go upstairs into a room. He brings a bottle of port. I'm on one bed, he's on the other bed. And he said, 'Now, sing for me. Sing a song.' I was blown away, because now it's just me and him. And I played him a song of my own. He takes the guitar. 'What do you want to hear?' I said, 'Anything?' And he said, 'Yeah.' I said 'One Irish Rover'. He plays it.

"What was amazing is I'm sitting there, watching Van Morrison, watching his fingers and watching his throat, and watching his mouth and watching how his mouth moves, getting to see a master at work right up close—watching everything and just drinking the experience in. I can't believe my luck. He finishes the song, hands me the guitar. 'Sing another.' I swear to God, I got to hear 'Madame George', I got to hear 'Sweet Thing', I got to hear 'Astral Weeks'. All the songs I've ever loved. And we passed the guitar back and forth. I ran out of songs after an hour and a half, because I wasn't old enough to have written that many! Van kept going and kept going, all these songs. And the sun came up and eventually a knock on the door, and Van's girlfriend at the time said, 'Van, we have to go.' And he stood up and he said to me, 'Nice voice, nice songs, blah, blah, blah', and just walked out!

"That was all he said to me all night. We just sang to each other. There was no dialogue, nothing, no talk. Just sing, sing, sing. And he left. I sat there feeling like I'd just won the lottery. And that experience deepened me so much, because had I walked away on that first challenge, I'd have lost that whole night. And somehow—not even through my own volition, but through someone else's—I stayed and it's an experience I will take to my grave as in being one of the great experiences of being with a master and him taking you all the way in and letting you see. His only gift to me could have been, 'Here's what I do, and here it is up close.' And his rhythm style, I picked it up. The moment he left I was, like, working out. He has this style of rhythm that's so addictive, so powerful, and so him. I came away from that experience not only a bigger fan, but a changed musician, changed forever."

○

Dublin wasn't just where the object of Morrison's awkward affection resided—it was where he could let loose and get loaded with his mates. These included various members of The Rolling Stones and a legendary rock'n'roller about to declare himself an honorary Irishman: Jerry Lee Lewis, who—in March 1993—moved latest wife Kerrie and son Lee to Dublin.

"I've always been Irish," The Killer—never one to allow the triviality of truth to trump the kind of hyperbolic declaration guaranteed to win over the locals—announced to Eamonn Carr in *The Evening Herald*. "I've learned to love, Dublin, man. This is one of the finest places I've ever been in my life."

That may have had something to do with his membership of a hard-drinking hardcore that included Morrison, Ronnie Wood, and Shane MacGowan. Such inebriated gatherings occasionally greased the wheels of hypothetical alliances. There was talk of Van and Jerry Lee doing a covers album. That came apart at the corporate level, though Morrison did eventually go on to record *You Win Again*, a duets album with Lewis's sister Linda Gail Lewis. There was talk, too, of Van producing an album of his own songs by MacGowan. Again, this foundered, mainly because of contractual complications.

MacGowan, on the face of it, seemed an unlikely acquaintance of Morrison's. Born on Christmas Day in Kent—the garden of England—to Irish parents, he spent his early years in rural County Tipperary, where he first developed his prodigious appetite for alcohol. "I was actually four when I started drinking," he told *The Daily Mirror*. "I just remember that Ribena turned into stout, and I developed an immediate love for it." Legend has it that he tried whiskey at the age of ten.

Back in England, MacGowan earned a literature scholarship and was accepted into the elite public school Westminster, close to the Houses of Parliament, only to be expelled in his second year when found in possession of drugs. The punk revolution was made for people like him, people disconnected from orthodox society. He became something of an ephemeral poster boy for the movement when, at a concert by The Clash in 1976, MacGowan's earlobe was damaged by Jane Crockford, later a member of The Modettes. A snap of him covered in blood made the papers under the headline 'Cannibalism At Clash Gig'. This first brush with notoriety wouldn't be his last. There was the formation of his own punk outfit, The Nipple Erectors (later truncated to The Nips), and then there was Pogue Mahone, soon to become The Pogues, with whom MacGowan wrote arguably some of the greatest songs in the Irish folk canon. Songs like 'Streams Of Whiskey', 'The Sick Bed Of Cuchulainn', 'A Pair Of Brown Eyes', and 'The Broad Majestic Shannon'. Songs heavily fuelled by booze and Irish nationalism.

MacGowan the public figure was given to speaking his mind, eschewing the diplomacy favoured by contemporaries. Many of the perspectives he shares in his memoir, *A Drink With Shane MacGowan* (co-authored by his missus, Victoria Clarke) are too intoxicated to be taken seriously. But many others emerge from the alcoholic haze to display an astute reading of personality. On Morrison, for instance, he says, "Van depressed me. I remember one time I had to pick him up off the floor of the Clarence [the Dublin hotel owned by U2], which is not an easy job, and I'm sure that's not the only time that's happened. I stayed up drinking with him many nights and I always tried to convince Van what a wonderful life it was and what a wonderful life he was living or could live if he stopped being such a miserable fuck, but it didn't work. There's a man who lived up to his public image. He was meant to be a miserable git and he is a miserable git, but he is capable of having a really good laugh."

MacGowan was among those whose paid tribute to Van upon his reception of the Outstanding Contribution to British Music Award at the 1994 Brit Awards. Sting described him as "musical mentor and spiritual mentor", Bob Geldof hoped that "long may you teach us what we're meant to be doing", Elvis Costello was "looking forward to listening when I'm a happy old man", while John Lee Hooker referred to him as "such a great person". Bob Dylan said there was no one more deserving of the accolade than Morrison, "for writing all those fine songs and giving us all that inspiration over the years". MacGowan was never going to be so reverential, and true to form, on a barnstorming 'Gloria' he subverted the chorus by singing "G-L-O-IRA", thereby turning Morrison's most famous song into "a Republican anthem", as Johnny Rogan put it.

Meanwhile, the title track of his most recent album, *Days Like This*, was, along with 'Brown Eyed Girl', co-opted by the Northern Ireland Office into a £1.2 million television campaign to back the paramilitary ceasefire that paved the way for the peace process brokered by US President Bill Clinton. When the latter made an historic visit to Northern Ireland on November 30 1995—the first sitting custodian of the White House to do so—Van The Man was his warm-up act.

The Irishness Morrison displayed that night "was different from his New Age Celticism or collaborations with The Chieftains", according to Lauren Onkey. Rather, this was an Irishness "deeply connected with America and black music: on the day when he represented hopes for new Northern Ireland identities to the world, Morrison's soulful sound and awkward look signified the profound and ambiguous impact of African American music on Irish culture. Morrison's singing demonstrated his lifelong facility with rhythm and blues and soul music".

In the same year, Morrison walked the streets of Dublin with thousands of others in a pro-divorce referendum march. But it was his dalliance with Rocca that continued to preoccupy the Dublin hacks, rather than his burgeoning role as something of a musical mascot for the end of the Troubles. The proliferation of newsprint about the affair, and Van's regular appearances in the gossip pages, prompted him to fire off an angry missive to *The Sunday Independent*, in which, bizarrely, he objected not to anything written about him and Rocca, but to his being referred to as a rock star:

"To call me a rock star is absurd, as anyone who has listened to my music will observe. For the benefit of the unenlightened it is not my nature to be a rock star. What I am is a singer and songwriter who does blues, soul, jazz etc etc etc.

"In fact, I have never claimed, in any shape or form, to be the above, and if anyone would care to do a bit of groundwork they would very easily discover what I have been saying for the last 30 years, that I am not that, and do not believe in it and never have.

"On the one hand I am flattered by the sudden attention of the rock star mythology, but on the other hand I do not need or want the attention, having spend most of my life living the role of an anti-hero and getting on with my job, so I tip my hat to the gods and goddesses of the media and say thanks but no thanks.

"Van Morrison, Chiswick, London."

He may not have wanted the attention, but Morrison was getting plenty of it. Each Sunday invariably brought lurid details of another embarrassing episode from the frontline of Dublin nightlife, such as the time Morrison and Rocca were at a gathering for Bono's wife Ali's birthday in the Chocolate Bar, and tempers became frayed. Rocca left hurriedly, while Morrison allegedly had to be restrained by Bono's minders. Or the time Morrison and Richard Gere became embroiled in a scuffle when Van accused the movie hearthrob of moving in on Rocca. A witness overheard Van's use of the words "Hollywood" and "cunt". And let's not forget the time Rocca was heard to tell her beau, in the presence of the hoi polloi at another Guinness soiree, "At least try to behave yourself in public. There are other people to consider."

Love on the rocks indeed. The denouement, when it came, was redtop heaven. Rocca, apparently engaged to Morrison at this stage, was, according to *The Daily Mirror*'s Northern Ireland edition, caught cheating with a horseracing magnate. Morrison felt "betrayed", declared the relationship over, and expressed disgust at "the behaviour of all parties involved. Michelle and I are finished".

Van lost the moral high ground the following week, when it emerged that he had shared a threesome with a couple of divorcees in a Wiltshire hotel. "I just felt lonely and rejected, and wanted something to hold on to," he confessed to a *Mirror* reporter after the scandal broke. This in itself was a strange tack for someone so media-averse to take. "I am so ashamed," he went on. "I was devastated about the breakup of my engagement to Michelle—who I loved—and I just went over the top. I have let my fans and myself down, but there's no excuse." It wasn't, he assured us, "the sort of thing I would normally do", but rather an uncharacteristic mistake. "But I have been to hell and back. Nobody knows the torment I have been through."

The episode represented an ignominious end to Van's heady Dublin period, though not, seemingly, an end to him and Rocca. A tawdry paternity story broke in 2010, forcing Morrison to issue a statement confirming that he was married to Rocca, and that they had two children.

CHAPTER 14
ONE OF US

Many of the column inches devoted to Van Morrison in the final years of the old millennium seemed more preoccupied with his and Michelle Rocca's on-off-on again relationship, and his omnipresence as a Dublin socialite—albeit an honorary Dubliner—than with his music. Indeed, his daughter Shana, according to diarist Katie Hannon, blamed Rocca for "ruining her father's career".

While such an accusation may have had something of the overstatement about it, there was something unseemly about how Morrison allowed his mid-life crisis—if that's what it was, although it could equally have been characterised as a postponed adolescence, given that, in his own telling, he was a working musician from the age of 15—to be conducted so publicly. When not carousing but composing, the songs mostly remained the same. He was working from tried and trusted templates. Admittedly, there were magical moments on *The Healing Game*, especially 'Rough God Goes Riding'— an image lifted from W.B. Yeats's 'The Second Coming'—'This Weight', 'The Waiting Game', and the title track, described by its author onstage as "a song about East Belfast, back in the days before everything got fucked up", while *Back On Top* boasted 'Philosopher's Stone'. Still, we expected more.

Van The Man's Irishness, a feature of his writing since *Astral Weeks* and particularly pronounced at certain points in the 70s, 80s and the early 90s, was largely conspicuous by its absence. He did make two appearances on Irish television, singing 'My Lagan Love', to Micheal O'Suilleabhain's piano accompaniment, on *River Of Sound*, a history of the country's musical journey, and then contributing a revamped, trad-heavy 'Saint Dominic's Preview' to *Sult* (which translates from Gaelic as 'Fun') with a backing band that included Donal Lunny, Steve Cooney, and Mary Black. But there are signs that Morrison is digging his roots again—not just his Irish roots, but his Scottish ones too—having expressed an interest in appearing on the Pelicula Films-produced BBC/RTE series, *Transatlantic Sessions*. First broadcast in 1995, the programme comprises collaborative live performances by leading folk and country artists from both sides of the Atlantic, playing music from Ireland, Scotland, and the United States, under the direction of fiddler Aly Bain and undisputed king of the dobro, Jerry Douglas.

On the set of the sixth *Transatlantic Sessions* in February 2013 in Loch Lomond outside Glasgow, Bain confirmed, "Van Morrison wanted to come this time, but he couldn't. He's since emailed to say that he wants to meet up in July to discuss it." It makes perfect sense for Morrison to involve himself in such a venture. Morrison fronting a house band featuring the likes of Danny Thompson on double bass, Donald Shaw on keyboards and piano, Russ Barenberg on guitar, fiddler John McCusker, and piper Michael McGoldrick is a mouth-watering prospect—The Chieftains eat your heart out.

In 1999, Morrison became the first inductee of the *Hot Press* Irish Music Hall of Fame. He was hailed by the magazine's editor, Niall Stokes, as "Ireland's greatest living legend", while Bob Geldof spoke eloquently (for a change) of his artistic merit:

"He is an extraordinary singer. No other person sounds like him. He is uniquely recognisable and he uses that beautiful thing to attempt to explore and examine areas and depths few have charted successfully. It is like some long journey for meaning. He is specific in location and mood, but the themes are universal and nearly always have a profound and troubled spiritual dimension. It seems to be music from another place that takes you somewhere else. The range of his musical influences transcends any limited sense of what contemporary music is."

The new millennium saw Van returning to his roots. Not his Irish roots, but his jazz and blues roots. The music on which he was weaned by father George in another century. Ever looking back to those halcyon days, he even penned 'Choppin' Wood', a sort of eulogy for George, on *Down The Road*. Not unlike Bob Dylan, late period Morrison evolved into the old venerable bluesman he always wanted to be, and perhaps—in spirit—he always was. But unlike Dylan, who found a new groove on 1997's *Time Out Of Mind* and has, during the intervening years, produced a series of intriguing albums, Morrison found himself stuck in a groove.

Liam Neeson talked earlier about the eager anticipation he used to feel at each impending Morrison release—an eager anticipation many of us have shared. However, there came a point in the noughties when this eager anticipation was supplanted by a kind of apathetic shrug with each underwhelming new collection. Van was running out of ideas—he was, claimed journalist Barney Hoskyns, "nothing more than a grotesque travesty of his former glorious selves". Hoskyns' use of the adjective 'grotesque' is perhaps severe, but it's difficult to disagree with his representation of Morrison's output at this time as that of an artist returning to the well only to find the well drained of inspiration.

Maybe Morrison himself knew it, which would explain why, in 2006, he went country with *Pay The Devil*, mainly a covers album—with the exception of 'Pay The Devil', 'Playhouse', and 'This Has Got To Stop'—featuring songs by Hank Williams, Webb Pierce, Leon Payne, and Rodney Crowell. Ireland has long had an affinity with country music, rooted, as Peter Mills puts it, "in the historic connections between Appalachian and British Celtic music; the original hillbillies were Irish immigrants. It's also been said that country music offers a kind of white man's blues, or white soul music, connecting the music of America and Morrison's upbringing". And let's not forget country & Irish, the hybrid musical sub-genre of which the chief protagonist was undoubtedly Daniel O'Donnell, before he crossed over into mainstream popular territory.

229

"When I started out, first started in music, I was singing songs like 'Half As Much', 'Your Cheatin' Heart', 'My Bucket's Got A Hole In It', 'More And More' ... there was Lead Belly, and there was that, you know?" Morrison said upon the album's release. "I think these songs are kind of similar to the blues in the fact that they are the true poetry of everyday life, really, a lot different than just pop songs. They actually mean something. It's the truth! It's something I can relate to, and it's very real. The lyrics are real. It's about real life experiences. It's very similar to the blues. In fact, they might be one and the same thing."

He had no truck with much of what constituted country in contemporary Nashville. But then, as he admitted to *The Independent*'s Paul Sexton, he was a man out of step with modernity.

"My musical sources come from way, way before any of this stuff existed. I'm coming from a more archaic, atavistic kind of source. It's almost pagan, almost folk music tradition before rock'n'roll, before electric. Like Ewan MacColl singing with a finger in the ear."

In 2009, Morrison returned to his own heritage on *Astral Weeks Live At The Hollywood Bowl*, a curious move given how, previously, he had disparaged the reverence in which the original has long been held. "I don't remember the last time I listened to it," he'd told Jon Wilde in 2005. "Why would I listen to an album like that? What it means to me is irrelevant, or should be irrelevant. It meant something to me when I was doing it. Now it doesn't matter to me in the slightest."

Three years later, Morrison maintained that this incarnation of *Astral Weeks* was "a totally different project. I had always wanted to do these songs fully orchestrated and live. I never got around to it. Then I thought, well, we have lost the great [drummer] Connie Kay already, and Larry Fallon, the original engineer, so I thought I should probably get to it now. Jay [Berliner] and Richard [Davis] have never done it fully orchestrated and live before either, so I see it as a new project".

The following year, interviewed by *Time* magazine, Morrison further explained why he had gone back to his magnum opus. "The main reason is I don't own the original record. Another reason is the songs are fresh because they haven't been performed that much. It's not like redoing the original, it's a completely different ball game."

In 2011, Morrison was feted by the US–Ireland Alliance—a proactive, non-partisan, non-profit organisation dedicated to consolidating existing relations between the United States and Ireland—when he received the Oscar Wilde: Honouring Irish Writing In Film award. Presenting the accolade, Oscar-winning actor Al Pacino jokingly remarked that, when he first met Van in London 20 years earlier, he couldn't understand a word of his thick Belfast brogue, but "somehow I could feel what he meant through his body language, and was taken by his sensitivity and kindness". Morrison was, Pacino added, "a descendant of a long line of Irish balladeers, poets, and writers whose lyrical words read like music—Wilde, Shaw, Yeats, Joyce, and [Sean] O'Casey". Van, in a typically brief acceptance speech, quipped that it was "a long way from Belfast to Hollywood", before treating invited guests to a 45-minute set that included appearances by the late great Solomon Burke (on a duet of 'Stand By Me'), Paddy Moloney, and Maura O'Connell.

O

Just when we thought that Van had nothing left to say, that he was resigned to letting his extensive catalogue do his talking for him as he entered his late sixties, he surprised us all in 2012 with *Born To Sing: No Plan B*. The majority verdict of the critics, for the first time in a bloody long time, was positive. The Man, they chorused, was back. That remains to be seen.

The Belfast in which *Born To Sing* was recorded, while still haunted by the ghosts of a post-conflict society, as well as suffering the effects of the global economic meltdown, is a markedly different place to the ominous years of the Troubles. A different place, too, to the Belfast that was central to the moulding of Van Morrison. It is very much a modern metropolis carving out a new identity as part of a global village—no bad thing when you consider how divisive an issue has been identity there. As Joshua Hammer wrote in a 2009 article for *Smithsonian* magazine:

"No town or city better illustrates how far Northern Ireland has come, and how far it has to go, than its capital, Belfast. Investment capital, much of it from England, has poured into the city since the coming of peace. The city centre, once deserted after dark, is now a jewel of restored Victorian architecture and trendy boutiques. A new riverside promenade winds past a renovation project that is transforming the moribund shipyards, at one time Belfast's largest employer, into a revitalised district, the Titanic Quarter, named for the doomed luxury liner that was built her in 1909-1912. The Lagan, once a neglected, smelly and polluted estuary, has been dramatically rehabilitated; an underwater aeration system has vastly improved water quality."

The Good Friday Agreement, even in its embryonic stages, "is increasingly regarded as a model of conflict resolution," Hammer added. "Politicians from Israel and Palestine, to Sri Lanka and Iraq, have studied the accord as a way to move a recalcitrant, even calcified, peace process forward."

Belfast's assimilation of chic European culture has made the city "unrecognisable", according to Brian Kennedy.

"Belfast is wealthy now," he said. "It's spread out, it's relaxed, it's sexy, it's funny. There are tables and chairs on the streets outside the cafes. That never existed before. Loads of the barriers you had to go through to get to the town to go shopping—you had to get searched—all those things have gone. It's come on in leaps and bounds, and it's great to see people consumed by other concerns."

Down south, meanwhile, the Republic of Ireland is on its knees after the unchecked avarice of the Celtic Tiger era. Ever since the international lenders bailed out the country in 2010 to the tune of 85 billion euros (£70 billion or $110 billion), the people have lived under a regime of punishing austerity and plummeting property prices. The rate of emigration is at its highest since the Great Hunger in the middle of the 19th century. The recovery is set to be protracted and painful. The country may never be the same again.

So how best to sum up Van Morrison's Ireland? In the opening chapter, I suggested that it's a mythical place, a place belonging to neither orange nor green, but common ground to both. A place where there is, as Morrison himself sang, no religion. Or at least no religion pernicious enough to rent asunder one body of people that inhabits the same island. No religion that exerts the kind of influence so terrible as to draw centuries of bloodshed from successive procession of martyrs that sacrificed themselves until peace brought the madness to its end. The Belfast that lies at the heart of Morrison's Ireland "provided a 30-year alternative to the dominant media image—a parallel Belfast of the imagination, insulated and isolated from the grim realities of the Troubles".

Morrison chose to write about the Belfast he knew—the Belfast he idealised, perhaps. And though he may have elicited criticism in some quarters because his Belfast wasn't the Belfast of guns and bombs and sectarian sociopaths, because it wasn't the Belfast with which we were confronted almost nightly on our television screens at the height of what was, let's face it, a grubby little war, as The Man himself said, he's no Pete Seeger. Besides, as Noel McLaughlin and Martin McLoone note, Morrison's Belfast "has a greater artistic and social integrity than any of the 'parachute' songwriters over the years who dropped in hoping for some street credibility or who dabbled with the city's problems out of a sense of political duty".

And then there's the other Ireland, the real Ireland that Van Morrison has done his bit to inspire. The Ireland that is separated, yes, but the Ireland that, rather than perpetuating mutual mistrust between north and south, cultivates a reciprocal respect of faith and culture and national identity.

Morrison—and here I write as a southerner raised a Catholic—allayed our suspicion of that other lot across the border in much the same way that George Best and Alex Higgins did. He may be one of them, but he's one of us, too. For all that he came from an East Belfast, with its pipes-and-drums soundtrack, its grave devotion to God and Queen, there's more than a whiff of the rakish Paddy about him in his fondness for the craic, his whimsy, his downright oddness. He's a Belfast Proddy who gets us—and we get him. Talk to any Irish person outside the Six Counties about Van The Man, and the majority will recognise him as an Irishman first—an Irish artist—and a Northern Irishman second. He is Ireland united in a way that it will never be.

SELECT DISCOGRAPHY

VAN MORRISON'S IRELAND ON ALBUM

Astral Weeks

It remains his masterpiece, the album against which all others are measured. As Noel McLaughlin and Martin McLoone write, Morrison "had to get out of Belfast to grow as an artist and a songwriter, but he is continually drawn back to his hometown for inspiration and emotional sustenance"—and never more so than on 'Cyprus Avenue' and 'Madame George', the explicit Belfast songs on this collection. But listen to the city's Sunday six-bells chime on 'Beside You', and the ferryboats pulling into Belfast Lough on 'Sweet Thing'.

Moondance

Local East Belfast landmarks abound on 'Into The Mystic' (the lough again), 'Everyone' (winding streams, pipes and drum), and 'Brand New Day' (the railroad track), though it's the childhood fishing trip to Ballystockert recalled on 'And It Stoned Me' that really gets you.

Saint Dominic's Preview

It's a long way from the United States, the place of Morrison's boyhood dreams, to Belfast city, but it's home and it's where the heart is on the title track and the sublime 'Listen To The Lion'.

Hard Nose The Highway

More nostalgia on 'Wild Children', Van channelling the spirit of his birth year, 1945, subliminal Irishness on 'Bein' Green', and a first foray into the folk heritage of his birthplace on 'Purple Heather'.

Veedon Fleece
Arguably as seminal a work as *Astral Weeks*, this is Morrison digging down into the soil of the south, a heretofore unknown Ireland to him. Killarney's lakes, the streets of Arklow, and Oscar Wilde are all evoked in his version of God's green land, though the spectre of the savagery up north is never far away, especially on 'Linden Arden Stole The Highlights' and 'Who Was That Masked Man'.

Beautiful Vision
More an exploration of Morrison's Celticism than his Irishness, the Northern Irish Protestant work ethic nonetheless comes through on 'Celtic Ray'. He finds his 'Northern Muse' in the County Down and reprises his days as a window cleaner on 'Cleaning Windows'.

Inarticulate Speech Of The Heart
New Age noodlings maybe, but the songs here are also thick with an emphatic Irish brogue yearning for the old country on 'Irish Heartbeat' and 'Cry For Home', and the instrumentals, 'Celtic Swing' and 'Connswater'.

A Sense Of Wonder
Back to Belfast on 'A Sense Of Wonder', with its cast of native characters (Wee Alfie, Johnny Mack Brown, McGimpsey), locations, and even dishes. Irish folk-rock stalwarts Moving Hearts feature as well, giving 'Boffyflow And Spike' a bit of welly and providing a teaser of what *Irish Heartbeat* might have sounded like if they, and not The Chieftains, had been Van's associates of choice on that particular project.

No Guru, No Method, No Teacher
'Got To Go Back' finds Van The Boy staring dreamily out of his Orangefield classroom window, before rushing home to Ray Charles on the turntable. Elsewhere, he's a self-proclaimed 'One Irish Rover', delves into Irish legend on 'Tir Na Nog', and playfully quotes W.B.

Yeats (whose estate had denied him permission to adapt 'Crazy Jane On God') on 'Here Comes The Knight'. And then there's the exalted 'In The Garden', which should be experienced rather than talked about.

Irish Heartbeat

On which Morrison finally brings it all back home. His rendition of 'Raglan Road' is, for my money, definitive. The same could be said for 'Carrickfergus', 'She Moved Through The Fair', and 'My Lagan Love'. Some of the material is predictable (for which the cute hoor Paddy Moloney must be credited/blamed), but still, you wouldn't begrudge Van having a laugh on 'I'll Tell Me Ma' and 'Marie's Wedding'.

Avalon Sunset

The God entity is, ahem, omnipresent, with even avowed Bible basher Cliff Richard drafted in to duet on 'Whenever God Shines His Light'. But this is all about the Irish triumvirate, 'Coney Island', 'I'm Tired Joey Boy', and 'Orangefield'.

Enlightenment

Dublin poet Paul Durcan and Limerick composer and piano virtuoso Micheal O'Suilleabhain are the Irish connections on 'In The Days Before Rock'n'Roll' and 'So Quiet In Here'. If it wasn't for the pair of them, you'd file *Enlightenment* under 'Rudimentary'.

Hymns To The Silence

These hymns are as much to Belfast as to the silence. 'On Hyndford Street' and 'Take Me Back' are memoirs of Morrison's infancy, while the traditional spirituals 'Just A Closer Walk With Thee' and 'Be Thou My Vision' recall his Protestant upbringing. The Chieftains lend their trad Irish weight to Don Gibson's country standard, 'I Can't Stop Loving You'.

The Philosopher's Stone

Morrison's attempt at replicating Bob Dylan's *The Bootleg Series* is confined to this one compilation of outtakes and previously unreleased material, featuring 'Drumshanbo Hustle' (inspired by an incident in County Letirim during his showband days), 'Crazy Jane On God' (finally), and the boisterous 'High Spirits' with The Chieftains.

Pay The Devil

Yes, it may be country, but country is just Irish music with a hillbilly twang.

IRISH EYES ARE SCOWLING
VAN MORRISON'S IRELAND, THE ALBUM

Indulge the author as he compiles his wishful anthology of Van's Irish songs. It's only a matter of time before a suit somewhere pilfers the idea for his own, kicks back, and watches the money roll in ...

Side One
'On Hyndford Street'
'Cyprus Avenue'
'Madame George'
'A Sense Of Wonder'
'Orangefield'

Side Two
'And It Stoned Me'
'Connswater'
'Coney Island'
'In The Days Before Rock'n'Roll'
'Purple Heather'

Side Three
'Star Of The County Down'
'Carrickfergus'
'Saint Dominic's Preview'
'Irish Heartbeat'
'One Irish Rover'

Side Four
'Linden Arden Stole The Highlights'
'Who Was That Masked Man'
'Bofflyflow And Spike'
'High Spirits'
'Raglan Road'

BIBLIOGRAPHY

Clancy, Liam *Memoirs Of An Irish Troubadour* (Virgin Books 2002)

Clarke, Victoria Mary & MacGowan, Shane *A Drink With Shane MacGowan* (Pan 2002)

Costello, Peter *The Irish 100: A Ranking Of The Most Influential Irish Men And Women Of All Time* (Simon & Schuster 2001)

DeGruy Leary, Dr Joy *Post Traumatic Slave Syndrome: America's Legacy Of Enduring Injury And Healing* (Uptone Press 2005)

Doherty, Harry & Gorham, Scott *The Boys Are Back In Town* (Omnibus Press 2012)

Dooley, Brian *Black And Green: The Fight For Civil Rights In Northern Ireland & Black America* (Pluto Press 1998)

Dudley Edwards, Ruth *Aftermath: The Omagh Bombing and the Families' Pursuit of Justice* (Vintage 2010)

Foster, R.F. *Modern Ireland 1600–1972* (Penguin 1989)

Flanagan, Bill *Written In My Soul: Conversations With Rock's Great Songwriters* (Contemporary Books 1987)

Glatt, John *The Chieftains: The Authorised Biography* (St Martin's Press 1997)

Heylin, Clinton *Can You Feel The Silence? Van Morrison: A New Biography* (Penguin 2004)

Hinton, Brian *Celtic Crossroads: The Art Of Van Morrison* (Sanctuary Music Library 1997)

Humphries, Patrick *Lonnie Donegan & The Birth Of British Rock & Roll* (The Robson Press 2012)

Lewis, C.S. *The Screwtape Letters* (HarperOne 2001)

Lyons, F.S.L. *Ireland Since The Famine* (Fontana Press 1985)

McKay, Susan *Northern Protestants: An Unsettled People* (Blackstaff Press 2005)

McLaughlin, Noel and McLoone, Martin *Rock And Popular Music In Ireland: Before And After U2* (Irish Academic Press 2012)

Marcus, Greil *Listening To Van Morrison* (Faber And Faber 2010)

Marcus, Greil *Rolling Stone Illustrated History Of Rock'n'Roll: The Definitive History Of The Most Important Artists And Their Music* (Random House 1992)

Marcus, Greil (ed) *Stranded: Rock And Roll For A Desert Island* (Da Capo Press 2007)

Mills, Peter *Hymns To The Silence: Inside The Words And Music Of Van Morrison* (Continuum 2010)

Negra, Diane (ed), *The Irish In Us: Irishness, Performativity, And Popular Culture* (Duke University Press 2006)

O' hAllmhurain, Dr Gearoid *The Pocket History Of Traditional Irish Music* (O'Brien Press 1998)

Prendergast, Mark J., *The Isle Of Noises* (St Martin's Press 1987)

Quinn, Antoinette *Patrick Kavanagh: A Biography* (Gill & Macmillan 2003)

Rogan, Johnny *Van Morrison: No Surrender* (Vintage 2006)

Turner, Steve *Van Morrison: Too Late To Stop Now* (Bloomsbury 1993)

Werner, Craig *A Change Is Gonna Come: Music, Race And The Soul Of America* (Canongate 2002)

ENDNOTES

The following provide references for sources other than interviews either conducted specifically for this book, or culled from archive interviews by the author.

Introduction
"usually to harangue somebody" *Uncut*, 2005
"Is it OK if I go to sleep?" Johnny Rogan, *Van Morrison: No Surrender*
"Well, in that case ... you're wrong!" *The Independent*, 2006.
"to the rough edge of the great man's tongue" *The Independent*, 2006
"heavy coat, scarf, shades, and a cap" *Mojo*, 2012
"the music is it", *Mojo*, 2012
"rude and bad-tempered" Clinton Heylin, *Can You Feel The Silence?*

Chapter One: Two Tribes
"the birthright of all the people of Northern Ireland" bbc.co.uk
"Northern Ireland's worst single terrorist atrocity" bbc.co.uk
"Irish men and women resisted British rule" Ruth Dudley Edwards, *Aftermath*
"the danger of trying to equate someone's religion" bbc.co.uk
"the rising of the moon" pbs.org
"the day... when all the people of Ireland" bobbysandstrust.com

"a kind of invented, artificial identity" *The Irish Times*, 2012
"don't feel culturally Irish" *The Irish Times*, 2012
"If that trend continues" *The Irish Times*, 2012
"a growth in people who feel politics" *The Irish Times*, 2012
"allow people to begin to recognise" Susan McKay, *Northern Protestants*
"an embattled minority" Susan McKay, *Northern Protestants*
"very, very much Irish" Susan McKay, *Northern Protestants*
"an extraordinary reflection on the social strictures" Susan McKay, *Northern Protestants*
"I feel I can be both" Susan McKay, *Northern Protestants*
"I always thought the Protestants" Susan McKay, *Northern Protestants*
"there is a real sense of a changing Northern Ireland" *The Irish Times*, 2012

Chapter Two: Funky Neighbourhood

"I come from a working-class background" Clinton Heylin, *Can You Feel The Silence?*
"You see that when you go away" *The Belfast Telegraph*, 2012
"Well, I go back to childhood" *The Belfast Telegraph*, 2012
"She was a free-thinker" Clinton Heylin, *Can You Feel The Silence?*
"totally Protestant" Clinton Heylin, *Can You Feel The Silence?*
"there wasn't any problems" Clinton Heylin, *Can You Feel The Silence?*
"I wasn't even aware" *Rolling Stone*, 1972
"a stand for truth in an age of sectarianism" grandorangelodge.co.uk
"so bare-faced and confident enough" Brian Dooley, *Black And Green*
"most Catholics are IRA sympathisers" *The Belfast Telegraph*, 2011
"are infused by a conservative social outlook" academia.eu
"When I was growing up" Johnny Rogan, *Van Morrison*
"couldn't get plugged in" *The Irish Times*, 1998
"upbringing in and association with the town" bbc.co.uk
"I can never remember talking about it" Clinton Heylin, *Can You Feel The Silence?*
"filled with angels, bright angelic wings" Clinton Heylin, *Can You Feel The Silence?*
"bleak, grimy ... windswept and cheerless" Peter Mills, *Hymns To The Silence*
"a beautiful landscape of small farms" Peter Mills, *Hymns To The Silence*
"He went to check things out" Brian Hinton, *Celtic Crossroads*
"I was lucky to grow up" *Mojo*, 2006
"just knew it was Ray Charles" *The Word*, 2007

"like the Bible" *The Word*, 2007
"It cost 1/6d in Smithfield" *The Irish Times, 1998*
"Memphis Slim had been in Belfast" *Rolling Stone*, 1972
"a pretty funky neighbourhood" Clinton Heylin, *Can You Feel The Silence?*
"incredible knowledge of Irish music" Clinton Heylin, *Can You Feel The Silence?*
"Relatives would come around on a Saturday evening" Clinton Heylin, *Can You Feel The Silence?*
"I can do little except teach you" mccormacksociety.co.uk
"wanted to hear him in little else" *John McCormack 1884–1945—Icon Of An Age: The Anthology*, 2006
"This and his support of the cause" Peter Costello, *The Irish 100*
"I live again the days and evenings" mccormacksociety.co.uk
"truly a singer for the people" mccormacksociety.co.uk
"He was a supreme example" mccormacksociety.co.uk
"My major influence was Lead Belly" Clinton Heylin, *Can You Feel The Silence?*
"I can remember when I started playing" *Now Dig This*, 1991
"your entrance into playing guitar" *Now Dig This*, 1991
"every night when I was a kid" vanmorrison.com
"That's when I became interested in it" vanmorrison.com
"brought the guitar in" *Now Dig This*, 1991
"For me, skiffle tapped into the Lead Belly thing" *Uncut*, 2005
"incredibly big-headed, conceited" Patrick Humphries, *Lonnie Donegan & The Birth Of British Rock & Roll*, 2012
"feeling it was too rough for public consumption" Johnny Rogan, *Van Morrison*
"Lonnie was difficult" Patrick Humphries, *Lonnie Donegan & The Birth Of British Rock & Roll*
"Everybody was in a skiffle group" thinkexist.com
"I decided I wanted a sax" Clinton Heylin, *Can You Feel The Silence?*
"It started off playing hospital stage productions" *No Guru, No Method, No Teacher* vinyl promotional interview album, 1986
"all sorts of names" *No Guru, No Method, No Teacher*
"It was mainly Jerry Lee" *No Guru, No Method, No Teacher*
"The development of the Orangfield school site" Johnny Rogan, *Van Morrison*
"had striking memories of him" Johnny Rogan, *Van Morrison*

"He slipped through school" Steve Turner, *Van Morrison*
"I wanted to be a vet" *Mojo*, 2012
"I didn't study poetry or read Irish writers" Johnny Rogan, *Van Morrison*
"I was just writing these songs instinctively" Johnny Rogan, *Van Morrison*
"There was no school for people like me" Johnny Rogan, *Van Morrison*

Chapter Three: Keep It Simple, Stupid
"musical desert" *From A Whisper To A Scream: The Living History Of Irish Rock* (DVD), 1999
"It's impossible to explain" Clinton Heylin, *Can You Feel The Silence?*
"In the beginning you had the showband" Mark J. Prendergast, *The Isle Of Noises*
"an enormous part in taking a closed Ireland" *Good Night, Safe Home And God Bless: The Story Of Irish Showbands* (DVD), 1998
"probably one of the biggest industries" *Good Night, Safe Home And God Bless: The Story Of Irish Showbands* (DVD), 1998
"part of the passage of the people" *Good Night, Safe Home And God Bless: The Story Of Irish Showbands* (DVD), 1998
"led 10 to 18 piece orchestras" irish-showbands.com
"Bands like Bill Haley And The Comets" irish-showbands.com
"They were wild" *Uncut*, 2005
"It was great training ground" *Mojo*, 2012
"We had a singer" *Uncut*, 2005
"strictly a rock'n'roll band" *Now Dig This*, 1991
"You had to have a horn section" *Now Dig This*, 1991
"That's how one got work" *Hot Press*, 2000
"might've worked us over" *Rolling Stone*, 1972
"Van became the basis of what he is today" Johnny Rogan, *Van Morrison*
"It was a completely different scene" *Rolling Stone*, 1972
"Ballrooms started to spring up" irish-showbands.com
"You paid cash into the ballrooms" *Good Night, Safe Home And God Bless: The Story Of Irish Showbands* (DVD), 1998
"The huge influx of copycat showbands" irish-showbands.com
"Immediately after the Miami killings" irish-showbands.com
"a terrible sense of reckoning" *Good Night, Safe Home And God Bless: The Story Of Irish Showbands* (DVD), 1998
"a very deep wound" *Good Night, Safe Home And God Bless: The Story Of Irish Showbands* (DVD), 1998

"Managers and ballroom owners' priorities" *R2/Rock'n'Reel*, 2012
"At a time when the church had an iron grip" irish-showbands.com
"operated a stranglehold in the way" Noel McLaughlin and Martin
  McLoone, *Rock And Popular Music In Ireland*

Chapter Four: Kicking Against The Pricks
"So I went out and found this club" *Now Dig This*, 1991
"I'd already been playing in bands" Danish radio interview, 1985
"earned a reputation on a par" ulsterhistorycircle.co.uk
"for kids of every religion and none" Lauren Onkey, *The Irish In Us*
"Who Are? What Are?" Johnny Rogan, *Van Morrison*
"We were playing for a certain bunch of people" Johnny Rogan, *Van
  Morrison*
"a hip, liberating, urban Irishness" Lauren Onkey, *The Irish In Us*
"I'm not Irish!" Noel McLaughlin and Martin McLoone, *Rock And Popular
  Music In Ireland*
"when we had a couple of hit records" *Rolling Stone*, 1970
"more spontaneous, more energetic" Steve Turner, *Van Morrison*
"Them lived and died" Johnny Rogan, *Van Morrison*
"Suddenly, it seemed like" *Uncut*, 2005
"They were the most boorish" *The Irish Independent*, 1965
"Irish rock music had not only arrived" Noel McLaughlin and Martin
  McLoone, *Rock And Popular Music In Ireland*
"some armed with bottles" Clinton Heylin, *Can You Feel The Silence?*
"I didn't want any of that stuff" *Uncut*, 2005
"Van Morrison was insane" waiting-forthe-sun.net
"slammed through several songs" Clinton Heylin, *Can You Feel The Silence?*
"They turned us into a pop group" *Uncut*, 2005
"The band were cooking" Steve Turner, *Van Morrison*
"I had the list of songs" Steve Turner, *Van Morrison*
"uncooperative and moody tendencies" Steve Turner, *Van Morrison*
"We had three hits" *Mojo*, 2012
"When I was with the group" *Rolling Stone*, 1970
"They were very close" Clinton Heylin, *Can You Feel The Silence?*

Chapter Five: Elegy For Belfast
"I saw a film version" Peter Mills, *Hymns To The Silence*
"you need a sense of the song" Greil Marcus, *Listening To Van Morrison*

"like starting again" *The Word*, 2007
"I was getting fed up" *The Word*, 2007
"This is not an exaggeration" *Mojo*, 2010
"That's one of the many myths" *Uncut*, 2005
"I wrote a couple of songs" *Hot Press*, 2000
"They are timeless works" *LA Times*, 2008
"I have probably always been more advanced in my head" *LA Times*, 2008
"If you listen to the album" Clinton Heylin, *Can You Feel The Silence?*
"He was remote from us" Clinton Heylin, *Can You Feel The Silence?*
"Morrison couldn't work with anybody" Lester Bangs, *Stranded*
"The songs came out of " *Select*, 1990
"with a lot of wealth" Brian Hinton, *Celtic Crossroads*
"the street that we would all aspire to" Clinton Heylin, *Can You Feel The Silence?*
"cause that's where all the expensive houses" Clinton Heylin, *Can You Feel The Silence?*
"the idea of another place" *The Irish Times*, 1998
"Just imagine we had a sponsor" *Rolling Stone*, 1970
"The song is actually 'Madame Joy'" *Hot Press*, 1977
"with its story-telling and repetitions" *The Irish Times*, 1998
"What Kavanagh saw" *The Irish Times*, 1998
"used the technique to show" Brian Hinton, *Celtic Crossroads*
"closer to the impressionistic style" Brian Hinton, *Celtic Crossroads*
"this double vision" Brian Hinton, *Celtic Crossroads*
"I want to give a picture of Dublin" jstor.org
"Genius it has I think" modernism.research.yale.edu
"a great comic vision" metaportal.com
"the iconographic site" *The Irish Times*, 1998
"which portrays a world of loss and gain" *The Irish Times*, 1998
"a portrait of a society" *The Irish Times*, 1998
"are textures of a recognisably 'ordinary' working class lifestyle" Noel McLaughlin and Martin McLoone, *Rock And Popular Music In Ireland*
"his most complete celebration of his Belfast roots" Noel McLaughlin and Martin McLoone, *Rock And Popular Music In Ireland:*
"Some of Astral Weeks is real" *Uncut*, 2005
"hung out and there was little aggro" *The Irish Times*, 1998
"the idea of the unfound door" Peter Mills, *Hymns To The Silence*
"in and through the ordinary" Peter Mills, *Hymns To The Silence*

"is a feeling for the emotional weight" Peter Mills, *Hymns To The Silence*

"We used to go to a place" Steve Turner, *Van Morrison*

"He wails as the jazz musician speaks of wailing" Johnny Rogan, *Van Morrison*

"just emerged from the Gaeltacht" Johnny Rogan, *Van Morrison*

"Northern, Orange-hued and urban" Johnny Rogan, *Van Morrison*

"in a misty-eyed romanticised Celtic twilight" Johnny Rogan, *Van Morrison*

Chapter Six: American Exile

"I didn't have a ranch" Clinton Heylin, *Can You Feel The Silence?*

"was very traumatic and horrible" Clinton Heylin, *Can You Feel The Silence?*

"a kind of odyssey" Greil Marcus, *Listening To Van Morrison*, 2010

"on his recent experiences in America" Johnny Rogan, *Van Morrison*

"I'm definitely Irish" Brian Hinton, *Celtic Crossroads*

"chosen exile, cunning and silence" Brian Hinton, *Celtic Crossroads*

"People not only ghettoised themselves" Johnny Rogan, *Van Morrison*

"definitely influenced by my childhood in Belfast" Johnny Rogan, *Van Morrison*

"I'd been working on this song" *Rolling Stone*, 1972

"I worked out in my head" *Hot Press*, 1977

"embraced Celtic mythology" Johnny Rogan, *Van Morrison*

"It used to be Scotland" *Stage Life*, 1977

"just a tag I came up with" *Uncut*, 2005

"a Francis Bacon equivalent" Micheal O'Suilleabhain, unpublished paper, 2013

"where a bellowing figure" Micheal O'Suilleabhain, unpublished paper, 2013

"a primal road. We can feel" Micheal O'Suilleabhain, unpublished paper, 2013

"a blast bag, a blowing bag" Micheal O'Suilleabhain, unpublished paper, 2013

"is an oil well belching up crude oil" Micheal O'Suilleabhain, unpublished paper, 2013

"digs with his pen" Micheal O'Suilleabhain, unpublished paper, 2013

"an attempt to shape" Greil Marcus, *Rolling Stone Illustrated History Of Rock'n'Roll*

"a spiritual descendant of the Irish prelate" Greil Marcus, *Rolling Stone Illustrated History Of Rock'n'Roll* "the Irish American relationship in Morrison's work" Lauren Onkey, *The Irish In Us*

"tried to get it on album for a long time" *Talk About Pop*, RTE Television, 1973

"at a party in Belfast" Peter Mills, *Hymns To The Silence*

"Irish music was nowhere" Peter Mills, *Hymns To The Silence*

"written for all the kids born" Clinton Heylin, *Can You Feel The Silence?*

"'Madame Joy' was something of a sequel" Clinton Heylin, *Can You Feel The Silence?*

"In a live setting" bbc.co.uk

"The Caledonia Soul Orchestra was so different" Clinton Heylin, *Can You Feel The Silence?*

Chapter Seven: God's Green Land

"We were delighted that he should want to appear" Johnny Rogan, *Van Morrison*

"It was dreadful television" Johnny Rogan, *Van Morrison*

"Let me elaborate" *Talk About Pop*, RTE Television, 1973

"How can you stand up an entire nation?" Johnny Rogan, *Van Morrison*

"after spending most of his life" Steve Turner, *Van Morrison*

"Take 'Purple Heather'" *Hot Press*, 1977

"I tell in detail of the enslavement" examiner.

"others acknowledge that the music" examiner.com

"Certainly, Irish folk music and African folk music" examiner.com

"is the gift of those slaves and virtual slaves" examiner.com

"I think a musician who gets involved in politics" Johnny Rogan, *Van Morrison*

"the hatred thing ... I don't have a specific country" Johnny Rogan, *Van Morrison*

"Van was finding fresh inspiration" Brian Hinton, *Celtic Crossroads*

"It reveals much about" Johnny Rogan, *Van Morrison*

"a poet and a musician" Johnny Rogan, *Van Morrison*

"comes from a different place" *The Independent*, 2006

"an instinctual thing" *The Independent*, 2006

"age-old oral and place name tradition" Brian Hinton, *Celtic Crossroads*

"that owes a lot to Calvinism" Johnny Rogan, *Van Morrison*

"Irish equivalent of the Holy Grail" Steve Turner, *Van Morrison*

"I told him that he could actually meet Van" Steve Turner, *Van Morrison*

"I haven't a clue what the title means" Brian Hinton, *Celtic Crossroads*

"a mad Irish poet" Steve Turner, *Van Morrison*
"in a very concrete way" scribd.com
"draws from Ireland from an outside perspective" Peter Mills, *Hymns To The Silence*
"a visitor, a guest in his own country" Peter Mills, *Hymns To The Silence*
"about an image of an Irish-American" Clinton Heylin, *Can You Feel The Silence?*
"It was a house I was staying in at the time" *Mojo*, 2012
"a cross between Desperate Dan" Johnny Rogan, *Van Morrison*
"'Who Was That Masked Man' does deal" Peter Mills, *Hymns To The Silence*
"the right of the people of Ireland" firstdail.com
"flashes of Ireland" Clinton Heylin, *Can You Feel The Silence?*
"about things that you remember happening to you" Brian Hinton, *Celtic Crossroads*
"an Irish mystical appreciation" Mark J. Prendergast, *The Isle Of Noises*
"to the body of work made by Irish artists in exile" Peter Mills, *Hymns To The Silence*
"to get a new perspective" Brian Hinton, *Celtic Crossroads*
"I got to the point" Brian Hinton, *Celtic Crossroads*
"been performing in bands since I was 12" *Stage Life*, 1977
"He went out there and really stormed the place" Johnny Rogan, *Van Morrison*
"He's written books that I can definitely connect with" *Stage Life*, 1977
"began to uncover more and more" F.S.L. Lyons, *Ireland Since The Famine*
"the coming of a new power into literature" F.S.L. Lyons, *Ireland Since The Famine*
"that he learned at first hand" F.S.L. Lyons, *Ireland Since The Famine*
"We propose to have performed in Dublin" R.F. Foster, *Modern Ireland 1600–1972*
"an unmitigated, protracted libel" guardian.co.uk
"a vile and inhuman story" guardian.co.uk
"In little more than ten years" F.S.L. Lyons, *Ireland Since The Famine*

Chapter Eight: Belonging To Ulster
"hoping for a work of primeval vocal aggression" Johnny Rogan, *Van Morrison*
"a masterclass in mediocrity" Johnny Rogan, *Van Morrison*
"It's good to see the Queen" Johnny Rogan, *Van Morrison*

"What I'm doing right now" Brian Hinton, *Celtic Crossroads*
"I have never done an interview that bad" Johnny Rogan, *Van Morrison*
"simple streams-of-consciousness" *Stage Life*, 1977
"You're like an instrument" *Stage Life*, 1977
"We might think" *Stage Life*, 1977
"It's no secret that you were" *Stage Life*, 1977
"When I was growing up in Belfast" *Rolling Stone*, 1978
"People expected him to walk on water" Clinton Heylin, *Can You Feel The Silence?*
"one way or the other" Steve Turner, *Van Morrison*
"How the hell can I live in Ireland?" Johnny Rogan, *Van Morrison*
"the missing link" Brian Hinton, *Celtic Crossroads*
"I was born in a Christian environment" Steve Turner, *Van Morrison*
"plucked, plonked and squawked" Brian Hinton, *Celtic Crossroads*
"In the days when I met him" Clinton Heylin, *Can You Feel The Silence?*
"In the mid-60s, Belfast was a switched-on town" politico.ie
"For a while he managed Van Morrison" politico.ie
"one of the smartest people I've ever met" politico.ie
"demonstrated that he had an appetite" Steve Turner, *Van Morrison*
"where Van Morrison leaves rock" Clinton Heylin, *Can You Feel The Silence?*
"with nothing to say and a limitless interest" Brian Hinton, *Celtic Crossroads*
"colossally smug and cosmically dull" Clinton Heylin, *Can You Feel The Silence?*
"was making holy music" Clinton Heylin, *Can You Feel The Silence?*
"for works of lyrical beauty and ethical depth" nobelprize.org
"poetry, like the soil" nobelprize.org
"in which can still be detected echoes" Peter Costello, *The Irish 100*
"on a level where he talks about weather reports" *Hot Press*, 2000
"Mr Heaney ... I read your book" Peter Mills, *Hymns To The Silence*
"read the landscape as a kind of manuscript" Peter Mills, *Hymns To The Silence*
"that relatively rare thing" Peter Mills, *Hymns To The Silence*
"to a specifically Northern Irish song tradition" Peter Mills, *Hymns To The Silence*
"very mellow" Johnny Rogan, *Van Morrison, No Surrender*, 2006
"He's discovered an Irish bar" Johnny Rogan, *Van Morrison*
"where it's going, and the force that's behind it" Clinton Heylin, *Can You Feel The Silence?*

"Irish music was going on all around me" Johnny Rogan, *Van Morrison*
"is that he embraces a Celtic vision" Lauren Onkey, *The Irish In Us*
"a vision of one place, one people" Lauren Onkey, *The Irish In Us*
"a Celtic invocation" Lauren Onkey, *The Irish In Us*
"a complex set of relations" Peter Mills, *Hymns To The Silence*
"The Greeks with their art" books.google.co.uk
"soul, personality, mind" Clinton Heylin, *Can You Feel The Silence?*
"a citizen of Europe and America" Bill Flanagan, *Written In My Soul*
"much closer to Belfast" Danish radio interview, 1985

Chapter Nine: Hollywood Glockamorra
"a very Protestant artiste" Johnny Rogan, *Van Morrison*
"Irish ambient music often incorporated uilleann pipes" Lauren Onkey, *The Irish In Us*
"I belong specifically to Ulster" Johnny Rogan, *Van Morrison*
"little direct relevance" Johnny Rogan, *Van Morrison*
"the latest incarnation of The Van Morrison Band" Brian Hinton, *Celtic Crossroads*
"rendered his new material almost inaccessible" Steve Turner, *Van Morrison*
"who had been drafted in" Clinton Heylin, *Can You Feel The Silence?*
"He very consciously tried to destabilise us" Clinton Heylin, *Can You Feel The Silence?*
"He was always just there" *Q*, 1997
"We were told by the Yeats estate" *New Age*, 1985
"I never asked him why the change was made" Clinton Heylin, *Can You Feel The Silence?*
"takes you through the meditation programme" *No Guru, No Method, No Teacher* vinyl promotional interview album, 1986
"at the young Van on Hyndford Street" Steve Turner, *Van Morrison*
"takes us ... to the world of Astral Weeks" Brian Hinton, *Celtic Crossroads*
"a beautiful young woman with long red hair" horseoftirnanog.com
"Approaching the sea" horseoftirnanog.com
"It was a Loyalist pub" Clinton Heylin, *Can You Feel The Silence?*
"A number of judges, spies and police officers" Johnny Rogan, *Van Morrison*
"as deprived as any in inner city Belfast" Susan McKay, *Northern Protestants*
"You couldn't sit down" Clinton Heylin, *Can You Feel The Silence?*
"to advance education and learning" wrekintrust.org
"with the purpose of awakening" wrekintrust.org

"an exploration into the power of music" Steve Turner, *Van Morrison*
"His passion for music" Johnny Rogan, *Van Morrison*
"engaged in a sort of battle" Clinton Heylin, *Can You Feel The Silence?*
"A lot of serious musicians" youtube.com

Chapter Ten: From Backward To Cool

"like idiots from Ireland" Lauren Onkey, *The Irish In Us*
"to be from Ireland" *Q*, 1993
"There was a barrier there" *Q*, 1993
"They thought people would feel proud of their culture" *Folk Hibernia*, BBC
    Television, 2008
"had a complex with their own music" *Folk Hibernia*, BBC Television, 2008
"The ideal Ireland that we would have" *Folk Hibernia*, BBC Television, 2008
"He took the orchestral concept" *Folk Hibernia*, BBC Television, 2008
"He managed to tape traditional musicians" Dr Gearoid O' hAllmhurain,
    The Pocket History Of Traditional Irish Music
"on a mission to collect songs and stories" *The Irish Independent*, 2009
"the rebirth of Irish music" *The Irish Times*, 2009
"his generation's Jerry Garcia" *R2/Rock'n'Reel*, 2013
"was in the vanguard" *R2/Rock'n'Reel*, 2013
"I'd never miss *Donagh MacDonagh's Song Bag*" Liam Clancy, *Memoirs Of An
    Irish Troubadour*
"On a more homespun level" Liam Clancy, *Memoirs Of An Irish Troubadour*
"one foot in the 20th century" Liam Clancy, *Memoirs Of An Irish Troubadour*
"I saw sights and heard music" Liam Clancy, *Memoirs Of An Irish Troubadour*
"Tommy's mother had worked" Liam Clancy, *Memoirs Of An Irish Troubadour*
"the great America had given their nod of approval" *Folk Hibernia*, BBC
    Television, 2008
"the undisputed leaders" *Time*, 1967
"a bullfrog with a hangover" *Time*, 1967
"The Clancys were on a different level" *Folk Hibernia*, BBC Television, 2008
"I was a middle class Dublin individual" *Folk Hibernia*, BBC Television, 2008
"We went out in a sociological context" *Folk Hibernia*, BBC Television, 2008
"used to play acoustic and electric guitars" *Folk Hibernia*, BBC Television,
    2008
"vision of a new folk folk music" Mark J. Prendergast, *The Isle Of Noises*
"You could come out as being a fan" *Folk Hibernia*, BBC Television, 2008
"It was cool" *Folk Hibernia*, BBC Television, 2008

"part of a younger generation" Mark J. Prendergast, *The Isle Of Noises*
"We were doing what any normal rock'n'roll band was doing" *Folk Hibernia*,
    BBC Television, 2008
"in another place, a voice in his head" Harry Doherty & Scott Gorham, *The
    Boys Are Back In Town*
"a strange musical brew" *Folk Hibernia*, BBC Television, 2008
"touted a strong national element" *Folk Hibernia*, BBC Television, 2008
"Celtic first and Irish second" *Folk Hibernia*, BBC Television, 2008
"Music and culture eased the way" *Folk Hibernia*, BBC Television, 2008
"the character of Irish folk" Mark J. Prendergast, *The Isle Of Noises*
"The music has been used" *Folk Hibernia*, BBC Television, 2008
"Truth is, Ireland is somewhat diverse" *Folk Hibernia*, BBC Television, 2008

Chapter Eleven: The Inner Paddy Revealed
"an inspiration in terms of some of the songs" Peter Mills, *Hymns To The
    Silence*
"I felt if they can get away with it" *Folk Hibernia*, BBC Television, 2008
"to place Irish traditional music on a par" Dr Gearoid O' hAllmhurain, *The
    Pocket History Of Traditional Irish Music*
"a comfortable niche" Brian Hinton, *Celtic Crossroads*
"Paddy, Paddy, we've got to do an album together!" Clinton Heylin, *Can You
    Feel The Silence?*
"Van's not really a great one" Clinton Heylin, *Can You Feel The Silence?*
"I started meditating and doing sounds" Clinton Heylin, *Can You Feel The
    Silence?*
"It was always part of the picture" Clinton Heylin, *Can You Feel The Silence?*
"soul Irish music ... a serious album of Irish music" Clinton Heylin, *Can
    You Feel The Silence?*
"The studio was decked out in Celtic emblems" Brian Hinton, *Celtic
    Crossroads*
"made explicit what had been implicit" Brian Hinton, *Celtic Crossroads*
"I said, 'Look, Van'" Clinton Heylin, *Can You Feel The Silence?*
"There's no fiddling around" Clinton Heylin, *Can You Feel The Silence?*
"a very curious person" John Glatt, *The Chieftains: The Authorised Biography*,
    1997
"an aspect of the Irish conundrum" Peter Mills, *Hymns To The Silence*
"When we were doing *Irish Heartbeat*" Johnny Rogan, *Van Morrison*
"straight off John McCormack" Peter Mills, *Hymns To The Silence*

"unmistakably Irish" Peter Mills, *Hymns To The Silence*
"The Chieftains don't know them" Peter Mills, *Hymns To The Silence*
"With her black wavy shoulder-length hair" Antoinette Quinn, *Patrick Kavanagh*
"On one occasion I dared to actually speak to the man" Peter Mills, *Hymns To The Silence*
"a wiping clean of the slate" Peter Mills, *Hymns To The Silence*
"of the high intensity of 'Linden Arden Stole The Highlights'" Peter Mills, *Hymns To The Silence*
"as a reminder of the unifying power" Peter Mills, *Hymns To The Silence*
"They're all Irish songs" Johnny Rogan, *Van Morrison*
"a bloody considerable marvel" *Melody Maker*, 1988
"Awesome" *NME*, 1988
"a marriage of convenience" *Evening Standard*, 1988
"splendour and intense beauty" *Rolling Stone*, 1988
"It is a breakthrough" Clinton Heylin, *Can You Feel The Silence?*
"It's a classic" John Glatt, *The Chieftains*
"every single Irish song we've done" Peter Mills, *Hymns To The Silence*
"It was a very simple album" Clinton Heylin, *Can You Feel The Silence?*
"trouble in the Dublin pubs" *The Belfast Telegraph*, 1988
"brings together the two finest poets" *Magill*, 1988
"Both northerners—solid ground boys" *Magill*, 1988
"All of Kavanagh and Morrison" *Magill*, 1988
"the top 30 of Morrison's poems" *Magill*, 1988
"And I'd state in my Leaving Certificate essay" *Magill*, 1988
"is a maestro of the improvised line" *Magill*, 1988
"the spiritual adventure of Morrison's poems" *Magill*, 1988
"Morrison's visit to the Church of Ireland" *Magill*, 1988
"part of an age-old oral" *Magill*, 1988
"an interesting example of cultural pluralism" Noel McLaughlin and Martin McLoone, *Rock And Popular Music In Ireland*
"I never think about music in terms of categories" *Uncut*, 2005
"a time to reflect" Johnny Rogan, *Van Morrison*
"He came out of himself a bit" Clinton Heylin, *Can You Feel The Silence?*
"For a while neither of them wanted to give way" Clinton Heylin, *Can You Feel The Silence?*
"a mismatch" Clinton Heylin, *Can You Feel The Silence?*
"We were all sitting about" Clinton Heylin, *Can You Feel The Silence?*

"too much under Moloney's apron strings" Clinton Heylin, *Can You Feel The Silence?*
"all these books about these masters" Clinton Heylin, *Can You Feel The Silence?*
"There were times when he would get into a mood" Johnny Rogan, *Van Morrison*
"he'd had enough of The Chieftains" Clinton Heylin, *Can You Feel The Silence?*
"So I lean over to Paddy" Clinton Heylin, *Can You Feel The Silence?*
"He does this for the whole song" Clinton Heylin, *Can You Feel The Silence?*
"from ancient Ireland, written out by monastic scribes" Peter Mills, *Hymns To The Silence*
"is strongly performative" Peter Mills, *Hymns To The Silence*

Chapter Twelve: The Hill Of Silence
"You're joking, aren't you?" *NME*, 1989
"I now play music for pure love" Steve Turner, *Van Morrison*
"shot through with contemplations about Christ" Clinton Heylin, *Can You Feel The Silence?*
"zigzags from the coast of County Down up to Belfast" Peter Mills, *Hymns To The Silence*
"From a sociological point of view" guardian.co.uk
"is to find a small, quiet stony beach" Peter Mills, *Hymns To The Silence*
"fell in love" *The Belfast Sunday Telegraph*, 2007
"may well have been intrigued" Peter Mills, *Hymns To The Silence*
"an Irish writer" Peter Mills, *Hymns To The Silence*
"in which to receive" Brian Hinton, *Celtic Crossroads*
"might be a way out of belonging" Brian Hinton, *Celtic Crossroads*
"As with James Joyce's imaginative remapping of Dublin" Peter Mills, *Hymns To The Silence*
"and particularly those of County Down" Peter Mills, *Hymns To The Silence*
"I have here discovered" C.S. Lewis, *The Screwtape Letters*
"perhaps is appeal is purely Irish" C.S. Lewis, *The Screwtape Letters*
"Basically Irish writers" *NME*, 1989
"beneath the skin music" Brian Hinton, *Celtic Crossroads*
"blackness and Irishness are inseparable" Lauren Onkey, *The Irish In Us*
"Irish version of the gospel impulse" Craig Werner, *A Change Is Gonna Come*
"I felt a transformation come over me" Johnny Rogan, *Van Morrison*

"made the album called Enlightenment" Johnny Rogan, *Van Morrison*
"a committed born-again Christian" guardian.co.uk
"let bygones be bygones" guardian.co.uk
"a signal on the organ" Johnny Rogan, *Van Morrison*
"in the best of faith" Johnny Rogan, *Van Morrison*
"Belfast chidhood and the city's atmosphere" Johnny Rogan, *Van Morrison*
"do it tomorrow" Johnny Rogan, *Van Morrison*
"was excitedly offering the singer" Johnny Rogan, *Van Morrison*
"In ancient Ireland there were four ways" Peter Mills, *Hymns To The Silence*
"When I started writing songs" Peter Mills, *Hymns To The Silence*
"You find out what you've been searching for" Peter Mills, *Hymns To The Silence*
"asserts his sense of belonging" Peter Mills, *Hymns To The Silence*
"appeal to the Irish in all of us" thegatheringireland.com
"Ireland is opening its arms" thegatheringireland.com
"Over 70 million people worldwide" thegatheringireland.com
"to shake them down for a few quid" bbc.co.uk
"The other day" *The Irish Times*, 2012
"as good examples of this" Peter Mills, *Hymns To The Silence*
"for his writing" nobelprize.org
"the old sow that eats her farrow" *The Observer*, 2010
"suicide to be abroad" *The Observer*, 2010
"I read a lot of Yeats myself" Clinton Heylin: *Can You Feel The Silence?*

Chapter Thirteen: Dublin's Fair City

"They live on beasts" irishhistorylinks.net
"People begin to doubt themselves" Dr Joy DeGruy Leary, *Post Traumatic Slave Syndrome*
"the most exciting city in Europe" Johnny Rogan, *Van Morrison*
"a strangely paradoxical statelet" Johnny Rogan, *Van Morrison*
"In hotel lounges and trendy diners" Johnny Rogan, *Van Morrison*
"the most unlikely coupling in human history" Johnny Rogan, *Van Morrison*
"having an intensely platonic relationship" *The Sunday Independent*, 1993
"When it comes to protesting" Johnny Rogan, *Van Morrison*
"designed to disguise" Johnny Rogan, *Van Morrison*
"trying to persuade him to relax more" Johnny Rogan, *Van Morrison*
"Rocca: The contemporary poet, Paul Durcan" *Vox*, 1994
"Catholic, falsetto-voiced and gay" Johnny Rogan, *Van Morrison*

"A rancid fog of blind reverence" *NME*, 1995
"an annoyingly enthusiastic horn section" *NME*, 1995
"She was a slightly older woman than me" youtube.com
"I went in and Van and Jerry Lee were singing" youtube.com
"He resembled a man" Johnny Rogan, *Van Morrison*
"I've always been Irish" Johnny Rogan, *Van Morrison*
"I was actually four when I started drinking" *Daily Mirror*, 2007
"Van depressed me" Victoria Mary Clarke & Shane MacGowan, *A Drink
    With Shane MacGowan*
"musical and spiritual mentor" Johnny Rogan, *Van Morrison*
"was different from his New Age Celticism" Lauren Onkey, *The Irish In Us*
"To call me a rock star" Clinton Heylin, *Can You Feel The Silence?*
"At least try to behave yourself" Clinton Heylin, *Can You Feel The Silence?*
"the behaviour of all parties involved" Clinton Heylin, *Can You Feel The
    Silence?*
"I just felt lonely and rejected" Clinton Heylin, *Can You Feel The Silence?*

Chapter Fourteen: One Of Us
"ruining her father's career" Clinton Heylin, *Can You Feel The Silence?*
"a song about East Belfast" Johnny Rogan, *Van Morrison*
"Ireland's greatest living legend" Johnny Rogan, *Van Morrison*
"nothing more than a grotesque travesty" Johnny Rogan, *Van Morrison*
"Country music's popularity in Scotland and Northern Ireland" Peter Mills,
    Hymns To The Silence
"My musical sources" *The Independent*, 2006
"I don't remember the last time I listened to it" *Uncut*, 2005
"a totally different project" *LA Times*, 2008
"The main reason is I don't own the original record" time.com
"somehow I could feel what he" vanmorrisonnews.blogspot.co.uk
"No town or city better illustrates" smithsonianmag.com
"is increasingly regarded as a model" smithsonianmag.com
"provided a 30-year alternative" Noel McLaughlin and Martin McLoone,
    Rock And Popular Music In Ireland
"has a greater artistic and social integrity" Noel McLaughlin and Martin
    McLoone, *Rock And Popular Music In Ireland*

INDEX

Unless otherwise stated, words in *italics* indicate album titles; words in 'quotes' indicate song titles.

ACKNOWLEDGEMENTS

Van Morrison once complained that, even though he's been the subject of several books, none of the writers have ever asked him for his say. Well, I did. An email outlining the brief of A Sense Of Wonder: Van Morrison's Ireland, was sent to his publicist, forwarded to his management and eventually to his assistant. "To be honest, you may or may not get an answer. However, it will be put in front of him," I was assured. I never did get a response. Shame. So, without The Man guiding me through his Ireland, I've had to rely on the available resources out there, as well as original and archival interviews of my own.

Getting people to talk wasn't easy. One particular individual (who shall remain nameless) initially agreed to discuss his working relationship with Van, only to change his mind after being "contacted by people with more money than me, who asked me not to be interviewed". Clannad's Moya Brennan and her brother, Ciaran, weren't comfortable taking part unless the project was officially endorsed by Morrison. And then there was Brian Kennedy who, when he found out there wouldn't be a fee involved, decided "not to go ahead".

But let's forget about those who weren't co-operative and instead concentrate on those who were. Profuse thanks, in alphabetical order, to Colin Bateman, Paul Bew, Aisling Bowyer, Brendan Bowyer, Gabriel Burke, Rupert Burley, Joanna Cannon, Gerald Dawe, Keith Donald, Garbhan Downey, Ruth Dudley Edwards, Marianne Elliott, Colin Eustace, Tommy Fleming, Gerry Gallagher, Anna Graham, Shay Healy, Declan Heeney, Trevor Hodgett, Patrick Humphries, Ken Hunt, Sean McGhee, Monica McWilliams, Mike Nesbitt, Alan Nierob, Joe O'Connor, Micheal O'Suilleabhain, Glenn Patterson, Stephen Pillster, Peter Robinson, Declan Sinnott, and Tom Seabrook.

Those quotes attributed to Aly Bain, Paul Brady, Liam Clancy, Damien Dempsey, Brian Kennedy, Philip King, and Paddy Moloney, which aren't referenced in the notes section, are from my own interviews conducted with each down the years.

Grateful appreciation also to Shirley, Francesca, and Dylan for their love and support.

Jacket photograph by Ken Sharp. Title page photograph by Joe Fox. 'Blues For Van Morrison' is reproduced exactly as it was written, complete with author's spellings of 'Cypress Avenue' (Cyprus Avenue) and 'St Dominick's' (St Dominic's). Many thanks to Joseph O'Connor for kindly granting permission to use it.

MILLION DOLLAR
BASH: BOB DYLAN,
THE BAND, AND THE
BASEMENT TAPES
by Sid Griffin

ISBN 978-1-906002-05-3

HOT BURRITOS:
THH TRUE STORY OF
THE FLYING BURRITO
BROTHERS
by John Einarson with
Chris Hillman

ISBN 978-1-906002-16-9

BOWIE IN BERLIN:
A NEW CAREER IN A
NEW TOWN
by Thomas Jerome
Seabrook

ISBN 978-1-906002-08-4

TO LIVE IS TO DIE:
THE LIFE AND DEATH
OF METALLICA'S
CLIFF BURTON
by Joel McIver

ISBN 978-1-906002-24-4

MILLION DOLLAR
LES PAUL: IN SEARCH
OF THE MOST
VALUABLE GUITAR IN
THE WORLD
by Tony Bacon

ISBN 978-1-906002-14-5

THE IMPOSSIBLE
DREAM: THE STORY
OF SCOTT WALKER
AND THE WALKER
BROTHERS
by Anthony Reynolds

ISBN 978-1-906002-25-1

JACK BRUCE:
COMPOSING
HIMSELF: THE
AUTHORISED
BIOGRAPHY
by Harry Shapiro

ISBN 978-1-906002-26-8

FOREVER CHANGES:
ARTHUR LEE AND THE
BOOK OF LOVE
by John Einarson

ISBN 978-1-906002-31-2

RETURN OF THE
KING: ELVIS PRESLEY'S
GREAT COMEBACK
by Gillian G. Gaar

ISBN 978-1-906002-28-2

A WIZARD, A TRUE
STAR: TODD
RUNDGREN IN THE
STUDIO
by Paul Myers

ISBN 978-1-906002-33-6

SEASONS THEY
CHANGE: THE STORY
OF ACID AND
PSYCHEDELIC FOLK
by Jeanette Leech

ISBN 978-1-906002-32-9

WON'T GET FOOLED
AGAIN: THE WHO
FROM LIFEHOUSE TO
QUADROPHENIA
by Richie Unterberger

ISBN 978-1-906002-35-0

THE
RESURRECTION OF
JOHNNY CASH:
HURT, REDEMPTION,
AND AMERICAN
RECORDINGS
by Graeme Thomson

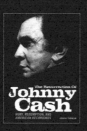

ISBN 978-1-906002-36-7

CRAZY TRAIN: THE
HIGH LIFE AND
TRAGIC DEATH OF
RANDY RHOADS
by Joel McIver

ISBN 978-1-906002-37-4

JUST CAN'T GET
ENOUGH:
THE MAKING OF
DEPECHE MODE
by Simon Spence

ISBN 978-1-906002-56-5

GLENN HUGHES:
FROM DEEP PURPLE
TO BLACK COUNTRY
COMMUNION
by Glenn Hughes

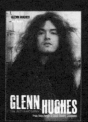

ISBN 978-1-906002-92-3

ENTERTAIN US:
THE RISE OF NIRVANA
by Gillian G. Gaar

ISBN 978-1-906002-89-3

MIKE SCOTT:
ADVENTURES OF A
WATERBOY
by Mike Scott

ISBN 978-1-908279-24-8

SHE BOP: THE
DEFINITIVE HISTORY
OF WOMEN IN
POPULAR MUSIC
by Lucy O'Brien
Revised Third Edition

ISBN 978-1-908279-27-9

SOLID
FOUNDATION: AN
ORAL HISTORY OF
REGGAE
by David Katz
Revised and Expanded
Edition

ISBN 978-1-908279-30-9

READ & BURN:
A BOOK ABOUT WIRE
by Wilson Neate

ISBN 978-1-908279-33-0

BIG STAR: THE STORY
OF ROCK'S
FORGOTTEN BAND
by Rob Jovanovic
Revised & Updated
Edition

ISBN 978-1-908279-36-1

RECOMBO DNA: THE
STORY OF DEVO: OR
HOW THE 60s BECAME
THE 80s
by Kevin C. Smith

ISBN 978-1-908279-39-2

TOUCHED BY
GRACE: MY TIME
WITH JEFF BUCKLEY
by Gary Lucas

ISBN 978-1-908279-45-3